FREE DVD   FREE DVD

CWOCN DVD from Trivium Test Prep!

Dear Customer,

Thank you for purchasing from Trivium Test Prep! We're honored to help you prepare for your CWOCN exam.

To show our appreciation, we're offering a **FREE *CWOCN Essential Test Tips* DVD by Trivium Test Prep**. Our DVD includes 35 test preparation strategies that will make you successful on the CWOCN Exam. All we ask is that you email us your feedback and describe your experience with our product. Amazing, awful, or just so-so: we want to hear what you have to say!

To receive your **FREE *CWOCN Essential Test Tips* DVD**, please email us at 5star@triviumtestprep.com. Include "Free 5 Star" in the subject line and the following information in your email:

1. The title of the product you purchased.
2. Your rating from 1 – 5 (with 5 being the best).
3. Your feedback about the product, including how our materials helped you meet your goals and ways in which we can improve our products.
4. Your full name and shipping address so we can send your **FREE *CWOCN Essential Test Tips* DVD**.

If you have any questions or concerns please feel free to contact us directly at 5star@triviumtestprep.com. Thank you!

- Trivium Test Prep Team

CWOCN Study Guide:
CWOCN Exam Prep and Practice Test Questions for the WOCNCB Certified Wound, Ostomy, and Continence Nurse Exam

Copyright © 2019 by Trivium LLC.
ALL RIGHTS RESERVED. By purchase of this book, you have been licensed one copy for personal use only. No part of this work may be reproduced, redistributed, or used in any form or by any means without prior written permission of the publisher and copyright owner.

Questions regarding permissions or copyrighting may be sent to
support@triviumtestprep.com.

Table of Contents

Introduction to the Nursing Process — 7
The Nursing Process — 7
The Psychosocial, Spiritual, Cultural, Developmental and Functional Assessment of an Individual — 15
The Physical Assessment — 17

Wound Care
General Principles of Assessment — 45
General Principles of Management — 97
Pressure Ulcers — 125
Lower Extremity Ulcers — 129
Other Types of Wounds — 145

Ostomy Care
General Principles of Assessment — 161
General Principles of Management and Patient Teaching — 179
Fecal and Urinary Diversions (Colostomy, Illeostomy, Urostomy) — 223
Continent Fecal and Urinary Diversions — 227
Fistula and Percutaneous Tubes and Drains — 229

Continence Care
General Principles of Assessment — 231
Differentiate and Manage Types of Urinary Incontinence — 261
Types of Bowel Dysfunction — 273

Practice Test — 279

Exclusive Test Tips — 303

About Trivium Test Prep

Trivium Test Prep uses industry professionals with decade's worth of knowledge in the fields they have mastered, proven with degrees and honors in law, medicine, business, education, military, and more to produce high-quality test prep books such as this for students.

Our study guides are specifically designed to increase ANY student's score, regardless of his or her current scoring ability. At only 25% - 35% of the page count of most study guides, you will increase your score, while significantly decreasing your study time.

How to Use this Guide

This guide is not meant to reteach you material you have already learned or waste your time on superfluous information. We hope you use this guide to focus on the key concepts you need to master for the test and develop critical test-taking skills. To support this effort, the guide provides:

- *Practice questions with worked-through solutions*
- *Key test-taking tactics that reveal the tricks and secrets of the test*
- *Simulated one-on-one tutor experience*
- *Organized concepts with detailed explanations*
- *Tips, tricks, and test secrets revealed*

Because we have eliminated "filler" or "fluff", you will be able to work through the guide at a significantly faster pace than other prep books. By allowing you to focus ONLY on those concepts that will increase your score, study time is more effective and you are less likely to lose focus or get mentally fatigued.

Introduction to the Nursing Process

The nursing process is a form of problem solving. The nursing process is a systematic, ongoing cyclical, dynamic, goal directed, client centered problem solving approach to nursing care. It provides nurses with a systematic, logical, coherent and complete framework to address patient care needs.

This process has a series of interrelated and interconnected phases that move seamlessly toward identifying and meeting the needs of clients and/or their significant others. Every phase of the nursing process impacts on and affects all of the other phases of the nursing process. Data collected during one phase provides information and data that must be considered during the next phase. For example, data collected during the assessment phase is used by the nurse during the analysis phase; and evaluation phase, the fifth phase of the nursing process, provides data and information that is input into the assessment, or the first phase of the nursing process.

The Nursing Process

The five dynamic phases of the nursing process are:

1. Assessment
2. Diagnosing
3. Planning
4. Implementation
5. Evaluation

All phases of the nursing process are done with the active collaboration and participation of the client, and others as the client chooses.

Assessment

Data, that is related to the client, family members and significant others, is collected during the assessment phase of the nursing process. This data is also organized, validated with the client and others, and documented.

Diagnosis

This phase of the nursing process involves professional critical thinking in order to:

- *Analyze the data and information that was collected during the assessment phase*
- *Identify any health related risk factors*
- *Determine health related concerns and problems*
- *Determine the strengths, as well as the weaknesses, of the client and others*

- *Identify and generate accurate and appropriate nursing diagnoses relating to both actual and potential health problems.*

Planning

During the planning phase of the nursing, the registered nurse determines and establishes priorities, generates the expected outcomes of care, or goals, and selects scientifically sound interventions to meet these goals.

Implementation

Implementation is the actual performance of interventions. However, during this phase, the registered nurse delegates some aspects of care to others, supervises the care rendered by others and assesses and reassesses client responses to the planned interventions.

Evaluation

The evaluation phase, closely similar to the assessment phase, cyclically returns data and information into the assessment phase of the nursing process. Evaluation data, which reflect the client's current condition, is compared and contrasted to the pre-established expected outcomes of care, which were established during the planning phase of the nursing process. The registered nurse then makes a determination about goal achievement. Were the goals completely met? Were the goals only partially met? Were the goals not met at all? After these determinations, the nurse decides to continue, modify, or discontinue part of the plan of care.

Collecting Data for the Health History

During the interview process, the healthcare professional must establish trust, inform the client and their significant others about the purpose of the health history, insure patient confidentiality, maintain patient privacy and ensure a comfortable environment.

During the interview, open-ended questions and closed ended questions are used. Open ended questions elicit full and meaningful answers from the client that reflect the client's own beliefs, knowledge and feelings; closed ended questions do not elicit the same rich information and data. Closed ended questions simply elicit as "no" or "yes" response and no other information. An example of an open-ended question is "Tell me about your pain"; and an example of a closed ended question is "Are you in pain?"

Demographic and Biographical Data

The following biographical and demographic data is collected during the health history.

- *Name*
- *Address*
- *Telephone Number*
- *Emergency Contact Information*
- *Age*

- *Gender*
- *Marital status*
- *Occupation or Avocation (Hobby)*
- *Cultural Values and Beliefs*
- *Spiritual/Religious Preference(s)*
- *Health Insurance*
- *Client's Access to Healthcare Services in the Community*

Chief Complaint

The chief complaint is elicited from the patient by asking a question such as, "What has brought you to the emergency room today?" or "What has brought you to the hospital today?" These questions are open ended. The responses to these questions will reflect the patient's perception of their current situation. Please note: The client's response may or may not be accurate, but nonetheless, these perceptions are helpful to the healthcare professional even when they are inaccurate.

Past Medical History

This component of the health collects data relating to:

- *Immunization status*
- *Childhood illnesses*
- *Acute illnesses*
- *Chronic illnesses*
- *Past injuries and accidents*
- *Current medications, including over the counter medications, herbs and supplements*
- *Prior surgical procedures*
- *Previous hospitalizations*
- *Allergies (medications, foods, environmental sources)*
- *Previous healthcare adverse events like medication toxicities and the adverse effects of anesthesia*

Current Medical History

Some of the questions that are asked during this phase of the health history include:

- *Describe your symptoms.*
- *When did the symptoms begin?*
- *What precipitates it?*
- *What relieves it?*
- *What makes it worse?*
- *How often does this problem or the symptoms occur?*
- *Where is the pain or distress?*
- *Tell me the character (crushing, sore, etc.), intensity (on a pain scale from 1 to 10), the quality (color of the sputum, etc.), the quantity (amount of drainage, etc.) of the presenting symptom or concern.*

Family Medical History

During this phase of the health history, the healthcare professional collects data and information about:

- *The family's presence or absence of common disorders, such as genetic disorders (bleeding, clotting, etc.), alcoholism, hypertension, cancer, diabetes, heart disease, in addition to other psychological and social disorders and concerns, both acute and chronic*
- *The ages, current states of health or age and cause of death for grandparents, parents, siblings and children*

Lifestyle Choices

The healthcare professional collects this data and information in order to identify possible risk factors and to provide a foundation for future teaching and health promotion activities.

- *Diet including any dietary restrictions, the quality and quantity of food consumed, cultural preferences, and religious modifications*
- *Strengths and weaknesses in terms of the client's performance of the activities of daily living, such as dressing, eating, grooming, bathing and hygiene*
- *Consumption patterns in relationship to illicit drugs, alcohol, and tobacco*
- *Sleep and rest patterns*
- *Exercise*
- *Occupational and vocational preferences*

Patterns of Health Care

The purpose of eliciting data and information about the client's patterns of health care is to determine what type of healthcare resources they utilize. For example, does the client use a primary care physician, a community clinic, specialists, etc.? Are these resources adequate and accessible for the client?

Other assessment data, in addition to the client history, that is collected and/or reviewed upon first contact or upon admission include:

- *The present illness*
- *Medication history*
- *DNR status*
- *Admission notes*
- *Progress notes*
- *Previous patient education*
- *The client's diagnoses*

Present Illness

The present illness, and the chief complaint, provides healthcare providers with critical information in terms of the onset, duration, severity, precipitating factors, alleviating factors and the progression of the current illness or disorder.

The current illness can be classified in a number of different ways. It can be classified, or categorized, as an acute illness such as a pulmonary embolus, pneumothorax or the aspiration of a foreign body. The present illness can also be classified as a repeated but intermittent illness such as pneumonia, congestive heart failure and asthma, as a progressive disorder like chronic bronchitis, heart failure and emphysema, and, lastly, as a mixed pattern of illness such as chronic obstructive pulmonary disease and neuromuscular lung disease.

The Medication History

Medication reconciliation and the medication history of the client is one of the most important aspects of the admission process. Simply stated, medication reconciliation is a systematic and formal process for creating the most accurate and complete list possible of a client's current medications and comparing this list to the medications ordered in the client's medical record. For obvious reasons, all prescription medications, vitamins, over the counter medications, herbal remedies, nutritional and dietary supplements, vaccinations, blood derivatives, diagnostic and contrast agents, and radioactive medications are included in this list.

The five steps of this formal medication reconciliation process are as follows:

1. *Generate and document a list of current medications*
2. *Generate a list of newly prescribed medications*
3. *Compare and contrast the two lists*
4. *Employ critical thinking and professional judgments during the comparisons of the two lists*
5. *Communicate and document the new list of medications to the appropriate healthcare providers*

It has been reported by the Institute of Medicine's Preventing Medication Errors report, that hospitalized clients are highly prone to medication errors under our care, and greater than 40 percent of these errors are the result of the lack of medication reconciliation and the lack of communication and documentation when the client is admitted, transferred, and discharged. Medication errors are a very commonly occurring medical error that can, and should be, prevented.

The primary purpose of medication reconciliation is to avoid a number of different errors including those related to omissions, faulty dosages, incorrect timing, duplications, drug-drug interactions and adverse interactions between the current illness and a current medication.

Do Not Resuscitate Status (DNR)

The Do Not Resuscitate, or DNR status, of the client is also reviewed. As you know, all clients should have end of life decisions, including the desire to not be resuscitated, documented prior to the end of life.

Admission Notes

All healthcare providers must review the admission notes that are documented upon first contact or admission to a healthcare facility. These admission notes provide the client's current state of illness, or disease, and a brief description of the progression of this illness and disease that has led to the current admission.

Progress Notes

Like admission notes, progress notes should also be reviewed on a regular basis. At times these notes should be reviewed on an hourly or more frequent basis when the client's condition is unstable and frequently changing; at other times, these notes should be reviewed every shift when the client's condition is relatively stable.

Previous Patient Education

Although data relating to previous patient education should be determined, previous patient education does not necessarily mean that the client and family members have achieved and maintained the knowledge, skills and abilities that were addressed in the previous patient educational activity. For example, barriers to learning may have negatively impacted the success of this previous education, and the knowledge or skill that was addressed in the previous education may have been forgotten. For these reasons, among others, all healthcare professionals must establish the client and family members' baseline level of knowledge in order to plan future patient educational activities that meet these needs.

Diagnoses

These diagnoses should be reviewed and integrated into the care of the client throughout the course of treatment.

Medical diagnoses reflect the specific diseases or illnesses that are currently causing the client's signs and symptoms. Medical diagnoses can include both primary medical diagnoses and any existing comorbidities. For example, clients may be admitted with the diagnosis of pulmonary embolism but they may also be affected with other disorders and diseases such as heart disease and peripheral vascular disease. Comorbidities impact on the client's current physical status, and they also alert healthcare professionals to the possibilities of complications and challenges in terms of the treatment of the client.

Medical diagnoses are based on the client's medical history, the findings of a complete and thorough physical assessment and a number of different diagnostic tests. Medical diagnoses can be definitive, or certain, when the signs and symptoms are nonspecific to a particular disorder, but instead, representative of a number of possible disorders that must be ruled out or eliminated in order for the physician to arrive at a definitive medical diagnosis.

Nursing diagnoses, on the other hand, are differentiated from medical diagnoses. The North American Nursing Diagnosis Association International (NANDA-I) is an international nursing association that develops and refines nursing diagnoses that are highly beneficial for the nursing profession. It provides a standardized, consistent communication and nursing documentation.

The Psychosocial, Spiritual, Cultural, Developmental and Functional Assessment of an Individual

Psychological Assessment

Some of the psychological data collected include things like the client's:

- *Attitude, mood, affect, thought processes and coherence*
- *Coping skills and mechanisms and their successes or failures*
- *Stress and stressors*
- *Communication patterns*

History of a chronic or acute psychological disorder, such as depression, abuse, neglect, violence, apathy, suicidal thoughts, and panic disorders

Cultural Assessment

Some of the cultural data that is collected include the person's ethnic and cultural customs, beliefs, practices and preferences. Similar to age/development status, personal preferences, personal beliefs, and religious/spiritual needs, care is modified according to the client's cultural history. More information about culture and cultural diversity will be found below.

Spiritual Assessment

Some of the data and information that is collected include the person's religious and spiritual customs, beliefs, practices and preferences. Spirituality and religiousness are different concepts.

Developmental Assessment

Developmental stages are assessed not only to determine if the client is at the expected level of development but also to modify all aspects of care, and communication, according to the client's specific needs.

Functional Assessment

Some of the specific factors and forces that impact on the client's level of functioning include the client's:

- *Overall state of health, wellness and illness including the presence of comorbidities*
- *Status of the central and peripheral nervous systems*
- *Level of cognition and level of consciousness*
- *Status of the musculoskeletal system*
- *Perceptions*
- *Level of motivation*
- *Fears*
- *Methods of coping*
- *Social, cultural and economic status*

- Age
- Level of development
- Environment

Some of the components of this assessment include the client's ability to perform the activities of daily living, the factors that have led to a functional decline, the assessment of the musculoskeletal and nervous systems and level of cognition.

Some of the tests that can be used for this assessment include the:

- *Functional Independence Measure*
- *The Get up and Go Test*
- *The Barthel Index, Klein-Bell Scale and the Assessment of Motor and Process Skills*
- *Mini Mental Status*
- *Physical Assessment*

The Physical Assessment

Physical Assessment Techniques

The four basic methods or techniques that are used for physical assessment are inspection, palpation, percussion and auscultation.

1. *Inspection*: Inspection is the purposeful and systematic visual inspection and examination of the client. Inspection is typically the first aspect of assessment when performing a total, head to toe assessment of the client.

2. *Palpation*: The palpation technique employs the sense of touch. Palpation can be categorized, or classified, as light palpation and deep palpation. Light palpation is used more often than deep palpation because deep palpation must be used with caution. The person who is performing the assessment applies the fingertips to the body to assess temperature, mobility, degree of distention, pain points, texture, position, size, symmetry, tenderness, any vibrations, pulses and the presence or absence of any abnormalities, including masses and asymmetry.

3. *Percussion*: Percussion is used to assess the size and shape of internal organs and tissue in addition to the assessment of underlying structures, in terms of its solidity, regularity/irregularity, and the presence or absence of fluid and air, for example.

    Percussion is performed by striking the client's body in order to determine what sounds and vibrations their body will produce. The two types of percussion are indirect and direct percussion.

    The five types of sounds that are elicited during percussion are flatness, resonance, hyperresonance, tympany and dullness. Flatness is normally assessed over muscles and bones; resonance is a hollow sound that is heard, for example, over the air filled lungs; and hyperresonance, which is a booming sound that is heard over abnormal lung tissue, as occurs among clients with chronic obstructive pulmonary disease (COPD). Lastly, tympany is heard over the stomach with air as a drum like sound; and dullness is normally heard over solid organs, such as the spleen, heart and liver. It is a thud like sound.

4. *Auscultation*: is performed by using a stethoscope, the person who is performing the assessment listens to the sounds that are produced in the body. The four types of sound that are auscultated are pitch, duration, intensity and quality.

    Pitch is the frequency of vibrations. The pitch can be high pitched or low pitched. Duration is the length of time from the beginning to the end of the sound; and intensity is characterized along a continuum from softness to loudness. Lastly, subjective sound characteristics can include such things as irregularity, regularity, grating, booming and other characteristics.

A thorough physical assessment can be done with the following components:

- *General survey*
- *Vital signs*
- *Oxygen saturation*
- *The integumentary system assessment*
- *The assessment of the head*
- *The assessment of the neck*
- *The assessment of the thorax and lungs*
- *Lung sounds*
- *The assessment of the cardiovascular system*
- *Heart sounds*
- *The assessment of the peripheral vascular system*
- *The assessment of the breast and axillae*
- *The assessment of the abdomen*
- *The assessment of the musculoskeletal system*
- *The assessment of the neurological system*
- *The assessment of the male and female genitalia and inguinal lymph nodes*
- *The assessment of the rectum and anus*

The General Survey

The general survey is an overall look at the client, their appearance and general state of health. Some of the components of this general survey are not done for the neonate and infant. For example, gait and balance are assessed only among young children, children, adolescents and adults. Some of the things that the person who is performing the assessments assesses as part of the general survey include:

- *Weight, height and body build*
- *Posture, gait, and balance*
- *Hygiene and grooming*
- *The person's actual age as compared to their appearance and how old they appear*
- *Oral and bodily odors*
- *Signs of distress and/or obvious signs of illness or deformity, such as dyspnea, swelling and reddened skin*

Vital Signs

The vital signs include the assessment of the pulse, body temperature, respirations, blood pressure and oxygen saturation, which is the newest of all the vital signs.

Pulses

Pulse can be assessed at a number of sites including the apical area, using a stethoscope, near the radius, the temporal area of the head, the carotid area of the neck, in the groin area (femoral), the lower legs behind the knee (popliteal), on the inner aspect of the arm in the brachial area, on the front of the foot (dorsalis pedis) and near the ankle (posterior tibial), using the index and middle fingers.

Pulses are assessed for rate, volume, intensity, rhythm, and bilateral equality. The parameters of a normal pulse for an adult are from 80 to 100 beats per minute. Infants and children have different "normal" parameters.

Temperature

Bodily temperature results from the differences between heat production and heat losses. The normal oral bodily temperature is 98.6 degrees F, or 36.7 to 37 degrees centigrade. Temperature can be taken at a number of sites including the mouth, rectum, ear and axillae.

The oral route is contraindicated among unconscious and uncooperative patients, infants, and small children. The ear is the preferred site for infants and young children. The rectal route is contraindicated when a client is affected with a seizure disorder, heart disease or any kind of rectal disorder.

Respirations

Respiratory rate is the only vital sign that humans have some conscious control over, at least until the point when carbon dioxide builds up in the body and one is forced to breathe.

Respirations are assessed, and documented, in terms of rate, regularity, depth and quality, which can include some assessment findings like stridor, dyspnea, and shortness of breath. An increased respiratory rate can occur as the result of fear, anxiety, pain, acidosis and a fever; a decreased respiratory rate can result from alkalosis, sedation, central nervous system depression and a coma.

Normal and abnormal breath signs are discussed below under the section entitled "Assessment of the Thorax and Lungs".

Blood Pressure

Blood pressure results from the pressure of the blood flow as it moves through the arteries. The systolic blood pressure indicates the amount of pressure exerted on the arteries during the heart's contractions; and the diastolic blood pressure indicates the pressure exerted on the arteries when the heart is at rest. Blood pressure is most often measured over the upper arm just above the antecubital space although it can also be measured on other sites such as the legs.

Pulse pressure is defined as the mathematical difference between the systolic and diastolic blood pressures. For example, a client who has a systolic blood pressure of 197 and a diastolic blood pressure of 110 has a pulse pressure of 87.

Oxygen Saturation

Oxygen saturation reflects the amount of oxygen saturation in arterial blood. It is measured by placing a sensor on the person's finger. At times, the forehead, nose, or ear can be used for these measurements.

The Assessment of the Integumentary System

The integumentary consists of the hair, skin, fingernails and toenails.

- *The hair is inspected and thoroughly assessed in terms of distribution, amount, the presence of any alopecia or baldness, hair thickness, and the presence of any abnormalities like an infestation or infection.*
- *The Nails are assessed in terms of texture, blanching and shape (curvature and angle). The skin around the nails is also observed, as well as the color of the nail beds.*
- *The skin is assessed with inspection and palpation and the components of this assessment include the skin's color, moisture, turgor, temperature, and the presence of any edema and/or skin lesions.*

The Assessment of the Head

The assessment of the head consists of the following assessments:

- *Face and Skull*
- *The face and facial expressions are inspected for abnormalities and a lack of symmetry as can occur with neurological damage, such as that which occurs with a cerebrovascular accident.*
- *The skull is assessed for shape, size and symmetry, and the presence or absence of any tenderness, nodules, or depressions are also noted.*
- *Nose and Sinuses*
- *The external nose is assessed for its size, shape, color, symmetry and the presence of any nasal flaring and/or discharge. The interior nasal passages are assessed for intactness and patency, the presence of any masses, and any abnormalities of the cartilaginous and/or bone tissue. The frontal and maxillary sinuses are assessed for any tenderness.*
- *Eyes and Vision*
- *The person who is performing the assessment assesses the conjunctiva, the lacrimal glands and ducts, the clarity of the corneas, the eyelashes, eyebrows, eyebrow movement, eye movement, blinking, and the pupils for color, shape, size, symmetry of size, accommodation and reactions to light. Visual acuity is assessed using the Snellen chart.*
- *The eyes are also inspected for any signs of infection and irritation, such as discharge and redness, hollowness, and abnormalities, such as a sunken or protruding appearance.*
- *Pupil reflexes and their assessment are fully discussed below under the section entitled "Reflexes".*
- *Ears and Hearing*
- *The ear structures and the sense of hearing are assessed with this portion of the physical assessment. The ear lobes, or auricles, are assessed in terms of symmetry, texture, position, color, elasticity and any areas of tenderness. The tympanic membrane is examined for intactness and color. The external ear canal is assessed in terms of the amount of cerumen, and the presence of any blood, pus, abnormal structures and/or lesions.*
- *In order to test for gross hearing, the client is asked to listen and respond by telling if they hear both whispered and normal words.*
  Bone conduction is assessed using Weber's test. The Rinne test compares air conduction to the bone conduction. A tuning fork is needed to perform these two tests.

- *Mouth and Throat*

    The lips are assessed for color, texture and symmetry; missing loose and damaged teeth are noted; the gums are assessed for color and the presence of any sores or other lesions; the cheeks, or buccal membranes, and the inner lips are assessed for in terms of moisture, and the presence or the absence of any lesions.

The color, movement, and the presence of any lesions are assessed on the tongue and all of its surfaces. In order to perform this assessment, the client sticks their tongue out while the person who is performing the assessment pulls it forward using a dry gauze pad.

The soft and hard palates are assessed for color, texture and the presence of any lesions; the salivary glands are examined for any swelling or redness; and the uvula is assessed for position, movement and color. Lastly, the gag reflex is checked and the tonsils and oropharynx are assessed for size, color and the presence of any lesions or swelling while using a penlight and tongue blade.

The Assessment of the Neck

During this phase of a complete physical assessment, the following are assessed:

- *Thyroid gland*
- *This butterfly shaped gland is inspected for symmetry, movement during swallowing, and the presence of any lesions or masses. The thyroid gland is auscultated for bruits and it is additionally palpated in order to determine its size and smoothness.*
- *Neck muscles*
- *The neck muscles are assessed by observing head movements, muscular strength, and observing for the presence of any swelling or masses.*
- *Lymph nodes*
- *The entire neck area is palpated for any lymph node swelling.*
- *Trachea*
- *Any deviation of the trachea from normal centrality of position is noted.*

The Assessment of the Thorax and Lungs

The person who is performing the assessment assesses the thorax and lungs, including the lateral, posterior and anterior thorax, during this phase of the physical assessment. The lateral, posterior and anterior thoraxes are inspected for size, shape, symmetry, and any signs of spinal misalignment and abnormality. The posterior chest is palpated for fremitus and respiratory excursion; the thorax is percussed, using a zigzag pattern; diaphragmatic movement is visually assessed and the lungs are auscultated for breath sounds, as discussed below.

Lung and Breath Sounds

Go to the below link:

http://www.easyauscultation.com/lung-sounds.aspx?gclid=CNmq3u3ru60CFRAq7AodSwJtA Q

Then go into Basic Sounds, read each Description and listen to each Waveform, as listed below:

1 *Vesicular - Normal*

2 *Crackles - Fine (Rales)*

3 *Crackles - Coarse (Rales)*

4 *Wheeze*

5 *Rhonchi - Low Pitched Wheezes*

6 *Bronchial*

7 *Pleural Rubs*

8 *Bronchovesicular*

Now, go back to this site, http://www.easyauscultation.com/lungsounds.aspx?gclid=CNmq3u3ru60CFRAq7AodSwJtAQ

Then, enter Intermediate Sounds, read the Description and listed to each Waveform, as listed below:

1 *Vesicular - Diminished*

2 *Bronchophony - Healthy*

3 *Bronchophony - Abnormal*

4 *Egophony - e*

5 *Egophony - a*

6 *Whispered Pectoriloquy - Healthy*

7 *Whispered Pectoriloquy - Abnormal*

8 *Wheeze - Expiratory*

9 *Wheeze - Monophonic*

10 *Wheeze - Polyphonic*

11 *Crackles - Early Inspiratory (Rales)*

12 *Crackles - Late Inspiratory (Rales)*

13 *Stridor*

The normal breath sounds are:

- *Bronchovesicular breath sounds*
- *Bronchovesicular breath sounds are heard during both inspiration and expiration between the scapulae and between the 1st and 2nd intercostal spaces.*
- *Vesicular breath sounds*
- *These sounds are typically best heard during inspiration over the base of the lungs or over the peripheral lung area.*

The abnormal, or adventitious, breath sounds are:

- *Tubular or bronchial breath sounds*
- *Tubular, or bronchial, breath sounds have a shorter inspiratory phase than expiratory phase. They are louder than vesicular sounds and it is NOT normal to hear these sounds over normal lung tissue.*
- *Wheezing*
- *Wheezes are squeaky, high-pitched breath sounds that are most typically heard during expiration and they can be heard over all lung fields. Coughing does not diminish or decrease wheezing like it does with rhonchi. Tumors and other forms of enlargement, such as occurs with swelling, create secretions that can lead to these adventitious breath sounds.*
- *Rales or crackles*
- *Rales, or crackles, are most often heard over the bases of the lungs. This sound is similar to the sound that can be created by rolling a small amount of hair next to your ear. They are fine and short, crackling sounds that are produced when fluid or mucus is present in a lung passage.*
- *Friction rub sounds*
- *Friction rub sounds are grating sounds. They occur when the pleural surfaces are inflamed and rub together. These sounds can be heard during both the inspiratory*

and expiratory phases of respiration and are most often over the lateral or lower anterior chest. These sounds can indicate that an infection affecting the heart.
- *Gurgles or rhonchi*
- *These sounds are harsh, low pitched and gurgling in nature. They are produced when airways are narrowed by such abnormalities as tumors, swelling, or secretions. They are heard most often over the trachea and the bronchi. Gurgles can be diminished when the client coughs.*
- *Stridor*
- *Stridor can be heard as a squeaking, high pitched sound upon inspiration. It closely mimics the sound of wheezing so the person performing the assessment should place the stethoscope over the neck and listen. It is most likely stridor, rather than wheezing, when the sound is louder over the neck area. Stridor results from a large upper respiratory airway obstruction.*
-

The Assessment of the Cardiovascular System

Cardiovascular assessment, in addition to the vital signs discussed above, includes:

- *Inspection*
- *Auscultation*
- *Palpation*
-

Heart Sounds and Murmurs

Heart sounds occur as the result of the heart valves opening and closing. Heart sounds are classified and characterized as systolic heart sounds and diastolic heart sounds.

The systolic heart sounds are:

- *S1 or the first heart sound*
- *Clicks*
- *S1 in combination with S2, which is a diastolic heart sound, are the normal heart sounds that we hear as "lub dub."*
- *S1 begins when systole begins and it results from primarily mitral valve closure, but it can occur to a lesser extent by the tricuspid valve closure. This heart sound may be high pitched and split; however, when it is loud, it can indicate mitral stenosis; and it can be absent or soft sounding with mitral regurgitation. It is also asynchronous normally because left ventricular systole occurs slightly before right ventricular systole.*
Clicks are only heard during systole and at different phases of systole. They can be singular or multiple and they are differentiated from S1 and S2 heart sounds with their briefer duration and higher pitch than the S1 and S2 heart sounds.

Congenital pulmonic and aortic stenosis as well as severe pulmonary hypertension is marked with clicks at the very beginning of S1, and it is believed that these clicks occur as the result of ventricular wall tension that is not normal. Clicks that occur during the middle or later phases of systole are heard among clients affected with tricuspid or mitral valve prolapsed, and it is believed that these clicks occur as the result of abnormally high tension against valve leaflets or an elongated chordae tendinae.

The diastolic heart sounds are:

- *S2*
- *S3*
- *S4*
- *Diastolic knocks*
- *Mitral valve sounds*
- *Diastolic heart sounds are of lower pitch, softer and longer in duration than the systolic heart sounds. All of these heart sounds are not normal with the exception of S2 and a sometimes present S3 during and among some clients less than 40 years of age.*
- *S2, which begins at the beginning of diastole, is heard when the pulmonic and aortic valves close; the aortic valve typically closes prior to the closure of the pulmonic valve closure with the exception of occasions where the aortic valve closes late or the pulmonic valve closes early. The former often occurs with the presence of aortic stenosis or left bundle branch block cardiac arrhythmia; the latter often occurs when the client is affected with a pre-excitation disorder, which is a condition where the ventricles of the heart become depolarized too early, which leads to their partial premature contraction. Additionally, a late pulmonic valve closure can occur as the result of an increase of blood flow through the right ventricle, as occurs with an atrial septal defect, or complete right bundle branch block.*
- *S3, when it occurs, is heard early during diastole at the time when the heart's ventricle is dilated and not compliant. It can indicate serious abnormal ventricular functioning among adult clients, and it can be normal among pregnant women, some children and adults up to about 40 years of age.*
Right ventricular problems are signaled when the S3 heart sound is heard best and only during inspiration when the client is in the supine position; left ventricular S3 is best heard during expiration and when the client is in the left lateral decubitus position.

Similar to the S3 heart sound, the S4 heart sound is only heard or heard best using the bell of the stethoscope; it is more often auscultated than the S3 heart sound but it typically indicates less ventricular dysfunction than an S3 heart sound. The right ventricle S4 heart sound increases and the left ventricle S4 heart sound decreases during inspiration. S4 heart sounds are most typically found after a myocardial infarction and with myocardial ischemia. S4 heart sounds without any S3 heart sounds occur most often in diastolic left ventricular dysfunction; S3 heart sounds accompanied and not accompanied with S4 heart sounds are typically found among clients affected with systolic left ventricular dysfunction.

A diastolic knock, when present, occurs during the early diastolic phase. It is characterized as a thudding loud sound, which results from an abrupt cessation of ventricular filling as the result of a constricting and noncompliant pericardium.

Mitral valve opening snaps, which are heard during early diastole most often when the client is affected with mitral stenosis and, to a lesser extent, clients affected with tricuspid stenosis, are short, high pitched sounds that are best auscultated with the stethoscope's diaphragm.

An opening snap may occur in early diastole in mitral stenosis or, rarely, in tricuspid stenosis. Mitral opening snap is very high pitched, brief, and heard best with the diaphragm of the stethoscope at the left lower border of the sternum, although, at times, they can be heard at the heart's apex. The greater and more severe the mitral stenosis, the closer any opening snap will be to the pulmonic aspect of S2. Snap sounds are loudest when valve leaflets remain somewhat elastic but they progress to soft sounds and then to their disappearance when fibrosis, calcification and/or sclerosis of the valve occurs.

Murmurs

Murmurs are of longer duration than heart sounds, and they can be characterized as systolic, diastolic or continuous. They are also characterized by their location and they are graded according to their intensity as below.

- *Grade 1: Barely audible*
- *Grade 2: Soft but easily audible*
- *Grade 3: Loud but without a thrill*
- *Grade 4: Loud and with a thrill*
- *Grade 5: Loud and audible with minimal stethoscope chest contact*
- *Grade 6: Loud and audible without any stethoscope chest contact*

The timing of murmurs provides information about the cause and etiology of the murmur, as summarized in the table below.

The Timing of the Murmur	The Cause of the Murmur
A mid systolic ejection murmur	Obstruction of the aorta

	Pulmonic obstruction
	Dilation of the ascending aorta or the pulmonary artery
	Increased flow across the aortic or pulmonic valve
A mid to late systolic murmur	Papillary muscle impairment
	Mitral valve prolapse

A holosystolic murmur	A ventral septal defect
	Regurgitation of the tricuspid or mitral valve
An early diastolic regurgitant murmur	Regurgitation of the aortic valve or the mitral valve
	A congenital abnormality of the bicuspid valve with or without the presence of a ventricular septal defect
	The Tetralogy of Fallot
	A dilation of the valve ring as that which occurs with Marfan syndrome and pulmonary hypertension
A mid diastolic murmur	Mitral stenosis and/or regurgitation
	Patent ductus arteriosus

	Complete heart block
	A ventricular or atrial septal defect
	Tricuspid stenosis or regurgitation
	Atrial tumors or thrombi

A continuous heart murmur	An aortic septal defect
	Patent ductus arteriosus
	Pulmonary artery coarctation
	Multiple other causes

Pericardial friction rubs can also be auscultated during the physical assessment of the cardiopulmonary system. This high pitched, scratchy, extra heart sound occurs when the pericardial sac rubs as the heart moves during contractions. It is heard best with the stethoscope's diaphragm when the client is in an upright position and leaning forward. This sound is associated with infiltrations, infections and inflammations such as pericarditis.

Sinus Bradycardia and Sinus Tachycardia

Sinus bradycardia occurs when the SA node takes longer than normal to depolarize as the result of some parasympathetic stimulation. The duration of diastole increases while the cardiac output decreases. This arrhythmia is often found among patients affected with coronary artery disease, during a myocardial infarction, secondary to increased intracranial pressure, and the result of some medications, such as digitalis and beta-blockers.

Some of the general signs and symptoms of bradycardia are:

- *Fainting*
- *Weakness*
- *Dizziness*
- *Fatigue*
- *Shortness of breath*
- *Chest pain*
- *Confusion*

The treatment depends on the type of electrical conduction problem, the severity of symptoms, and the cause. The treatment of choice is the treatment of the underlying causal condition.

Sinus tachycardia is associated with sympathetic nervous system stimulation, such as occurs with strenuous exercise, stress, pain, hyperthyroidism, caffeine use, and a cardiovascular response to hypovolemia and hypotension.

Some of the general signs and symptoms of tachycardia are:

- *Palpitations*
- *Chest pressure or tightness*
- *Dizziness*
- *Lightheadedness*

Like sinus bradycardia, the treatment of sinus tachycardia depends on the type of electrical conduction problem, the severity of symptoms, and the cause. Treatment choices include treatment of the underlying condition.

Sinus bradycardia and sinus tachycardia both have all the features of a normal sinus rhythm other than a normal rate of from 60 to 100 beats per minute.

Atrial Flutter

Atrial flutter occurs when rapid atrial depolarization occurs. The cardiac rate may be regular or irregular. The danger of thrombosis is present but not to the extent that it can occur with atrial fibrillation.

Some of the causes of atrial flutter are heart failure, chronic pulmonary disease and right sided heart enlargement. This cardiac arrhythmia is treated with digitalis, beta-blockers, calcium channel blockers, amiodarone, and cardioversion when it is needed.

Atrial Fibrillation

Atrial fibrillation is a relatively common arrhythmia among those affected with pulmonary embolus, hypoxia, a mitral valve disorder, congestive heart disease and also among the elderly.

Cardiac output is decreased with this dysrhythmia. Emergency cardioversion may be indicated immediately after the administration of heparin or low molecular weight heparin to prevent thromboembolism.

Premature Atrial Contractions

Premature atrial contractions occur as the result of atrial cells taking over the role of the SA node. Normal QRS complexes occur but the QRS is preceded by a premature P wave. This arrhythmia can result from a number of causes including nicotine, fatigue, alcohol, digitalis, electrolyte imbalances, ischemia and hypoxia.

Paroxysmal Supraventricular Tachycardia

With this arrhythmia, the atria or the AV junction takes over the pacemaker role from the body's natural pacemaker, which is the SA node. It usually appears and disappears in a rather rapid manner.

Some of the causes of paroxysmal supraventricular tachycardia are nicotine, caffeine, alcohol, stress, electrolyte imbalances, hypoxic episodes and ischemia.

This cardiac arrhythmia is sometimes short lived and self-limiting. Simple coughing or carotid massage may readily resolve it. Other treatment interventions include adenosine intravenously and cardioversion when the client is unstable as a result of this dysrhythmia.

First-Degree Atrioventricular Block

First-degree atrioventricular block occurs when the AV node impulse is delayed, thus leading to a prolonged PR interval. The P wave is present before each QRS complex.

It is very often asymptomatic; and treatment is typically not indicated unless the client is symptomatic. However, it should be noted that first-degree atrioventricular blocks can lead to more severe types of heart block.

Second-Degree Atrioventricular Block, Type I

Second-degree atrioventricular (AV) block type I is also referred to as Wenckebach and Mobitz type I arrhythmias. This dysrhythmia is characterized with progressive delays of conduction through the AV node, which progressively lengthens the PR interval until it results in a missing QRS interval and a non-conducted P wave.

Again, treatment may not be necessary unless the client is symptomatic. Some cases may be caused by digoxin toxicity.

Second-Degree Atrioventricular Block, Type II

Second-degree AV block type II, also referred to as Mobitz type II, occurs when the AV node impulses are intermittently blocked and do not reach the heart's ventricles. Second-degree AV block type II can lead to complete heart block. Treatment includes supplemental oxygen, intravenous atropine, and a temporary pacemaker.

Complete Heart Block (Third Degree Heart Block)

Third-degree heart block, or complete AV disassociation, occurs arises when no atrial impulses reach the ventricle so a ventricular or junctional pacemaker takes over. This causes a lack of coordination between the ventricles and the atria; the ventricular and atrial rates are different and the QRS complex is wide.

Some of the risk factors associated with complete heart block are medications like beta-blockers and digoxin, a myocardial infarction, coronary heart disease, an atrial septal defect, and acute rheumatic fever.

The signs and symptoms include an altered level of consciousness, syncope and chest pain.

Emergency treatment is necessary. Cardiac failure and cardiac arrest can occur as the result of this cardiac arrhythmia. Cardiac pacing should be immediately started and preparation for basic and advanced life support should begin.

Premature Ventricular Contractions

Premature ventricular contractions are also referred to as extrasystole, premature ventricular complexes, and premature ventricular ectopic beats. It is a life-threatening emergency.

Ventricular irritability causes abnormal impulses from an ectopic area in the ventricle. This life threatening arrhythmia can be caused by electrolyte imbalances, acidosis, hypoxia, ischemia, and digitalis toxicity.

Premature ventricular contractions can occur in isolation (single focus) or in clusters (multifocal). Multifocal patterns are called bigeminy and trigeminy, respectively. A couplet is two PVCs in succession; and a triplet is when three PVCs occur in succession.

Ventricular Tachycardia

NO cardiac impulses come from the atrium with life threatening ventricular tachycardia. This arrhythmia often leads to ventricular fibrillation and asystole unless it is immediately treated.

The QRS complex is broadened and the rate is dangerously fast and inefficient. Significant and life threatening hemodynamic compromise occurs very rapidly.

Emergency interventions include cardioversion, intravenous lidocaine and magnesium sulfate, and antiarrhymic medications, such as amiodarone.

Ventricular Fibrillation

Ventricular fibrillation occurs when there are chaotic and rapid signals from ectopic ventricular sites. All of the ventricular contractions are ineffective; therefore, no cardiac output occurs.

Death is very likely when this arrhythmia persists for more than 6 minutes.

The treatment involves immediate advanced life support, including defibrillation, intravenous adrenaline and 100% supplemental oxygen. A lack of treatment leads to asystole.

Asystole

Asystole, or a flat line, is the total and complete absence of any ventricular activity, despite the fact that atrial impulses and P waves may be present.

Immediate advanced life support is necessary. Intravenous adrenaline, sodium bicarbonate and atropine, as well as 100% oxygen are done in hopes of saving the person's life.

The Assessment of the Peripheral Vascular System

The peripheral vascular system is assessed by palpating the bilateral pulses to determine volume, equality, and other characteristics such as regularity. The carotid pulse is auscultated for bruits. The jugular veins are inspected for any signs of distention or abnormal pulsation while the patient is in the semi Fowler's position.

The peripheral veins in the legs and arms are inspected for their general condition and for any signs of tenderness, swelling, phlebitis, particularly in the lower extremities. Perfusion is assessed by inspecting the color and temperature of the skin, which assesses the adequacy of blood flow.

The Assessment of the Breast and Axillae

During this phase of the physical assessment, the person who is performing the assessment also uses the surfaces of all fingertips and palpates the lymph nodes and the breasts for any tenderness or masses.

The breast and the axillae are assessed using both palpation and inspection, among both males and females. The breasts and the areola are assessed for shape, size, contour, color, and the presence or absence of any lumps, lesions, dimpling, retraction, swelling, edema, and/or hyperpigmentation. The nipples are examined for any discharge, which is an abnormal finding unless the female is lactating.

The Assessment of the Abdomen

The abdomen is inspected for size, movement, contour, size, movement and skin integrity. Any fluid buildup, or ascites, and any aortic pulsations are abnormal. The abdomen is auscultated for the presence or absence of bowel sounds in all four of the quadrants- the upper right, upper left, lower right and lower left quadrants.

Additionally, all 4 quadrants are palpated, using light palpation initially, for any tenderness, guarding or masses. Later, deep palpation is done to determine the presence or absence of the same findings done during light palpation.

The bladder is also palpated to assess for any urinary retention.

The Assessment of the Musculoskeletal System

The muscles of the body are bilaterally assessed for size and symmetry. Contractures, tremors, weakness, paralysis, tremors, spasticity and/or flaccidity are identified and documented.

The bones, and the areas around the bones, are assessed for any swelling, tenderness and deformities. All bodily joints are inspected for full range of motion, tenderness and lesions.

The Assessment of the Neurological System

There are a number of areas of concern that are assessed as part of a complete neurological system assessment:

- *Gross motor function and balance*
- *Fine motor function for both the upper and lower extremities*
- *Temperature sensation*
- *Kinesthetic sensation*
- *Sensory function*
- *Tactile sensation*
- *Cranial nerves*
- *Reflexes*

Gross Motor Function

There are several tools and methods that can be used to accomplish this task. The Romberg test is commonly used. This test involves having the client stand with their arms to their sides while closing their eyes. Another alternative is to simply have the client walk as you are monitoring their balance, coordination, gait and gross motor movement.

Having the client stand on one foot with the eyes closed is a common test to assess the client's balance. Toe to heal and heal to toe walking can be used to assess the client's gait.

Fine Motor Function

Fine motor function of the upper extremities is assessed by observing the client's fine motor function and coordination in the hands and fingers; lower extremity fine motor function is assessed by having the client place each of their heels on the opposite shin, as close to the knee as possible, and then run the heel down the leg, while in a supine position.

Temperature Sensation

Temperature sensation is assessed by touching various areas of the body, bilaterally, using warm and cool objects.

Kinesthetic Sensation

Kinesthetic sensations allow a person to perceive their bodily positioning without the use of any visual cues. This is assessed by the person who is performing the assessment moving the client's fingers and toes in different directions while the client's eyes are closed. The client is then asked whether the digit is up, down or straight out as the person who is performing the assessment changes the positions without the help of visual cues.

Sensory Function

Using a pen, or another device, the person who is performing the assessment gently touches the surfaces of the body to determine whether or not the person is able to feel the object.

The perception of pain is also assessed as part of sensory function. For this aspect of the physical assessment, the person who is performing the assessment uses a both a sharp and a dull object to touch the client's body and to determine if the client can correctly identify a dull or a sharp object. At times, the client may feel no sensation whatsoever.

Tactile Sensation

Tactile sensation and discrimination is the person's ability to perform the following while their eyes are closed:

- *One and two point discrimination. During this phase of testing, the person who is performing the assessment touches the skin with either one or two pin pricks and the client states how many pricks they feel.*
- *Stereognosis. A familiar item like a button, a pen or a paper clip is placed in the person's hand with their eyes shut. The person who is performing the assessment then asks the person to identify the familiar object.*
- *Extinction. This test is performed by the person who is performing the assessment by simultaneously touching two symmetrical bodily areas, like both knees and both ear lobes, and asking the client if they feel one or two touches.*

The Cranial Nerves

The twelve cranial nerves can be easily remembered using this mnemonic: On Old Olympus Tippy Top, A Fat Armed German View A Hop, as below:

1. *Olfactory*

   This nerve is purely sensory; it transmits the sense of smell from the nasal cavity's olfactory foramina in the cribriform plate of the ethmoid.

2. *Optic*

   This nerve is also purely sensory. It sends or transmits visual signals from the retina of the eye to the brain. This nerve is located in the optic canal.

3. *Oculomotor*

   This nerve is primarily motor; it innervates various muscle groups which, in concert with each other, collectively perform most eye movements. It also innervates the ciliary body muscles and the sphincter papillae, which are located in the superior orbital fissure.

4. *Trochlear*

   The trochlear nerve is a motor nerve that controls the superior oblique muscle. It is located in the superior aspect of the orbital fissure and it rotates and moves the eyeballs.

5. *Trigeminal*

   This nerve is both motor and sensory. It receives stimulation from the face and it innervates the muscles of mastication, or chewing muscles.

6. *Abducens*

   This nerve is primarily motor. This cranial nerve is located in the superior orbital fissure. It innervates the lateral rectus which abducts the eye.

7. *Facial*

   This nerve is both motor and sensory. This nerve originates in the internal acoustic canal and it innervates a variety of muscles that control facial expressions, the sense of taste from the anterior portion of the tongue; and it provides secretomotor innervation to all of the salivary glands, with the exception of the parotid salivary gland and the lacrimal, or tear producing, glands.

8. *Acoustic*

   This sensory nerve, that originates in the internal acoustic canal, senses gravity, sound, and rotation. It is necessary for bodily movement and balance. The vestibular branch carries impulses for equilibrium and the cochlear branch carries impulses for hearing.

9. *Glossopharyngeal*

   This motor and sensory nerve, that is located in the jugular foramen, provides us with our sense of taste from the posterior aspect of the tongue. It provides secretomotor innervation to the parotid gland and motor signals to the stylopharyneus.

10. *Vagus*

    The vagus nerve is both motor and sensory and it is located in the jugular foramen. The vagus nerve innervates the laryngeal and pharyngeal muscles; it also provides parasympathetic activity to virtually all of the abdominal and thoracic viscera; and it controls the resonance of the voice. Swallowing disorders like dysphasia originate from a disorder of this cranial nerve.

11. *Spinal accessory*

    The spinal accessory nerve is a motor nerve that innervates the trapezius and sternocleidomastoid muscles in concert with the vagus nerve. This cranial nerve is also anatomically located in the jugular foramen.

12. *Hypoglossal*

    This motor nerve, located in the hypoglossal canal, is essential for swallowing and speech. It provides motor innervation to the tongue muscles with the exception of the palatoglossus muscle, which is innervated by other glossal muscles and the vagus cranial nerve.

Reflexes

A reflex is a muscle reaction that automatically occurs in response to a certain type of stimulus, or stimulation. Exaggerated, distorted, and absent reflexes can indicate serious nervous system pathology even before other abnormal neurological signs and symptoms appear.

When reflexes are assessed, they must be assessed bilaterally in short succession so any differences can be noted. For example, when the person who is performing the assessments assesses the plantar reflex of the right limb, the same assessment should be done for the left limb immediately thereafter.

There are two types of reflexes. Some reflexes are present at the time of birth but they disappear shortly thereafter; other reflexes are present at the time of birth and they remain active throughout the person's entire life.

Some of the most common reflexes are the:

- *Plantar reflex*
- *Biceps reflex*
- *Triceps reflex*
- *Patellar tendon reflex*
- *Calcaneal reflex*
- *Pupil reflexes*

The plantar reflex involves plantar flexion of the foot. Normally, a stroke on the foot will cause the toes to move together and curl downward. An abnormal plantar reflex, referred to as the Babinski sign, occurs when the foot dorsiflexes, and the greater, or big toe, curls upward and the other toes flare out.

The person who is performing the assessment elicits the plantar reflex by drawing the handle of a Taylor hammer, or another blunt object, along the lateral side of the client's sole, starting at the heel and ending on the ball of the foot near the big toe. A positive Babinski sign can indicate the presence of a life threatening disorder, such as deep vein thrombosis.

The biceps reflex is assessed by having the client sit with their hands resting on their legs, and the person who is performing the assessment then places their thumb on the biceps tendon while simultaneously tapping the thumb with the Taylor hammer. Similarly, the triceps reflex is elicited bilaterally by having the client sit with their hands resting on their legs as the person who is performing the assessment lightly holds the client's forearm when simultaneously tapping the triceps tendon, which is located just above the elbow.

The patellar tendon reflex, often referred to as the knee-jerk reflex, is assessed by sharply tapping or striking the patellar. The calcaneal reflex, also referred to as the ankle-jerk reflex and the Achilles reflex, is elicitedby sharply tapping the calcaneal tendon ankle with the base of a Taylor hammer.

Pupil reflexes include pupil dilation and accommodation. The mnemonic "PERLA" is useful for the assessment. PERLA stands for Pupils Equally Reactive to Light and Accommodation.

Pupil dilation is assessed while having the client in a dimly lit room. Place the edge of your hand on the bridge of the client's nose to separate each eye and its field of vision. Then bring a flashlight from the side of the face to within 5 to 10 cm of the subject's face while shining the light into each eye to assess and determine the pupils' responses to light.

Did the pupils normally constrict with the light? Did the pupils constrict equally and identically for both eyes?

Asking the patient to look into the distance and then look at an object close to their face is done to assess pupillary accommodation. The pupils normally constrict when an object is close to their face; and the pupils should normally dilate when an object is further away. Do the pupils constrict and dilate, as they should? Are the responses the same for both eyes?

Other reflexes that are present at birth and last throughout the entire lifetime include the:

- *Gag reflex: Gagging when the throat or back of the mouth is stimulated*
- *Sneeze reflex: Sneezing when the nasal passages are irritated*
- *Blinking reflex: Blinking the eyes when they are touched or when a sudden bright light appears*
- *Cough reflex: Coughing when the airway is stimulated*
- *Yawn reflex: Yawning when the body needs more oxygen*

Infant Reflexes

Infant reflexes, also referred to as primitive reflexes, are a highly important signs of nervous system development and function among infants. These primitive reflexes will normally disappear, as the child grows older. When an infant reflex remains past the expected age of disappearance, it can be a sign of brain damage and damage to the nervous system.

Some examples of these reflexes are the:

- *Sucking reflex*
- *Rooting reflex*
- *Moro or startle reflex*
- *Step reflex*
- *Tonic neck reflex*
- *Galant or truncal incurvation reflex*
- *Grasp reflex*
- *Parachute reflex*

The infant reflexes are described in the table below.

Primitive Reflexes	Description
Sucking Reflex	This reflex is linked to the rooting reflex. The infant instinctively sucks anytime something, like a finger or a nipple, touches the area around the mouth or on the roof of the mouth.
Rooting Reflex	The infant will turn toward the side that is stroked and begins to make sucking motions with the mouth.
Moro or Startle Reflex	The Moro, or startle reflex, is elicited with sudden noises and other sudden changes like environmental temperature occur. The legs and head extend while the arms jerk up and out with the palms up and thumbs flexed. Then the arms are brought together, the hands clench into fists, and the infant cries. This reflex usually, and normally, disappears in about 3 or 4 months of age.
Step Reflex	When the soles of the infant's feet touch a flat surface they will attempt to 'walk' by placing one foot in front of the other. The step or walking reflex also begins at birth and it disappears at about six to eight weeks of age.

| Tonic Neck Reflex | The tonic neck reflex occurs when you move the head of a child to the side and the arm on the side where the head is facing reaches straight away from the body with the hand partly open.

The arm on the side away from the face is flexed and the fist is clenched tightly. Turning the baby's face in the other direction reverses the position.

The tonic neck position is often described as the fencer's position because it looks like a fencer's stance. |
|---|---|
| The Galant or Truncal Incurvation Reflex | The Galant, or truncal incurvation reflex, occurs when you stroke or tap along the side of the spine while the infant lies on the stomach. The infant will twitch his or her hips toward the touch in a dance like movement. |
| The Grasp Reflex | Newborn infants have strong grasps and can almost be lifted up if both hands are grasping your fingers.

The grasp reflex is elicited when you put a finger on the infant's open palm. The hand will close around the finger. Trying to remove the finger causes the grip to tighten. |
| The Parachute Reflex | When you hold the child upright and then rotate his or her body quickly, the child will face forward as if they are falling.

The baby will extend his arms forward as if to break a fall, even though this reflex appears long before the baby walks.

The parachute reflex begins in slightly older infants than most primitive reflexes. |

The Assessment of the Male and Female Genitalia and Inguinal Lymph Nodes

For both genders, the person who is performing the assessment assesses the inguinal lymph nodes, the skin around the pubic hair for any swelling, infection, inflammation and/or infestation, and they assess the pubic hair for characteristics, amount and distribution.

For the male, the person who is performing the assessment also assesses the penis, urethral meatus, and the scrotum. These genitalia are examined for swelling, any signs of inflammation, tenderness and any discharge. When the person who is performing the assessment assesses the female, the person who is performing the assessment separates the labia, examines the skin, the clitoris, the vagina and the urethral opening.

The Assessment of the Rectum and Anus

The anal sphincter is palpated to determine tone, masses, tenderness or nodules with a finger of a gloved hand. The glove is then examined for any signs of obvious blood.

Anatomy and physiology of skin structures

The anatomy and physiology of the skin structures are as follows:

- *The epidermis*

    The outer avascular layer of skin, which is composed of stratified squamous epithelial cells or keratinocytes, and it regenerates every 4-6 weeks. The epidermis is made up of four to five layers, which include the following:

    - *Stratum corneum or cornified layer*

        This outer layer is flattened dead keratinized cells or corneocytes, which provide a waterproof barrier against microorganisms and injury. It is made up of ten to thirty layers, of which the palms of the hands and the soles of the feet have the most layers.

    - *Stratum lucidum or clear/translucent layer*

        This layer is one to five translucent cells, which are thick and found in the palms and soles of the feet where the skin is thicker.

    - *Stratum granulosum or granular layer*

        This layer is one to five cells thick and contains keratinocytes with granules that contain proteins.

    - *Stratum spinosum or spinous layer*

        These prickly layers contain spiny desmosomes that join cube-like cells in multiple layers, and provide structure and support.

    - *Stratum germinativum/stratum basale or basal/germinal layer*

The basal layer contains melanocytes, which provide pigmentation and protection from sunlight. It is one layer of active undifferentiated basal cells, which is attached to a basement membrane zone beneath it. Cells ascend into the stratum spinosum and become keratinocytes. It can take 2-3 weeks for a cell to leave the basal layer and move upward to the stratum corneum, replenishing the various layers.

- *The basement membrane zone*

    This is the junction of the epidermis and dermis, and it provides support for those cells that are above it. This zone is made up of two layers, which include:

    1. *Lamina lucida or because of translucent electrons contains glycoprotein laminin*
    2. *Lamina densa or because of dense electrons comprises type IV collagen*

- *The lamina reticularis*

    This is found between the basement membrane and the underlying connective tissue, which is the bottom portion, and it serves as the interface between them. It is synthesized by cells in connective tissues beneath and contains fibronectin. It contains Type I, II, III and sometimes IV collagen.

- *The anchoring structures*

    The anchoring structures are made up of hemidesmosomes, which attach anchoring filaments and fibrils, by the basal keratocytes.

- *The dermis*

    This layer is located beneath the epidermis and basement membrane zone. The dermis contains nerves, sebaceous glands, sweat glands, hair follicles as well as lymphatic vessels, veins and arteries. The proteins of this layer, collagen and elastin are produced by fibroblasts. A protein substance, known as ground substance is found in the area between these. The dermis also contains mast cells, macrophages and lymphocytes, which are all involved in the immune system of the skin. There are two areas of the dermis, they include the following:

    - *Papillary dermis*

- Blood flow is regulated in the papillary dermis and it also contains sensory nerve endings. The vascular networks that support the epidermis with oxygen and nutrients *are also found here.*

- *Reticular dermis*

This layer contains blood vessels, hair follicles and glands. It is also made up of connective tissue with collagen and elastic fibers that provides elasticity and strength to the skin.

- *The hypodermis comprises*

  This is a layer of subcutaneous tissue below the dermis, which provides vasculature, cushioning, and insulation.

Primary functions of the skin

The primary functions of the skin include the following:

- *Immunity*

  The skin promotes tissue repair and wound healing, the immune system along with the Langerhans cells protect the skin, and the mast cells and macrophages destroy pathogenic microorganisms

- *Sensation*

  The skin contains nerve endings which allow for a number of sensations including tactile sensations and the sense of heat and cold.

- *Metabolism*

  Ultraviolet rays convert 7-dehydrocholesterol to cholecalciferol (one of the D vitamins); Vitamin D is then transmitted to other parts of the body, following it blending within the skin; calcium and phosphate are metabolized as well, and all of those are vital for our existence, health and healing

- *Appearance*

  Our skin is what is shown and seen by others therefore the care of skin is very important

- *Thermoregulation*

- *Protection*

  The skin is our first line of defense against the environment. It protects against microorganisms, chemicals and it serves as a barrier against moisture and other environmental contents.

Wound Care

This section reviews factors that affect the healing process, including end of life issues, comorbidities, age, medications, differential essential, etc. The different assessments and how they affect wound care and healing are discussed as well. Factors affecting the care of patients and the overall wound care processes and interactions.

Factors Affecting Healing

End of Life Issues

Like so many biological events, death is a process. The perideath experience consists of the preparation for death, the death itself and the third phase which is after death. The nurses play an important role in all three of these phases of perideath.

Some of the signs and symptoms that occur during phase 1, the preparation for death, impact on the client's skin and also on urinary and fecal continence include:

- *Bodily coolness*
- *Excessive sleeping*
- *Decreases of food and fluids*
- *Incontinence*
- *Congestion*
- *Changes in breathing patterns, including Cheyne-Stokes respirations*
- *Disorientation*
- *Restlessness*
- *Withdrawal*
- *Vision like experiences*
- *Letting go*
- *Saying goodbye*

Skin care goals are focused on prevention and healing of wounds, but when the patient is nearing the end of their life, there are other factors and patient care needs that also have to be considered and addressed. These end-of-life issues, such as hospice care, advance directives, and the best interest of the patient, have to be addressed on a case-by-case basis.

If a patient is being cared for in a hospice setting, whether it be in their home or in a residential facility, they are treated with palliative care, however, curative wound care continues to be provided in order to increase the client's comfort and to decrease associated pain in many cases.

When a patient is competent to make decisions whether or not to refuse treatment as well as making advanced directives, the Patient Self-determination Act allows them to do so. It can at times be a difficult decision when it comes to wound care. As a patient's health deteriorates, they are prone to pressure sores; therefore it is vital to make sure that patients are turned frequently to avoid any added pain or discomfort.

Trivium Test Prep

Some of the legal and ethical issues that impact client care at the end of life include health care proxy, advanced and informed consent.

Guardianship and Health Care Proxy

Guardianship is the legal process with which another person makes decisions for a person who is not competent to make sound decisions on his or her own, as previously discussed.

Advance Directives and Living Wills

Advanced directives and living wills contain the wishes of the client in terms of treatments and interventions that the client does and does not want to be carried out when the client is no longer able to competently provide these consents and rejections of treatment. For example, a young male person with no history of disease may elect to NOT have CPR or a ventilator in the event of sudden death. Another client with cancer may choose to have tube feedings but no IVs in the advanced directive.

Informed Consent

All clients have the legal right to accept or reject all treatments and interventions. Patients must be fully informed and knowledgeable about the risks, benefits, and alternatives for all interventions and aspects of care. The client will then consent to, or reject, the treatment. Parents will consent for their minor child; a legally appointed guardian or health care proxy will consent when the client is not competent to do so.

Cultural Diversity

Some of the cultural data that is collected include the person's ethnic and cultural customs, beliefs, practices and preferences. Similar to age/development status, personal preferences, personal beliefs, and religious/spiritual needs, care is modified according to the client's cultural history.

Culture is a set of established beliefs held by a certain group of people that has been handed down from generation to generation. Other definitions relating to culture are below.

- *Race – a group of people that share one or more biologically distinct physical features, or characteristics, such as skin color*
- *Ethnocentricity – an intolerance of other cultures and ethnic groups other than one's own.*
- *Acculturation - the adaptation to most or all of the values, beliefs and behaviors of another culture*
- *Cultural Competence – the knowledge and skills necessary to care for and modify the care of people and groups of diverse cultures*
- *Cultural Awareness – the reflective exploration of one's own values and beliefs and how they influence others of a different culture*
- *Cultural Blindness – a lack of a person's ability to understand and recognize the fact that others hold different cultural values, beliefs and practices than one self*

- *Cultural Humility – self awareness of one's own biases and prejudices.*
- *Culture bound syndromes – illnesses and disorders recognized by various cultures that are not present in the professional literature*
- *Prejudice – judging people based on their belonging to a particular group without regard for the individual as a unique being*
- *Xenophobia – fear of those that are different from a different culture, race, religion, etc.*
- *Values – beliefs about the relative worth and importance of something like health*
- *Stereotyping – seeing groups of people as a category rather than individuals*

Culturally sensitive care, according to Leininger's Transcultural Nursing theory, enables the nurse to:

- *Have respect of diversity*
- *Welcome human diversity*
- *Apply cultural client assessments and understand the impact that these cultural assessments have on wellness, illness, suffering and death*
- *View the client as a whole person rather than viewing the patient as simply a set of symptoms or an illness*
- *Apply cultural assessments to the individualized plan of care*

- Madeleine Leininger's theory supports three nursing modes of intervention necessary in order for nurses to care for clients with diverse cultures. These nursing modes are:

- *Cultural care accommodation, negotiation or both*
- *Cultural preservation and maintenance*
- *Cultural care repatterning and restructuring*

Leininger's Modes of Culturally Competent Care: The Transcultural Nursing Model	
Preservation	Supporting and maintaining the client's cultural preferences and resources to prevent illness and to promote health and wellness

Example:

The nurse assesses traditional dietary values, beliefs and practices and then modifies the client's diet accordingly. |

Accommodation	Nursing care is modified, adapted or adjusted to meet the needs of the client in respect to their cultural beliefs and practices.

Example:

Chinese clients are encouraged to breast feed and then bottle feed the neonate after birth because this culture does not believe that colostrum has enough nutritional value for the neonate. |

Re-patterning	The attitudes and beliefs of a culture change when this change is necessary for the group to be able to function in another more dominant culture.

Example:

Health insurance reimburses for alternative and complementary treatments and therapies as a result of repatterning. |

Some of the other models that address cultural competency include the:

- BE SAFE Model
- ASKED Model
- Culturally Competent Community Care Model

Nurses collect cultural data and information from the client and family members including the person's ethnic and cultural customs, values, beliefs, practices and preferences.

Social and cultural characteristics directly and indirectly impact health and how we deliver healthcare services. For example, cultural and ethnical dietary preferences high in calories and fats may lead to adverse heart disease, and a cultural preference for fruits and vegetables leads to positive outcomes in terms of health. An indirect effect, like a physiological disease or disorder, can result from a cultural belief in internal forces like yin and yang and not poor lifestyle choices, for example.

Some of these cultural factors assessed and accommodated for are cultural values, beliefs and practices, social networks and support, biological and psychosocial factors, interpersonal relations, sexuality, reproduction, birth control, perceptions of health and illness, biological considerations such as genetics, psychological considerations such attitudes about change, extrinsic factors like interpersonal relationships, behavioral factors such as consumption patterns and sociocultural factors such as language and methods of communication.

Normal Changes of the Aging Process: The Integumentary and Other Bodily Systems

Some of the normal skin changes associated with the aging process are:

- *The skin becomes more fragile. Skin tears may happen.*
- *The skin loses turgor and elasticity.*
- *Rashes are more common. Contact with some soaps and "make up" can lead to rashes.*
- *The skin may become paler. The person may be more prone to bad sunburn.*
- *"Age spots" or "liver spots" may appear.*
- *Skin tags may appear, mostly on the neck.*
- *The skin may become thinner. Wrinkles appear.*
- *Dry skin may occur.*
- *The hair gets gray and faded.*
- *Hair thins on the head, under the arms and in the pubic area.*
- *Nose and ear hair becomes thicker and more visible.*
- *Facial hair for women may appear.*
- *Finger nails and toe nails get thick.*
- *The sweat glands in the skin slow down. The person may not tolerate hot rooms because their "cooling" (sweat) slows down.*

As people age their skin goes through changes. At birth the dermis layer of the skin is only sixty percent of that of an adult, and if the neonate was born premature, it is even thinner. The thickness of the dermis increases about twenty percent during adolescence, and as one ages the amount of Langerhans' cells decrease; this change can be accompanied with skin cancer and a decrease in inflammatory reactions.

With aging, vascularity and subcutaneous fat decrease; these changes interfere with thermoregulation and they lead to dryness and irritation of the skin. With solar exposure over time, the elastin in the skin degrades and the hypodermis thins, which can lead to a higher risk for pressure sores.

Exposure to the sun, which is referred to as photoaging or dermatoheliosis, is one of the most common causes of skin aging.

During the assessment, the following photoaging affects should be noted:

- *Benign lesions, such as actinic and seborrheic keratoses*
- *Malignant lesions, such as basal cell and squamous cell carcinoma*
- *Fine veins present on the face and/or ears*
- *Dry, rough, and/or wrinkled skin*
- *Skin elasticity and strength decreased*
- *Freckles and large sized brown colored maciles, known as liver spots, or solar lentigines, present on the face, and/or any other exposed areas on the upper and/or lower extremities, such as the hands, arms, legs, etc*

Other normal changes associated with the aging process include a decrease in the stroke volume and the cardiac output, a risk for hypertension secondary to atherosclerosis, diminished venous return, incompetent venous valves, a slower insulin response to glucose, decreased sensory perception, a loss of body weight and poor dentition.

Older adults are at risk for fluid and electrolyte imbalances as well, particularly if they have hypertension or heart disease and are using diuretics. Additionally, the elderly are also at risk for fluid and electrolyte alterations as the result of some of the normal changes associated with aging, such as:

- *The loss of thirst sensation*
- *Less ability of the kidneys to concentrate urine*
- *Changes in intracellular fluid and total body water*
- *Altered response to hormones that help to regulate fluid and electrolytes*
- *Less intake of food and water*

Medication dosages may be decreased somewhat among the elderly because the normal physiological changes of the aging process make this age group more susceptible to side effects, adverse drug reactions, toxicity and over dosages.

Absorption is reduced because of the decrease of small intestinal surface area and the increase of gastric acid pH. Distribution of drugs changes among the elderly as the result of decreases of serum albumin as well as total body water, in addition to increases in the percentage of the elderly person's body fat.

The renal function among the elderly is affected with diminished renal blood flow, reduced creatinine clearance, decreased drug clearance, lower renal mass and decreased glomerular and tubular functioning.

Hepatic function is also altered as the result of the normal aging process. Decreased hepatic blood flow, which results in reduced hepatic metabolism and increased concentrations of medications, as well as a smaller hepatic mass, impact the medications that this population takes.

Older adults can experience problems in urinary elimination due to the aging process. Older men can have enlarged prostate glands, which can lead to urinary incontinence and urinary retention because they may be unable to empty their entire bladder.

Older women, such as those who have already experienced menopause, can experience urgency and stress incontinence as a result of a decrease in perineal tone and support of the bladder, vagina and supporting tissues.

Medications

Some of the effects of medications, in addition to the expected and desired effects include:

- *Side effects: All medications have side effects. Unlike a therapeutic effect, a side effect of a medication is a secondary, not primary, effect of a medication. Some side effects are desirable, others are minor, and still more can be harmful and/or distressing to the client.*
- *Adverse effects: Adverse effects are the most serious of side effects. These effects can even be life threatening; they typically lead to the discontinuation of the medication.*
- *Idiosyncratic effects: An unexpected side effect of the medication that is peculiar to a particular client. For example, when a sedative makes a person agitated instead of sedated, this is an idiosyncratic effect.*
- *Anaphylactic reactions: This is the most severe and life threatening adverse reaction of all medication allergy responses. The symptoms include shortness of breath, tachycardia, hypotension and swelling of the throat and tongue.*
- *Drug toxicity: Drug toxicity is an unintended over dosage of a medication, most often due to the cumulative effect of the drug because of poor metabolism and/or excretion.*
- *Drug allergy: An antigen- antibody immunologic response to a medication. Some allergic responses are minor; others are life threatening.*
- *Drug interaction: Drugs can interact with a number of things including other prescribed drugs, over the counter drug, foods, herbs, and other natural substances.*
- *Drug tolerance: Drug tolerance occurs as the result of the repeated use of a drug like an opioid. The client needs increasing doses of the drug in order to achieve the therapeutic effect.*
- *Cumulative effects: An accumulation or buildup of the medication in the client's system as a result of impaired excretion or metabolism of the drug. It can lead to drug toxicity.*
- *Potentiating effect: A potentiating, or synergistic, effect is one that results from the combination of two or more drugs where the effects of one, or both, are increased.*

- *Inhibiting effect: The opposite of a potentiating, or synergistic, effect. An inhibiting effect is one that results from the combination of two or more drugs where the effects of one, or both, are decreased.*

The integrity of the skin can often be adversely affected by certain medications. During the assessment, the nurse assesses all of the client's medications, as discussed above. These factors can cause an allergic reaction, which can present as a rash, erythema, edema, and pruritus and it can also lead to a phototoxic reaction with which the drug can be converted into a toxin causing the patient to experience edema, pain, and pronounced erythema. Photosensitive reactions can result from thiazide diuretics and conjugated estrogens.

All medications can cause an allergic reaction, which can include a rash, urticaria, and serum sickness, particularly with amoxicillin and clavulanate. Drug allergies can also lead to life threatening anaphylactic shock, so all clients must be assessed upon admission for any drug allergies, which is also discussed earlier in the assessment section of the review.

Anaphylactic shock, a type of distributive shock, occurs when the body's immune system over reacts with systemic circulatory relaxation. Anaphylactic shock most often occurs as the result of an allergic response to a medication, such as penicillin. The signs and symptoms include massive relaxation of the blood vessels, decreased cardiac output, histamine release, a drop in blood pressure, pooling of venous blood, laryngeal edema, a rash, and a rapid bounding heart beat.

If the cause of the anaphylaxis is an IV antibiotic the IV must be immediately removed. Adrenaline or noradrenaline is also given to reduce laryngeal edema and to constrict the vasculature.

Calcium channel blockers, such as nifedipine, verapamil and diltizem, can cause erythema multiforme. Ranitidine and ciprofloxacin can cause toxic epidermal necrolysis with full thickness loss of the epidermis. Oral, topical or inhaled corticosteroids can lead to thinning of the skin and skin atrophy as the result of a loss of collagen and telangiectasia, also known as spider veins.

Conduct and interpret differential assessment to identify etiologic factors

A differential assessment of a wound should be done during the initial assessment, as it is used to rule out the wrong causes and determine the correct etiology of the wound. There are many different causes of wounds, and care and treatment rely on the knowledge of the etiology. It is pertinent that assumptions are not made and the proper differential assessment is performed.

To ensure proper treatment, it is necessary to evaluate wounds during the initial assessment to identify the etiology of the wound. There are a variety of different causes for wounds including:

- *Infection: An infection of a traumatic wound or surgical site can cause edema, pain, drainage, cellulitis, erosion of the sutures, and/or ulceration of the affected or surrounding tissue. All surgical and trauma sites must be carefully assessed and cared for, and all laboratory findings must be carefully reviewed to determine whether or not the signs and symptoms of infection are present. The signs and symptoms of infection are discussed below.*

- *Burns: Burns can be chemical or thermal and the assessment includes the depth of the burn, the percentage of the body that is burned, and the area where the burn is located. Third-degree burns are the most serious; they affect the underlying tissue, which includes nerves, muscles, and vasculture, whereas first degree burns affect only the epidermis and are superficial in nature. Second degree burns extend through the epidermis and the dermis. More information about burns will be found below.*
- *Trauma: When a trauma results in an injury the damage can vary greatly. Any degree of damage to the bone(s), tissues, organs, and circulation can result in contamination and extensive damage; therefore each trauma must be assessed and evaluated on a case-by-case basis.*
- *Diabetic Neuropathy/Ischemia: Injuries to the feet can go unnoticed with diabetic neuropathy because the client has a lack of sensation to pain. Ulcerations may also form because diabetes can cause damage to the small microcirculation vessels, thus leading to ischemia.*
- *Venous Stasis: A brown discoloration may form in the lower leg as a result of hemoglobin leaking into the tissues of that area when there is a decrease in venous circulation. Tissue is often edematous and it is most common for ulcers to form near the medial malleolus.*
- *Arterial Functioning: A decrease in pedal pulses and cool atrophic, shiny dry skin are associated with arterial insufficiency. This can cause small sized puncture type ulcers that are often seen on the dorsum of the foot.*
- *Pressure: Areas of skin over bony prominences, such as coccyx, heels, etc, can be affected by pressure sores, as a result of friction, shear or pressure. Compromise can be indicated by discolorations or texture change, therefore it is vital to carefully examine these areas. Pressure ulcers are discussed in full later in the review.*

Infections

Infection is defined as the physical invasion of a pathogenic organism that leads to an infection and an immune response by the affected individual.

The Chain of Infection

The chain of infection reflects the manner with which infections are transmitted and carried. The elements in the chain of infection include the agent, the reservoir, the environment, the mode of transmission, the portal of entry, the portal of exist and the susceptible host.

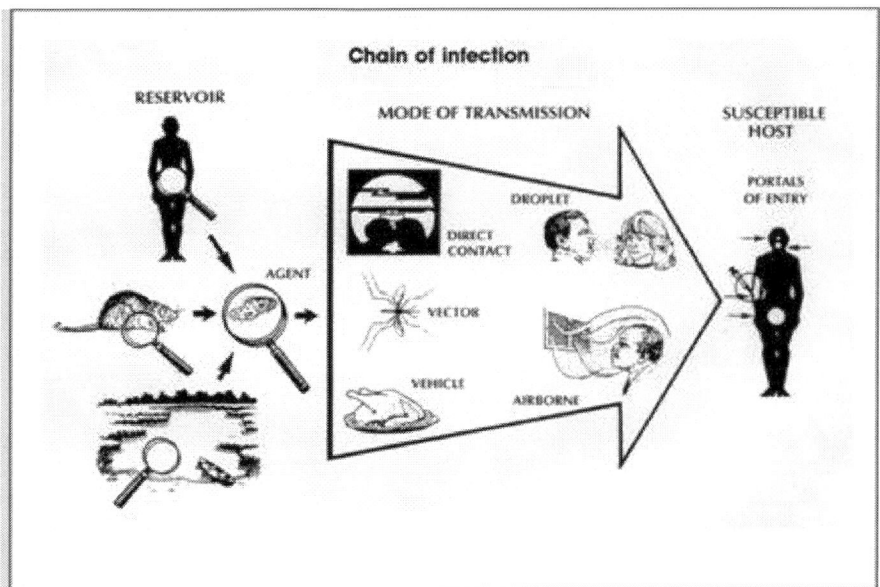

Source: Centers for Disease Control and Prevention. Principles of epidemiology, 2nd ed. Atlanta: U.S. Department of Health and Human Services; 1992.

Body Defenses against Infection

Some of the natural bodily defenses that protect humans from infection include nonspecific and specific defenses.

Some of the nonspecific defenses against infection include anatomical and physiological barriers to infection, such as the skin, and the inflammation process itself.

Some of the specific responses to infection include the immune systems' antibody mediated defenses and the cell mediated defenses or cellular immunity. Antibody mediated defenses include immunities including active immunity and passive immunity.

The Stages of Infection

The stages of infection are the incubation stage, the prodromal stages, the illness stage and the convalescence stage.

- *The incubation stage* is the stage that begins with the entry of the agent into the host and ends when the signs and symptoms of the infection begin.

- *The prodromal stage* is the stage that begins with the onset of general symptoms and ends when infection specific symptoms begin. It is during the prodromal period that the pathogen is replicating and reproducing. Some of the general symptoms that appear during the prodromal phase include malaise, joint and muscular aches and pains, anorexia, and headache.

- *The illness stage* is the period of time when specific symptoms begin and it continues until the symptoms are no longer present.

- *The convalescence stage* is the period of recovery during which time the symptoms completely disappear.

The Inflammatory Process

The inflammatory process is a naturally occurring protective response of the body when it is impacted with one of many possible causes of tissue damage. The goals of the inflammatory process are to defend against harm, to rid the body of damaged tissue and to promote the restoration of normal tissue.

The inflammatory process has five classical signs and symptoms including:

- *Pain: Pain results when chemicals are released from the damaged tissue and cells*
- *Redness: Redness occurs when the affected area's vessels vasodilate in response to the injury.*
- *Swelling: This occurs because bodily fluids go to the area of tissue damage.*
- *Heat and warmth: Because the blood flow to the area increases, the area becomes warm and hot*
- *Dysfunction of the area: Some degree of dysfunction occurs when the area is painful and edematous as the result of the inflammatory process.*

The stages of the inflammatory process include:

- *Tissue injury as the result of an infection or trauma*
- *The release of chemicals from the damaged cells, including histamine, prostaglandins and kinins, all of which facilitate vasodilation and an increased supply of blood.*
- *The migration of leukocytes, including macrophages and neutrophils, to the site of damage occurs as part of the body's natural defense mechanisms*

The Signs and Symptoms of Infection

The signs and symptoms of infection include both local and systemic signs.

- *The local signs of infection*, like the signs and symptoms of the inflammatory process, are site pain, redness, heat, swelling and a degree of local dysfunction.

- *The systemic signs and symptoms of infection* include fever, malaise, fatigue, chills, an increased respiratory and cardiac rate resulting from the fever, nausea, vomiting, anorexia, abdominal cramping and diarrhea, among other specific pathogenic signs and symptoms as based on the site of the infection. For example, respiratory infections are often characterized with a cough, dyspnea and adventitious breath sounds; urinary infections classically manifest with urinary frequency and urgency, dysuria and hematuria. Similarly, skin infections are typically marked with a rash, skin lesions and pruritis.

Some of the unusual and atypical signs of infection including confusion, incontinence and agitation can also occur. Additionally, the aging population may not present with the signs of infection until later than a younger person would because their protective inflammatory response may be decreased as a result of the aging process.

Diagnostic Testing for Infection

Some of the commonly used blood laboratory tests used for infections includes the erythrocyte sedimentation rate (ESR), C-reactive protein (CRP) and plasma viscosity (PV). All of these tests are sensitive to the increases in protein, which is a part of the inflammation process. The ESR, CRP and PV can be raised with primarily bacterial infections, abscesses and other disorders such as cancer, burns and a myocardial infarction. Some health problems like polycythemia, sickle cell anemia and heart failure can be signaled with a less than normal ESR.

The Erythrocyte Sedimentation Rate (ESR)

The erythrocyte sedimentation rate (ESR) measures the rate with which the red blood cells separate from the plasma and fall to the bottom of the test tube within a given period of time. A high erythrocyte sedimentation rate indicates the presence of infection because the proteins of infection cover the red blood cells thus causing them to fall more rapidly.

The normal erythrocyte sedimentation rate (ESR) for females is 0-20 millimeters per hour and the normal rate for males is 0-15 millimeters per hour. The normal sedimentation rate among elders can be slightly higher.

C Reactive Protein

C reactive protein sometimes referred to as the acute phase of inflammation protein, can rise as high as 1000 times normal when infection and inflammation occur. It can also rise with burns, surgery and cancer.

The normal C reactive protein is < 1.0 mg/dL or less than 10 mg/L

Plasma Viscosity

Simply stated, blood viscosity is the thickness of the blood. Some of the factors that impact on the viscosity of blood include plasma viscosity, or thickness, the hematocrit, the level of red blood cell aggregation and temperature. Higher temperatures lead to lower viscosity and lower temperatures lead to increase blood thickness and viscosity. The normal viscosity of the blood, at 37 °C, is 3×10^{-3} to 4×10^{-3}.

Cultures and Sensitivity Tests

Cultures and sensitivity testing is frequently done for a wide variety of samples, including those relating to wound infections, gastrointestinal infections, urinary tract infections and all other types of infections.

When a culture and sensitivity is indicated, as based on the client's clinical condition, the sample is microscopically examined, after which it is cultured in an appropriate medium such as a nutrient broth or agar. Cultures are useful for the identification of the microorganism, to determine whether the wound, for example, is colonized or infected and also to get a numeric values for the colony. For example, a urine specimen may have 123 colony-forming units per mL (123 cfu/mL).

Sensitivity testing entails subjecting the culture to a number of different antibiotics in order to confirm whether or not the pathogen is treatable and sensitive to specific antibiotics or it is resistant to the antibiotic, as is the case with methicillin-resistant Staphylococcus aureus (MRSA).

Specimens for microbiology, culture and sensitivity must be collected correctly and processed as soon as possible after collection because some microorganisms may not survive prolonged lengths of time before the laboratory processes them.

Urine Tests

More than 100 different tests can be done on urine. A regular, or routine, urinalysis includes the color, clarity, odor, specific gravity, pH, proteins, glucose, ketones, nitrites, leukocyte esterase and microscopic evaluation.

Bacteria can make normally clear urine cloudy. Infections can also make urine odorous, In the presence of a urinary tract infection, nitrites will be present and the leukocyte esterase will show white blood cells or leukocytes in the urine.

Microscopic analysis is done after the urine is centrifuged to render sediment for analysis. Some of the things that can be found in urine with microscopic analysis include the abnormal presence of red and/or white blood cells which indicates inflammation and infection, casts which can also indicate infection, crystals in the presence of stones, and bacteria, yeast, and/or parasites when an infection is present.

Spinal Taps

Spinal taps, also referred to as a lumbar puncture, is also done to determine if the cerebrospinal fluid is infected, as is the case with meningitis.

Normal values for cerebrospinal fluid is:

- *A pressure of 70 - 180 mm H20*
- *A colorless and clear appearance*
- *15 - 60 mg/100 mL of total protein*
- *3 - 12% of the total protein is gamma globulin*
- *50 - 80 mg/100 mL glucose*
- *0 - 5 mononuclear white blood cells*
- *No red blood cells*
- *110 - 125 mEq/L chloride*

Increased CSF pressure occurs as the result of increased intracranial pressure secondary to a head injury, for example. Protein can increase with an infection or any other inflammatory process; glucose can be decreased with infections like meningitis and tuberculosis; increased white blood cells can indicate an acute infection; and red blood cells indicate bleeding.

The Limitations and Advantages of Tests to Diagnose Infections

All tests have limitations, advantages and disadvantages. Some tests are more effective than others for specific infections. Some are more costly and invasive than others. For example, endoscopic tests are more invasive and expensive than a blood or urine test. Additionally, some tests may have false negative and false positive findings.

For these reasons, and others, diagnostic tests are a part of the diagnostic process and not the entire diagnostic process.

Burns

A first degree burn is superficial that typically heals in a couple of days without scarring but they are painful. A second degree burn is a partial thickness injury consisting of the epidermis and the upper dermis. A third degree burn injury involves all layers of the skin and the underlying tissue including the bones, muscles, nerves. Virtually every organ of the body is affected by a major burn.

A burn is considered major if it the burn covers more than 25% of the total body surface area. The rule of nines is used as a quick estimate for burn size until a more thorough assessment is done. The anterior and posterior portion of each leg is considered 9% and all other areas are areas in multiples of 9%. For example, the anterior and posterior of each arm is 4.5%. The anterior and posterior chest is 18% and the anterior and posterior of the face/skull is 4.5%.

Respiratory alterations include hyperventilation, increased oxygen demand, pulmonary edema, initial respiratory alkalosis from the hyperventilation which is often followed with respiratory acidosis associated with pulmonary insufficiency.

Hemodynamic changes include less circulating blood volume resulting in lower cardiac output and tachycardia, decreased stroke volume, hyponatremia, increased blood viscosity, vasoconstriction, initial hyperkalemia followed by hypokalemia as the potassium is depleted by fluid shifts, and inadequate tissue perfusion which can lead to acidosis, renal failure and irreversible "burn shock".

Metabolic changes are the release of catecholamines in response to burn injury, hyperglycemia because insulin levels decrease early in the burn response, a need for 3,000-5,000 calories to reverse the negative nitrogen balance and to promote a positive nitrogen balance necessary for healing and increased metabolic needs.

Fluid changes include fluid shifts out of the vascular compartment, the hematocrit rises, blood flow is impaired in the micro-circulation, compensatory mechanisms for plasma volume losses include vasoconstriction, capillary permeability increases and hypovolemic shock can occur.

Renal changes can include a decrease in renal blood flow, high output failure or oliguric renal failure, decreased creatinine clearance, decreased glomerular filtration and the release of hemoglobin and myoglobin into the urine which could result in tubular necrosis unless increased fluids are given.

Hematological changes are thrombocytopenia, impaired platelet function, decreased fibrinogen levels, diminished fibrinolysis, the inhibition of plasma clotting factors and the destruction of red blood cells which can lead to anemia.

Gastrointestinal effects include decreased peristalsis, gastric ulcers and duodenal ulcers and gastrointestinal hemorrhage.

The client may have immunological changes including decreased immunoglobulins, serum albumin, cellular immunity, lymphocytopenia and signs of the inflammatory response.

The treatments, depending on the severity and the stage of the burn, include fluids like Lactated Ringer's, silvadene skin ointment, cool compresses and hydrocortisone cream for pain and perhaps a nonsteroidal anti-inflammatory drug (NSAID). The life threatening complications of major burns include infection and shock.

Assess and Interpret Nutritional Status, and Impact on Wound Healing

Nutritional Assessment

Within the first twenty-four hours of care a nutritional assessment is done. Data is collected with the health history and physical exam. This assessment is performed to insure that all nutritional requirements are met and it includes data over the last three months in order to determine the client's nutritional pattern.

The components of this assessment include the following:

- *Weight gain or loss*
- *Presence of any pressure sores or wounds*
- *Use of prescription or non-prescription drugs*
- *Living status which includes either living independently or dependently*
- *Body Mass Index (BMI) including the mid-arm circumference and the calf circumference*
- *Mental status*
- *Mobility*
- *Feeding ability which includes independent or assisted feeding methods*
- *Fluid intake on average which should include type, amount and frequency of fluids*
- *Food intake patterns which includes the number of meals consumed daily*
- *Stress or depression related to dietary intake*
- *Number of protein, fruit, grain and vegetable servings per day*

Creating an average daily menu with the client or family member can be helpful in giving the nurse a clear picture of the patient's daily nutritional routine.

The nutritional status of a patient is essential for maintaining the integrity of the client's skin. There are several different nutritional factors that affect the skin and its health including the following:

- *Vitamin A is used to help repair the tissue of the skin*
- *Vitamin B complex, especially biotin, is a vital for skin formation and it also helps to prevent itching and dryness of the skin*
- *Vitamins C and E have been known to help to reduce counteract the negative effects that the ultraviolet rays of the sun can cause to the skin*
- *Patients who are on some restrictive diets or who do not have an adequate amount of protein in their diet will lack the amino acids for protein synthesis*
- *Patients with a diet that is too low in fats can be deficient in the essential fatty acids that the skin cells require for the lipid barrier*
- *The basic functions of metabolism that the cells carry out require carbohydrates*

Malnutrition

Malnutrition and problems with self-feeding are extremely important to detect during the assessment phase. During the physical assessment the patient may show signs of malnutrition, which can be observed. The patient should be checked for problems affecting the skin, such as ulcerations, abrasions, pressure areas, ecchymosis, poor turgor, or tears, and nail problems, such as brittle nails or spoon-shaped or pale nail bed which can be indicative of low iron.

If a patient is observed to have crippled or arthritic hands it can cause difficulty self-feeding, and vision problems can also make it difficult for a patient to both prepare and consume their food. Patients with poor gross and fine motor skills as well as poor coordination can struggle with self-feeding. The use of special utensils and plates can help.

Patients suffering from mental impairments may be unable to remember to eat, or even how to prepare their meals. In some cases, patients may experience pain when eating because they have cuts or sores in their mouth or on their lips; they may also have problems with their gums, teeth or dentures, their tongue or any other oral issue.

Risk factors for malnutrition, which can leave the patient unable or unwilling to eat, include the following:

- *Changes in taste or smell*
- *Food intolerance*
- *Lack of teeth or dentures*
- *Restrictive diets*
- *Limitations functioning that affects their ability to self feed*
- *Loss of appetite*

Other factors for malnutrition include low body weight (less than 90% of ideal body weight for their age), or low body mass index (BMI) (less than 18.5), weight loss (10% loss of normal weight or more over 3 months), malabsorption, diarrhea, vomiting, the use of immunosuppressive drugs which interfere with the absorption of nutrients, and hypermetabolism which can result from diseases like AIDS, trauma, stress, or infection.

The Height and Weight

The height of the client can be determined by using the height measurement stick on a standard hospital scale or marking the wall with a strike at the top of the person's head and then using a measuring tape or yardstick to measure the distance from the floor to the mark on the wall where the top of the client's head was.

Weight is assessed using a scale. In order to accurately determine weight loss and weight gain, the client should be weighed at the same time of the day and wearing the same amount of clothing. When a drastic weight gain occurs, it is possible that the diabetic client is retaining water from kidney, or renal, complications rather than gaining body weight.

Failure to Thrive and Malabsorption

Failure to Thrive

Some symptoms of failure to thrive include avoiding eye contact, irritability, loss of interest in their surroundings and not reaching the developmental milestones, such as sitting up, crawling, walking, talking etc. among infants and children.

There are many reasons why one can suffer from failure to thrive, and they include the following:

- *Social factors like caregiver neglect*
- *Gastrointestinal problems, which include gastroesophageal reflux disease (GERD), chronic diarrhea, cystic fibrosis, chronic liver disease,, and celiac disease*
- *Chronic illness or an acute medical disorder, which can include different types of cancers or other serious diseases*
- *Infections, which include parasites, urinary tract infections, tuberculosis can force the body to expend excessive amounts of energy and also can cause a loss of appetite*
- *Metabolic disorders, which can limit the ability of the body to make use of all of the calories it ingests because of an inability to break down foods into energy.*

Treatment

The treatment for the failure to thrive depends on the underlying cause of this disorder. For example, a child who is experiencing difficulties feeding, such as problems with breastfeeding latching, a nursing coach can be helpful, as can an occupational and speech therapist, as they can help the mother and child with sucking and/or swallowing problems, because of their expertise in the muscular control that is necessary for eating. If the failure to thrive is due to a disease or disorder, it may be necessary to consult with a specialist, such as a cardiologist, neurologist, gastroenterologist etc.

When the failure to thrive is related to a caregivers neglect or similar issue, a social worker and, in some cases, a psychologist or other mental health professional can be involved in order to address the situation and to make sure that proper nutrients are included in the diet. High caloric foods are often recommended. More severe cases may require a feeding tube that can provide a steady amount of nutrition.

Malabsorption Disorders

If a disorder interferes with the digestion of food or if it interferes directly with the absorption of nutrients, malabsorption occurs. Disorders that prevent adequate mixing of food with digestive enzymes and acid from the stomach adversely affect digestion, as is the case when the patient has had a partial or complete gastrectomy.

Other causes include a lactase deficiency, decreased digestive enzyme production, decreased bile, increased digestive acid production and other insults to the gastrointestinal system including infections, drugs, such as cholestyramine, tetracycline, colchicine and alcohol, and disorders, such as celiac disease, Chron's disease, intestinal wall lymphoma and an inadequate supply of blood to the small intestine.

Symptoms

The most common symptom is chronic diarrhea. Steatorrhea results from the inadequate absorption of fats in the digestive tract. Explosive diarrhea, abdominal bloating and flatulence can all result from the inadequate absorption of sugars.

Deficiencies of all nutrients and selective deficiencies of minerals, fats, proteins, or sugars can be caused with malabsorption.

Weight loss, edema, dry skin, hair loss, anemia, fatigue and weakness can occur.

Body Mass Index

Simply stated, obesity occurs when the energy consumed (calories) exceed the energy expended and being underweight is the result of too few calories consumed. According to the Centers for Disease Control and Prevention, obesity and being overweight are defined as a high body mass index or BMI. The body mass index is calculated using the person's weight and height; adults with a BMI of less than 25 are not obese or overweight. A BMI of 25 to 29.9 is overweight, and adults with a BMI greater than 30 are considered obese.

The body mass index is calculated by dividing the weight of the client by the height of the client in terms of meters squared. For example, if the client weighs 70 kg, or 154 pounds, and the client is 165 cm or 1.65 m, the BMI is determined as follows.

70 divided by 1.65

70/2.72 = 25.73

This client's BMI is 25.73

Assess for pain

Pain

According to the International Association for the Study of Pain, pain is defined as "An unpleasant sensory and emotional experience associated with actual or potential tissue damage or described in terms of such damage. Pain is always subjective and is whatever the person says it is, existing whenever the person says it does. The clinician must accept the patient's report of pain"; and pain management is defined as "The use of pharmacological and non-pharmacological interventions to control the patient's identified pain. Pain management extends beyond pain relief, encompassing the patient's quality of life, ability to work productively, to enjoy recreation, to function normally in the family and society, and to die with dignity."(International Association for the Study of Pain, 2013)

Pain is a subjective, multidimensional biopsychosocial experience that only the affected person can fully and deeply describe and evaluate. Patient reports of pain are far more accurate and reliable than other pain assessments, like those related to physical and behavioral changes; client reports of pain are the most useful of all pain assessment data in terms developing an individualized and successful pain management treatment plan.

Pain is now described as the 5th vital sign because so much focus and attention is now placed on pain and pain assessment. It is now at the same level of importance as the other vital signs of pulse, respiration, blood pressure, and bodily temperature. Pain assessment has become, and should remain, a routine, ongoing part of client assessment.

Pain is all encompassing and it leads to many adverse physical, psychological, cognitive, social, and spiritual deleterious effects.

The Classifications of Pain

Pain can be classified and categorized in a number of different ways. It can be classified as nociceptive and neuropathic; it can be classified as acute and chronic; it can be classified as superficial, somatic, radicular, referred or visceral pain; it can be classified as localized or diffuse; and it can be classified as mild, moderate, and severe.

Nocicetive Pain

Nocicetive pain occurs as the result of an insult, such as a cut or broken bones, which with proper nervous system operation sends a signal to the brain that an injury has occurred. Nocicetive pain can be further categorized and classified as somatic and radicular.

Somatic pain is pain originating from deep tissue injuries like those affecting the bones and the muscles. Radicular pain, also referred to as radiculopathy, originates from the nerve roots of the spinal cord and it travels down the legs. This pain occurs with the herniation of a spinal disc.

Neuropathic Pain

Neuropathic pain, unlike nocicetive pain, occurs when the nervous system has been damaged and it is not functioning in a normal manner. The source of this type of pain cannot be readily identified and its characteristics are reported as sharp, severe, burning and spasmodic.

Central neuropathic pain occurs as the result of damage to the central nervous system, as occurs with spinal cord injuries. Peripheral neuropathic pain arises from the peripheral nervous system, as occurs with neuropathy, carpal tunnel syndrome and phantom pain after an amputation. Lastly, sympathetically mediated pain has it etiology in a pathological connection between the sympathetic nervous system and nerve pain fibers.

Acute and Chronic Pain

Pain can be classified as acute or chronic. At times, client can have both types of pain simultaneously. The treatments and management of acute and chronic pain vary and, at times, they may be difficult to distinguish from each other.

Acute pain is typically transient, self limiting and correctable. It is marked with a duration of less than 3 months, a sudden and abrupt onset, localized and identifiable locations, and signs of sympathetic hyperactivity like increased blood pressure, diaphoresis, tachycardia, adrenal hormone secretion and dilation of the pupils.

Acute pain is a predictable, physiological warning that something is wrong and this type of pain is more likely than chronic pain to be relieved completely with adequate treatment. Clients with acute pain experience anxiety, muscular tension and tightness, all of which increase the intensity of pain for the client.

Chronic pain, on the other hand, is prolonged and it can remain for extended periods of time from months to even years after the expected time of healing as well as when no healing was even needed. It may, or may not, be accompanied with physiological signs. Its intensity is more difficult to evaluate, and the pain areas are less definable than acute pain. Cancer pain, or malignant pain, which is often intractable, is an example of this type of pain. Chronic pain can also be subcategorized as nonmalignant pain. Additionally, chronic pain can be continuous or intermittent and its intensity can vary along the continuum or it can remain relatively constant over time.

There are typically no changes in vital signs because the body has adapted to the pain and, unlike acute pain, it usually cannot be completely relieved with adequate pain management. This type of pain serves no purpose in terms of warning the body that something is wrong. Chronic pain is accompanied with emotional responses, such as irritability, depression, and other changes, such as anorexia, insomnia and fatigue.

The Pain Process

The pain process consists of four phases or steps. These phases are transduction, transmission, modulation and perception.

Transduction

Simply stated, transduction is the stimulation of nociceptors. Nociceptors have unmyelinated or slightly myelinated afferent neurons and they are most frequently found in the mucous membranes and the skin, although they can also be found in some arterial walls, the viscera, joints and the bile ducts, to a lesser extent. These nociceptors respond to potentially harmful, as well as actually harmful stimuli, which can be chemical, mechanical or thermal.

These stimuli are transmitted from the peripheral nervous system to the central nervous system as an electrochemical impulse, or action potential. Examples of chemical noxious stimuli include acids, histamines, prostaglandins and bradykinin; swelling and edema are examples of mechanical stimuli (pressure); and excessive heat or cold are examples of thermal noxious stimuli.

Transmission

Transmission is the process with which pain impulses are sent, or transmitted, to the spinal cord, with two types of nervous system fibers- the slowly conducting, unmyelinated C nerve fibers and the rapidly conducting, thinly myelinated A delta fibers. Typically, C fibers transmit dull, burning, aching diffuse pain sensations; and A delta fibers transmit sharp localized pain.

The primary afferent nerve fibers enter the dorsal root of the spinal cord and they synapse in the substantia gelatinosa; the secondary afferent nerve fibers synapse in the dorsal horn of the spinal cord.

Modulation

Ekephalines are endorphin like and morphine type pentapeptides. Beta endorphins and other endorphins modulate and inhibit pain by suppressing the release of P, which is a neurotransmitting substance that is needed after synapse to produce pain.

These endorphins are located in relatively large amounts in the thalamus, brain ganglia, midbrain and the dorsal horn of the spinal cord.

Descending pathways, originating from the thalamus, mid brain, and medulla, conduct nociceptive inhibitory impulses as the fibers release serotonin, endorphins and norepinephrine presynaptically. Additionally, glycine and gamma aminobutyric, both amino acids, inhibit and suppress pain presynaptically.

Perception

Pain perception is a function of the transmission of pain stimuli from the ascending pathways to four regions of the cerebral cortex, namely, the insular cortex, the primary and secondary somatosensory cortices, and the anterior cingulate cortex. As these areas of the cerebral cortex interact with other areas of the brain, they produce the motivational-affective, motor, pain memory, cognitive and sensory discriminative dimensions of pain.

Pain is assessed with subjective and objective data. Pain is a subjective phenomenon, which cannot be empirically, or scientifically, proven to be true or false. Research indicates that subjective reports of pain, and its characteristics, are more reliable than objective, observable signs and symptoms. For example, a client's report of crushing chest pain is a more reliable indicator of pain than an observation such as crying, splinting and an inability to perform activities of daily living

Nonetheless, some of the other behavioral objective expressions of pain include the loss of appetite, loss of sleep, a lack of ability to perform activities of daily living, alterations of ambulation patterns, an inability to take deep breaths, guarding, muscular tension and rigidity, a narrowed, self centered focus of attention, and crying.

Some of the biological objective signs and symptoms of pain are increased pulse, diaphoresis, increased blood pressure, increased or decreased rate and depth of respirations, and dilation of the pupils.

Some of the questions that are asked of the client to assess pain include:

- *Describe your symptoms.*
- *When did the symptoms begin?*
- *What precipitates it?*
- *What relieves it?*
- *What makes it worse?*
- *How often does the pain occur?*
- *Where is the pain?*
- *Tell me the character (crushing, sore, etc.), intensity (on a pain scale from 0 to 10), the quality (color of the sputum, etc.), the quantity (amount of drainage, etc.) of the presenting symptom or concern.*

PQRST Method

The PQRST method of pain assessment is useful to nurses in order to insure that all pain related data is collected and assessed.

- *P: What provoked or precipitated the symptoms? What makes the pain worse or better?*
- *Q: What is the quality of the pain? Is it burning, aching, stabbing, sharp, dull, etc?*
- *R: In what region or area is the pain? Does the pain radiate to another area of the body like the jaw, arm or neck?*
- *S: What is the severity and intensity of the pain? What other symptoms occur with it?*
- *T: What triggers the pain? What makes it worse? Tell me about the timing of the pain. When did it begin? What is the duration, frequency and cause of the pain?*

Assessing the Quality of Pain

The quality of pain is described by clients using a wide variety of descriptive adjectives such as sharp, burning, throbbing, intense, miserable, piercing, pricking, shooting and crushing. Some of these descriptors can indicate a specific type of pain and the underlying etiology of the pain, and others do not. For example, burning, shooting and intermittent pain may be neuropathic in nature; and cramping, aches and pains may be musculoskeletal in terms of etiology.

The McGill Pain Questionnaire has a large number of descriptive adjectives to differentiate between neurogenic and musculoskeletal pain and it has three major classifications or descriptors. These descriptors include affective, sensory and evaluative descriptors and measures of pain intensity. For example, the descriptors of searing, hot, pricking, grueling and unbearable are used in this pain survey.

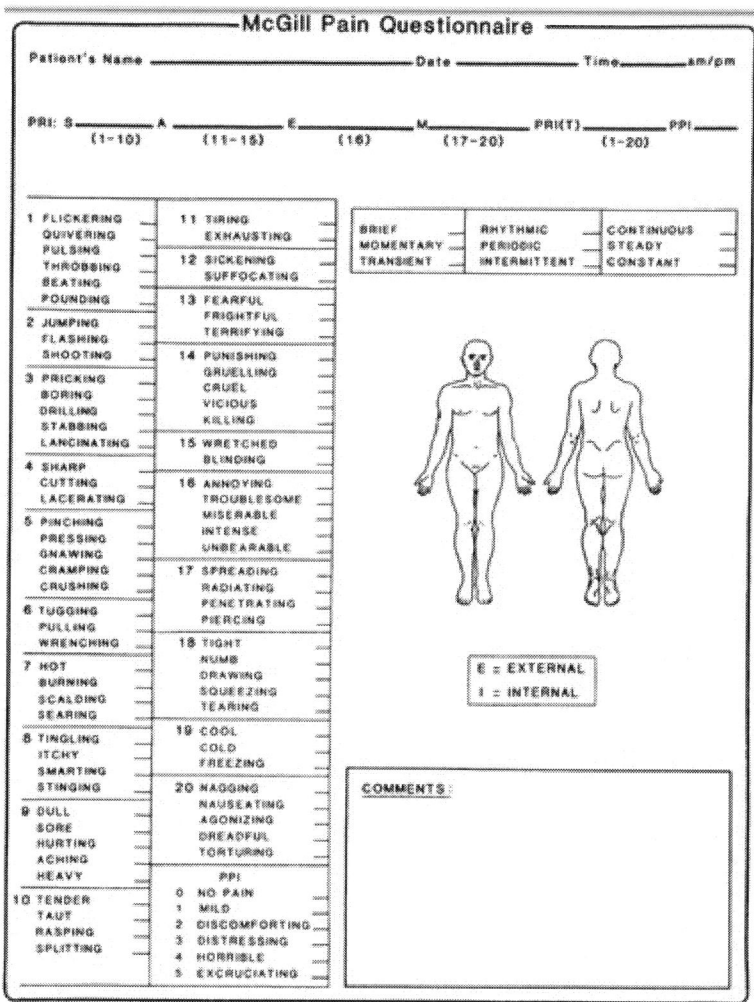

NIH/Warren Grant Magnusen Clinical Center

Assessing the Onset of Pain

Pain is also assessed in terms of its onset and when it began. For example, the client may state that the pain began an hour ago or they may state that the pain began a week ago and became progressively more severe during the week.

Assessing the Location of Pain

The location of pain is also determined. Some pain may be localized and easily identifiable by the client and other pain may be more diffuse and not amenable to determining its precise location.

Assessing the Duration of Pain

The duration of pain is the amount of time that the pain is experienced by the client. For example, the client may state that the pain lasts an hour or so.

Assessing the Radiation of Pain

At times, pain has a tendency to radiate to areas other than that of the injury. For example, cardiac pain may radiate to the shoulder, arm and jaw.

Assessing Aggravating and Alleviating Factors Relating to Pain

Pain can be precipitated and/or worsened with aggravating factors and it can be relieved and lessened with alleviating factors. For example, the nurse assesses the client to determine if physical factors, such as eating and exertion, psychological factors, such as stress and anxiety, and/or environmental factors such as humidity and cold environmental temperatures precipitate and aggravate pain; and nurses also assess the client to determine what factors relieve the pain. For example, the client may state that rest, over the counter pain medications and/or stress management techniques alleviate their pain.

Assessing the Intensity of Pain

At the current time, most nurses use a pain scale from 0 to 10 along the scale with 0 being the absence of pain and 10 being the worst possible level of pain. These 11 point scales offer nurses some consistency in their pain intensity assessments.

Other methods of pain intensity assessment for clients unable to use a numeric pain scale include a pictorial pain scale for children over three years of age and the nurse's assessment of a noncommunicative client's level of activity and functioning from 0 for no pain and 10 as intense pain that completely interferes with the client's level of functioning. These pain assessment scales are discussed below.

Assessing the Temporal Characteristics of Pain

Some studies indicate that there is a relationship between pain perception and time. It is believed that long duration pain is associated with more pain than short duration pain. It is also believed that the presence of pain impacts on one's perception of time. For example, the client's perception of time may be perceived as longer than it actually is when they are in pain.

Pain Assessment Scales

Pain assessment scales undergo the rigors of psychometric testing in terms of validity and reliability. In order for pain assessment scales, and all other scales including quality of life scales, must be psychometrically, or scientifically, valid and reliable in order to be scientific and usable in practice and research.

A tool, or scale, is considered valid when it actually measures what it is supposed to be measuring; and a measurement tool is considered reliable when it consistently and accurately measures the phenomenon despite the fact that measurement is done at different times and/or done by different people. A valid and reliable tool resists differences despite time and data collector variances. Specifically, pain assessment scales, ideally, should have the highest possible levels of validity and reliability.

In terms of validity, a pain assessment scale should measure pain and pain alone. It should not measure other extraneous or interfering variables such as other stressors.

Neonatal and Pediatric Pain Scales

The Pre-Verbal, Early Verbal Pediatric Pain Scale (PEPPS) is used to measure pain among toddlers. This scale has seven categories and the scores can range from 0 to 26. Other pain scales for the pediatric population include the Children's Hospital of Eastern Ontario Pain Scale (CHEOPS), Faces Legs Activity Cry Consolability Pain Scale (FLACC), Toddler Preschooler Postoperative Pain Scale (TPPPS), the observer Visual Analog Scale (VASobs) the Observation Scale of Behavioral Distress (OSBD), the FACES Pain Scale, the neonatal CRIES Pain Scale, the Neonatal Infant Pain Scale (NIPS) and the COMFORT Pain Scale.

Observational behavioral scales are used for children less than three years of age; and self reports of pain are used for pain assessments of children three years of age and older unless they are affected with a disorder, like a developmental disorder, or the inability to communicate their level of pain.

The Faces Pain Scale

The Faces Pain Scale contains cartoon like pictures of six faces ranging from 0, or "no hurt" to 10 which represents "the worst hurt". Most children 3 years of age and older can, typically, report their level of pain with the Faces Pain Scale.

http://www.wongbakerfaces.org/

The CRIES Pain Scale

The CRIES Pain scale has five behavioral and physical measurements that are scored from 0 to 2 and a total score of 0 to 10. Cries represents the neonate's Crying, Requires increased oxygen, Increased vital signs, Expression, and Sleepiness.

This scale is used for neonates and infants from 32 weeks of gestation to 6 months of age. It is NOT used for surgical related pain.

	DATE/TIME						
Crying - Characteristic cry of pain is high pitched. 0 – No cry or cry that is not high-pitched 1 - Cry high pitched but baby is easily consolable 2 - Cry high pitched but baby is inconsolable							
Requires O_2 for SaO_2 < 95% - Babies experiencing pain manifest decreased oxygenation. Consider other causes of hypoxemia, e.g., oversedation, atelectasis, pneumothorax) 0 – No oxygen required 1 – < 30% oxygen required 2 – > 30% oxygen required							
Increased vital signs (BP* and HR*) - Take BP last as this may awaken child making other assessments difficult 0 – Both HR and BP unchanged or less than baseline 1 – HR or BP increased but increase in < 20% of baseline 2 – HR or BP is increased > 20% over baseline.							
Expression - The facial expression most often associated with pain is a grimace. A grimace may be characterized by brow lowering, eyes squeezed shut, deepening naso-labial furrow, or open lips and mouth. 0 – No grimace present 1 – Grimace alone is present 2 – Grimace and non-cry vocalization grunt is present							
Sleepless - Scored based upon the infant's state during the hour preceding this recorded score. 0 – Child has been continuously asleep 1 – Child has awakened at frequent intervals 2 – Child has been awake constantly							
TOTAL SCORE							

NIH/Warren Grant Magnusen Clinical Center

Neonatal Infant Pain Scale (NIPS)

The Neonatal Infant Pain Scale (NIPS) rates behavioral variables as 0 or 1. 0 is the absence of a particular behavior and 1 is the presence of the behavior. The behaviors that are assessed include the infant's facial expression, crying, breathing pattern, arm movement, leg movement, state of arousal, heart rate, and oxygen saturation.

The Face, Legs, Activity, Crying, Consolability Scale (FLACC)

The Face, Legs, Activity, Crying, Consolability Scale (FLACC) can be used for infants 2 months of age and older up to 3 years of age. The FLACC Scale measures facial expressions, leg movements, overall level of activity, crying and consolability as 0, 1 or 2, with 2 as the behavioral indicators of great pain, 1 as the presence of pain behavior and 0 as the absence of the pain related behavior. A total score of 10 indicates severe pain in all categories.

Children's Hospital of Eastern Ontario Scale (CHEOPS)

The Children's Hospital of Eastern Ontario Scale (CHEOPS) pain scale is indicated for infants and children up to about 4 years of age. This scale measures pain as demonstrated by the child's cries, facial expressions, torso movement, verbalizations, touching the affected area of the body, and the positioning of the legs. Each behavior is rated from 0 to 2 with increasing intensity and a total score of 4 or more indicates the presence of pain.

		DATE/TIME					
ALERTNESS	1 - Deeply asleep 2 - Lightly asleep 3 - Drowsy 4 - Fully awake and alert 5 - Hyper alert						
CALMNESS	1 - Calm 2 - Slightly anxious 3 - Anxious 4 - Very anxious 5 - Panicky						
RESPIRATORY DISTRESS	1 - No coughing and no spontaneous respiration 2 - Spontaneous respiration with little or no response to ventilation 3 - Occasional cough or resistance to ventilation 4 - Actively breathes against ventilator or coughs regularly 5 - Fights ventilator; coughing or choking						
CRYING	1 - Quiet breathing, no crying 2 - Sobbing or gasping 3 - Moaning 4 - Crying 5 - Screaming						
PHYSICAL MOVEMENT	1 - No movement 2 - Occasional, slight movement 3 - Frequent, slight movements 4 - Vigorous movement 5 - Vigorous movements including torso and head						
MUSCLE TONE	1 - Muscles totally relaxed; no muscle tone 2 - Reduced muscle tone 3 - Normal muscle tone 4 - Increased muscle tone and flexion of fingers and toes 5 - Extreme muscle rigidity and flexion of fingers and toes						
FACIAL TENSION	1 - Facial muscles totally relaxed 2 - Facial muscle tone normal; no facial muscle tension evident 3 - Tension evident in some facial muscles 4 - Tension evident throughout facial muscles 5 - Facial muscles contorted and grimacing						
BLOOD PRESSURE (MAP) BASELINE	1 - Blood pressure below baseline 2 - Blood pressure consistently at baseline 3 - Infrequent elevations of 15% or more above baseline (1-3 during 2 minutes observation) 4 - Frequent elevations of 15% or more above baseline (> 3 during 2 minutes observation) 5 - Sustained elevations of 15% or more						
HEART RATE BASELINE	1 - Heart rate below baseline 2 - Heart rate consistently at baseline 3 - Infrequent elevations of 15% or more above baseline (1-3 during 2 minutes observation) 4 - Frequent elevations of 15% or more above baseline (> 3 during 2 minutes observation) 5 - Sustained elevations of 15% or more						
	TOTAL SCORE						

The COMFORT Scale for Pain Assessment

NIH/Warren Grant Magnusen Clinical Center

In addition to infants and young children, the COMFORT Scale can be for developmentally and cognitively impaired adults and older children as well as sedated adults who are unable to communicate their level of pain. Possible pain ratings using this scale can range from 9 to 45.

Successful pain management is not possible without a complete, accurate and timely assessment of pain and a complete pain history. This assessment should occur during the first client contact and in an ongoing manner as indicated by the client's condition. For example, some clients need a pain assessment every 1 to 2 hours and others may only need a pain reassessment every shift or every 8 hours.

Pain is assessed according to its quality, its onset, location, duration, radiation, intensity and also in terms of aggravating factors, alleviating factors and its temporal characteristics.

Some of the symptoms that often accompany pain include suffering, insomnia, anger, anxiety, depression, fear and distress.

Suffering is severe distress that results from events, like the pain experience, that threatens the person and their well being. In addition to physical symptoms, suffering entails all the person's dimensions including psychological and social dimensions. Many clients in pain and/or at the end of life experience anger and hostility. The North American Nursing Diagnosis Association (NANDA) defines anxiety as feelings of dread, discomfort, and apprehension. Anxiety leads to autonomic responses and the anticipation of danger. Fear is a feeling of dread and apprehension relating to some impending danger or threat. It can result from a real or unreal thereat, but, nonetheless, the client is adversely affected with it. Although fear and anxiety are highly similar and often occur simultaneously, they are also different. Fear is typically related to a current threat and anxiety is most often related to a future, anticipated threat. Lastly, anxiety is vaguer than fear; anxiety often arises from emotional conflict and fear is most often associated with a specific physical or psychological threat. Distress can be described as troubling feelings that can range from mild to severe and even disabling. A client can experience distress at anytime from diagnosis to the end of life. Its intensity can vary and become more severe as the client's disease or disorder progresses. It can impact on coping with even the least complex situations.

Behavioral Pain Cues along the Lifespan

Some examples of behavioral cues associated with pain perception for all age groups are discussed below.

- *Neonates and Infants*. Neonates and infants respond to pain with crying and other cues like turning away from the source of the pain.

- *Toddlers and Preschool Children*. These children begin to describe pain, its intensity and its location. They may believe that pain is a punishment and they may also respond to pain with anger, crying and blaming others.

- *The School Age Child*. This child is able to describe and identify the location of their pain in a somewhat detailed manner. They may attempt to remain brave when faced with pain and they can also regress as the result of the stressors associated with pain.

- *The Adolescent*. The adolescent may not report or relate their pain because they may feel that they should remain strong, brave and not weak.

- *Adults*. Adults may ignore and deny pain because it is viewed as a sign of weakness and they may also fear pain because of what it can mean.

- *Older Adults.* The elderly may view pain as a natural part of the aging process; they may not be as sensitive to pain as they had in the past and some of the behavioral indicators of pain among

Debunking Pain and Pain Management Myths

The consuming public has many misconceptions about pain, the pain experience, and pain management. Some believe that pain is expected during illness and hospitalization and that pain always has observable signs. Others, including nurses, may think that addiction is a major issue when clients take opioids for pain and they may also believe that one approach to pain management, rather than a multimodal approach, should be sufficient to effectively treat pain.

Still more may believe that infants, neonates and children do not experience pain and that older adults suffer pain as a normal consequence of the aging process, thus, the use of opioid pain medications are not indicated for the elders because they are too potent and powerful.

Other myths associated with pain management and addiction include:

Myth: Withdrawal, drug tolerance and physical dependence indicate addiction.

Fact: Although these responses occur with narcotics, but these responses alone do not indicate addiction.

Myth: Addiction can be accurately predicted.

Fact: It is not predictable but it can be diagnosed with established criteria, particularly among susceptible individuals.

Myth: Anxiety indicates addiction.

Fact: Anxiety and other psychological disorders exist with pain but not necessarily addiction.

Myth: Pain and anxiety medications should not be used with clients who have a substance abuse history.

Fact: Uncontrolled pain, anxiety and other emotional disorders may trigger an addiction relapse so a multimodal approach to pain should be initiated and this could consist of monitored pain medications.

Myth: Addiction is signaled when the client employs deception, stockpiling, preoccupation with the next dose and illicit substance abuse.

Fact: These clients are most often affected with pseudoaddiction, rather than addiction, and this is resolved with adequate pain relief.

Myth: Substance misuse is the same as substance abuse.

Fact: Substance misuse can occur from a variety of other factors that do not meet the established criteria of addiction and it does not indicate the need to cease opioids.

Assess and Interpret Wound Characteristics

Wound Characteristics

Wound characteristics including the wound's location, size, odor, drainage, margins, distribution, and bed tissue are assessed in an ongoing manner.

Location

While assessing the wound location, it is necessary to note the anatomic position as well as a landmark position, such as the umbilicus, sterna notch, etc. Proper medical terminology and directional terms are also used. The following are examples of directional terms:

- *Superior: Above*
- *Inferior: below*
- *Anterior: Front or towards the front*
- *Posterior: Back or towards the back*
- *Medial: Middle or towards the middle or center*
- *Lateral: Side or towards the side*
- *Proximal: Towards the center*
- *Distal: Away from the center*

Size

The size of a wound must be measured carefully in millimeters or centimeters by using a disposable ruler. Measuring a wound's depth should be performed by inserting a sterile cotton tipped applicator into the deepest part of the wound, and then marking the applicator at skin level. Once the applicator is removed, the measurement is done using a ruler from the end of the applicator that was inserted into the wound to skin level marked spot.

An association measurement, such as comparing to the size of the wound to an object like a coin, should not be used for the documentation of the wound size. Measurement includes length, width and depth of the wound. Complete accuracy is essential to wound assessments. Photographs of the wound with a ruler in place is helpful for insuring that the measurements are correct.

The dimension of a wound equals the length multiplied by the width multiplied by the depth of the wound.

Wound dimension = Wound length x wound width x wound depth

Wound dimension = 3 cm x 4 cm x 2 cm

Wound dimension = 24 cm

It is important to note that more than one measurement may be necessary, because wounds can be irregularly shaped, of different depths and widths at different parts of the wound. The correct measurement is at the part of the wound that is the greatest width and the part that is the greatest length and depth.

Odor

An assessment that is more subjective than other assessments is the odor of the wound. An odor can be helpful to diagnosis some infectious pathogens. For example, Pseudomonas has a distinctive odor.

Odor descriptions can be noted as foul, sweet, musty, etc.

Drainage

Wound discharge can vary greatly with different kinds of wounds. In some cases there can be no drainage and in other cases, it can have copious and excessive amounts of drainage, and some can fall anywhere between the two.

The characteristics of drainage fall into the following categories:

Purulent Discharge: Depending on the infective agent, the discharge can be green, brown, or yellow, and it can be thick and milky in consistency.

- *Sanguinous drainage*: The drainage is bloody.

- *Serosanguinous drainage*: This discharge is a mix of both blood and serous drainage.

- *Serous drainage*: This discharge is a slight yellow color and it consists of serum.

Wound Bed Tissue

It is important that the bed tissue of a wound is described with as much detail as possible. The intent is to allow the reader to visualize the tissue through the words. This enables all caregivers to treat the wound and treat any possible abnormalities in the healing process.

The observation of the bed tissue is interpreted as follows:

- *Wound healing that begins at the edges of the wound, then works itself across the wound until it covers the entire wound, and is a light shade of pink or violet in color and it is dry is the in process of epithelization.*

- *A viscous, soft and yellowish gray in color tissue that adheres to the wound is known as slough.*

- *Eschar appears with the death of tissue, and is hard necrotic tissue, that is brown or black in color.*

Deep pink to bright red moist tissue that appears slightly granular and is subject to easy bleeds, whereas clean non-granular tissue appears as deep pink or red tissue that is not healing. If proper epithelization is prevented, as the result of excessive granulating tissue (soft flaccid) raised above the periwound tissue, it is referred to as hypergranulation, and may mean that there is excess moisture present in the wound.

Margins

The margins of a wound, which includes its surrounding tissue, must be described carefully and be shared using the correct acceptable terminology. Assessment of the margins include descriptions of the color, the texture, state of the wound edges, and any presence of tunneling or undermining.

The wound color should include descriptive terms such as ecchymosed or yellow, purple, green, blanched, etc.

The wound texture can be described as edematous or swollen, indurated or hardened, normal, etc. If maceration or cellulitis is present it must be noted as well.

When describing the edges of a wound, there are several different terms to that are used. Some of these descriptive terms include an open wound, which can be seen with dehiscence or ulcerations, a closed wound such as a closed surgical incision site, a surgical incision site with attached or unattached edges, which can be indicative of undermining or tunneling; it can also be described as well defined with rolled or diffuse edges, and as a wound with a healing ridge that can indicate the beginning of granulation.

Tunneling and Undermining Wounds

Tunneling is caused by destruction of the fascial planes; adjacent structures slide relative to each other to create movements in our bodies resulting in a narrow passageway. Tunneling results in dead space that has the potential for abscess formation. Tunneling can occur in any wound, but it occurs most commonly in surgical wounds and wounds occurring from a neuropathic cause.

Undermining is caused by erosion under the wound edges, resulting in a large wound with a small opening. Much like an iceberg, what you see on the surface is not indicative of what lies below. Undermining generally includes a wider area of tissue than tunneling. Tunneling generally occurs in one direction, whereas undermining may occur in one or more directions. Undermining occurs most often in patient with pressure wounds or neuropathic ulcers.

A sterile moist cotton applicator is used to probe the margins of a wound in order to measure or estimate the size as close as possible. When measuring this way, the clock face terms are used. For example 12 o'clock is the location toward the patient's head and 3 pm is used to describe the area towards the client's arm.

Distribution

Distribution terms are used to explain how skin lesions are present on one's body. These descriptive terms are used to assist in diagnosing as well as following the progress of the lesion(s). Some terms include the following:

- *Localized: Limited to certain areas of the body*
- *Generalized: Lesions spread in many areas and there is no specific region that is not affected*
- *Acral: Lesions that present on protrusions of the body, such as buttocks, toes, ears, elbows, toes, knuckles, fingertips, elbows*
- *Extensor: Lesions that affect extensor surfaces of the limbs*
- *Symmetric: Lesions affecting matching regions on both the right and left side of the body*
- *Asymmetric: Affecting one side of the region or body and not the other*

If your patient has more than one lesion in an area, each must be clearly delineated and describe. At times wound distribution can assist in a terms of the patient's diagnosis and treatment(s). Arrangements can be seen as diffuse or scattered over an area, a satellite or one large lesion with small lesions around it and linear or in a line.

Use assessment data to determine phase of wound healing

Wound Healing

There are different types of wound healing, which include the following:

- *Primary healing*
- *Secondary healing*
- *Tertiary healing*

Primary Healing

The most common type of wound healing used for repairs, lacerations and surgeries is primary healing or healing by first intention. This type of healing involves the wound being covered completely with suturing, flaps or split or full-thickness grafts. Primary healing is done with wounds that are considered "clean" and not contaminated.

Secondary Healing

Wound healing in which the wound is left open and meant to heal through both granulation and epitheliazation is known as secondary healing, or healing by second intention. This form of healing is done in order to prepare the wound bed for healing; it is done when a wound is contaminated and considered "dirty" or infected. This type of healing is usually indicated in order to prevent the formation of an abscess and to allow the wound to drain before it closes over a draining and possibly infected area.

Tertiary Healing

Tertiary healing is also referred to as healing by third intention or delayed primary closure. With this type of healing, debriding the wound is performed after which it is left open to begin the healing process. This open wound is typically irrigated and packed to prevent healing from the top down. The healing pattern should be from the bottom up to the superficial layers of the skin.

Later suturing or grafts are used to close the wound and, at times, it is left to heal without these interventions. Contaminated wounds, such as animal bites or mixed trauma wounds often times are healed this way.

Phases of Wound Healing

There are phases in the wound healing process, which include the following:

- *Hemostasis*

    Homeostasis occurs in the few minutes immediately after an injury and bleeding; the vessels are sealed off and the circulatory system secrete substances that result in vasoconstriction and the formation of platelets. The clotting mechanism is stimulated by thrombin and it produces a fibrin mesh.

- *Inflammation (lag or exudative)*

    Inflammation occurs in about one to four days after the injury. Erythema, edema and pain occur as the result of plasma, neutrophils and polymorphonucleocytes being released by the blood vessels in order to start phagocytosis; this process removes any debris present and it prevents infection from forming and jeopardizing the wound.

- *Proliferative/granulation*

    Proliferative/granulation (fibroblastic) occurs during day five through day twenty after the injury. Production of collagen by the fibroblasts occurs during this phase; this process provides the structure and support of the wound. During this phase, granulation tissues begin forming, epithelialization occurs, as well as contracture of the wound.

- *Maturation*

    Maturation (differentiation, remodeling or plateau) phase begins after the twenty-first day and continues for an indeterminate amount of time. It can last for up to two years and the wound may break down easily during this phase because of this fragility. Tensile strength is gained in the tissue, the fibroblasts leave the wound, and scarring is reduced as a result of the collagen tightening.

Identify patient goals and factors affecting care

Patient Goals

After the assessment and diagnosis stage of the nursing, the planning phase begins. Establishing patient/client goals and expected outcomes is part of the planning phase.

The SMARTTA framework can be used for setting goals or expected outcomes. All goals have to be:

- *S= Specific*
- *M= Measurable*
- *A= Achievable*
- *R= Realistic*
- *T= Timeframe*
- *T= Trackable*
- *A= Agreed to by the client and significant other(s)*

All expected outcomes must be specific and well defined and not vague. Vague goals are not useful; they are too ambiguous to direct actions towards goals. Goals must also be achievable and realistic, as based on the client's current status. For example, ambulation two times a day may not be realistic and achievable for a client who has just had a cerebrovascular accident or stroke. A more realistic and achievable goal for this client may be that the "Client will transfer from the bed to the chair with assistance two times a day."

Expected outcomes, and goals, must be within a timeframe that is realistic, achievable, trackable and measureable. Goals without deadlines are rarely met. The evaluation phase of the nursing process, as stated previously, is based on the measurement of pre-established goals. For this reason, goals and expected outcomes must be trackable and measurable.

The components of a well phrased expected outcome consist of a:

- *Subject*

    The subject can be the client, spouse, caregiver or significant other but under no circumstances should it be the nurse.

    For example, it should start with the "The client will…", "The caregiver will…", or the "The spouse will…"

- *Verb*

    The verb is an action word that the subject will do, demonstrate or verbalize.

    For example, the verb can be "ambulate", "list" or "will be". The goal will begin with, "The client will be able to demonstrate wound dressing changes…", the "Caregiver will list the food groups…" or the "Spouse will demonstrate the procedure for taking blood glucose…"

- *Conditions*

    Conditions describe the when, how, and where of the action word or verb. For example, a condition may be "twice a day" or "with help".

- *Performance Criteria*

    Performance criteria describe exactly what is expected. It can precisely state what is expected in terms of accuracy, frequency, or time.

    For example, a performance criterion like 20 feet and twice a day can be inserted into an expected outcome, or client goal, like "The client will ambulate 20 feet with assistance two times per day". In this goal, 20 feet is the performance criteria; the subject is "client"; the verb is "ambulate"; and the condition is "with assistance".

The best way to author expected outcomes is to state, "The client will…" or the "The wife will…" and then follow this statement with what exactly you can expect the patient or spouse to do. For example, "The client will ambulate at least 20 feet three times a day with a walker" is a good expected outcome. It is client centered ("The client will"), specific in terms of exactly what you expect the client to do, measurable in terms of feet and frequency, in a timeframe, trackable, and presumably realistic and agreed to and understood by the client (the patient, spouse, caregiver, etc.).

Collaboration and the active involvement of the client, and significant others, must be in agreement with and must also fully understand all the client goals, or expected outcomes.

All treatments have benefits and risks; all treatment options and alternatives have to be decided upon by the client, and caregiver as indicated. Under all circumstances, we have the responsibility to educate our clients about these benefits and risks and then allow the client to make an informed decision about whether or not they want the treatment or the alternative. Most times, these decisions are difficult to make, so the nurse should assist the client to make decisions based on a sound decision making process.

Decision making can follow the paternalistic, patient sovereignty or a shared decision-making model. Paternalism and patient sovereignty do not respect client autonomy because the clinician makes decisions and the client makes decisions without guidance, respectively. The shared decision making model upholds client autonomy, because it includes the client, the nurse, and the other members of the healthcare team in a mutually respectful relationship, which enables them to make good decisions with the support of these healthcare professionals.

In order to help a patient in establishing goals for themselves begins with talking to them, and assisting them in recognizing both short- and long-term goals. Several factors can affect a patient's goals, as well as their care. Some of these factors are as follows:

- *Mental status*
- *Income*
- *Family support*
- *Community support*
- *Functional*
- *Disability*
- *Language barrier*
- *Smoking*
- *Diet*
- *Transportation*

Describe procedures and rationale for diagnostic testing

Diagnostic Testing and its rationale

There are many diagnostic tests available to detect factors that affect wound healing. Total protein levels are essential, as wound healing requires protein. The metabolic rate increases when a wound occurs, therefore, it is necessary to increase the protein intake when a wound occurs as well.

The normal values of protein are 5-9 g/kL, and the increased diet requirement for healing is approximately 1.25-1.5 g/kg per day.

The table below is a summary of the value ranges of a variety of proteins that are necessary to be monitored:

Protein Name	Normal Values	Mild Deficiency	Moderate Deficiency	Severe Deficiency
Albumin	3.5-5.5 g/dL	3-3.5 g/dL	2.5-3.0 g/dL	<2.5 g/dL
Prealbumin (transthyretin)	16-40 mg/dL	10-15 mg/dL	5-9 mg/dL	<5 mg/dL
Transferrin	200-400 mg/dL	150-200 mg/dL	100-150 mg/dL	<100 mg/dL
Total Lymphocyte Count	2000 cells/mm^3	1500-1800 2000 cells/mm^3	900-1500 2000 cells/mm^3	<900 2000 cells/mm^3

The liver produces a protein known as albumin which is necessary for the cells and tissues in the body to sustain them and to promote healing. Albumin levels are commonly used to test for protein levels; its half-life is 18-20 days. Renal disease, severe burns, and malnutrition cause decreased albumin; when the levels decrease to <3.2, it puts the patient at risk for morbidity and death.

Prealbumin is a protein made in the liver that is needed for transportation of vitamin A and thyroxine in the body. It has a half-life of 2-3 days, therefore, it is commonly used to indicate acute changes in the patient's nutritional status. The levels change very quickly in response to protein intake. Levels can rise due to Hodgkin's disease, the use of steroids, or the use of

NSAIDS. A decrease in this level can result as the consequence of liver disease, estrogen, and oral contraceptives.

Another protein made by the liver is transferrin. Transferrin transports iron from the intestines to the bone marrow, which allows for the production of hemoglobin.

Proper healing requires hydration. It is also needed to accurately measure nutrition. There are a number of diagnostic tests that can be used to check hydration. The table below includes different diagnostic tests and their uses.

Test Name	Normal Values	Dehydration	Use
Specific Gravity/Urine	1.003-1.028	>1.028	Measurement of the kidneys ability to concentrate or dilute urine following the changes in serum
Serum Osmolality	285-295 mill-osmoles per kilogram/H_2O	>295 mOsm/kg H_2O	Measures ion concentrations (glucose, potassium, urea, sodium, chloride, etc.) in the blood. With dehydration levels increase
Blood Urea Nitrogen (BUN)	7-23 mg/dL	>23 mg/dL	Protein by-product. Elevated BUN alone can be indicative of dehydration. Elevated BUN and creatinine can indicate kidney disease
BUN-Creatinine Ratio	10:1	>25:1	Renal failure monitored when there is enhanced reabsorption in the proximal tubules, resulting in an increase in urea level

Serum Sodium	135-150 mEq/L	>150 mE/L	Measures the level of sodium in the blood Medications can elevate or reduce levels

Blood Glucose Test

Diabetes mellitus is a disease that alters carbohydrate, protein and fat metabolism. It is the most common disease of the endocrine system. Type 1 diabetes mellitus, which is also known as insulin dependent diabetes mellitus, is associated with toxic chemicals, abnormal antibodies that attack the islet of Langerhans cells, some viruses and histocompatibility antigens. Type 2 diabetes mellitus, which is also known as non-insulin dependent diabetes mellitus, is associated with obesity. It results from defects in insulin secretion and action. Gestational diabetes mellitus during pregnancy is characterized with glucose intolerance and it usually disappears after the baby is delivered, but, at times, it can lead to either type 1 or type 2 diabetes. Other types of diabetes are associated with disorders such as certain genetic syndromes, insulin receptor disorder, endocrinopathies, pancreatic disease, and the use of drugs or chemicals, such as lithium, furosemide, epinephrine, corticosteroids and glucagon.

There classic signs and symptoms associated with diabetes mellitus including polyuria, polydipsia, polyphagia, weight loss, fatigue and somnolence.

The treatments include insulin, diet, exercise, and oral agents. Oral hypoglycemic agents include tolazamide, acetohexamide, glipizide and glyburide which stimulate insulin release and should be administered once or twice daily, chlorpropamide which is a long-acting agent used among clients who have low basal insulin secretion, and tolbutamide, which is a short-acting agent used among clients who have elevated basal insulin secretion, but cannot, with food intake, produce sufficient insulin.

Patients with diabetes mellitus and with higher than normal blood glucose levels are predisposed to skin injuries, slow healing, infection, and other skin issues. The fasting blood glucose test is used to diagnosis, confirm and to monitor the client who is affected with diabetes.

The normal parameters for a fasting blood sugar level are from 70 to 100 mg/dL, and an impaired fasting blood glucose level ranges from 100-125 mg/dL. A patient is considered to be diabetic if their fasting blood glucose level is >126 mg/dL.

Blood glucose levels can be affected as the result of a number of different reasons. A patient's blood glucose level can decrease due to starvation, hypothyroidism, liver disease, and adrenal insufficiency. An increase of the level of glucose in the blood can occur from stress, pancreatic disorders, hyperthyroidism, Cushing syndrome, renal failure, and as the result of medications, such as diuretics, tricyclic antidepressants, steroids, estrogen, phenytoin, or lithium, in addition to diabetes.

Other Diagnostic Tests

As nurses assess clients, they also collect and/or analyze the findings of laboratory and other diagnostic testing including those described below.

Complete Blood Count (CBC)

A complete blood count (CBC) determines the number of white blood cells (WBC), the number of red blood cells (RBC), the platelet count, the portion of the blood that contains red blood cells which is referred to as the hematocrit and the total amount of hemoglobin in the blood.

A complete blood count (CBC) is used to diagnose and monitor a wide variety of health disorders including anemia, infection, inflammation, leukemia, bleeding disorders, clotting disorders as well as abnormal blood cell destruction and production.

White Blood Cells

In addition to the white blood cell count (WBC), a CBC can also measure the white blood cell differential which counts the number of each of the five types of white blood cells in the blood, namely, the lymphocytes, neutrophils, monocytes, basophils and eosinophils and determine the number of band cells, which are immature neutrophils, T-type lymphocytes or T cells and B-type lymphocytes or B cells.

Leukopenia, or an abnormally low WBC count, can occur as the result of impaired bone marrow functioning, an autoimmune disease such as systemic lupus erythematosus, hepatic disease, viral infections and a disorder of the spleen. Clients with leukopenia, regardless of cause, are at greater risk for infection than other clients with a normal WBC count.

Leukocytosis, or an elevated WBC count, can result from inflammatory diseases such as arthritis, viral and bacterial infections such as tuberculosis and pneumonia, sepsis, leukemia, physical and emotional stress and extensive tissue damage such as that which occurs as the result of a burn.

The normal white blood count is 4,500 to 10,000 cells/mcL. With an acute and severe bacterial infection, this count can rise to 30,000 and a viral infection typically presents with a less than 4,000 white blood cell count.

The percentage of each different type of leukocyte is provided by the differential. Therefore, an increase in the white blood cell count is, in most cases, accompanied with an increase in one type of leukocyte and, in most cases, an increase in immature neurophils or bands. This phenomena is referred to as a shift to the left) and it is an indication of the presence of an infectious process.

	Normal Percentage	Increase or decrease with what
Immature neutrophils (bands)	1-3%	Increase with infection
Segmented neutrophils (segs) for adults	50-625	Increase with acute, localized, or systemic bacterial infections
Esoinophils	0-3%	Decrease with stress and acute infection
Basophils	0-1%	Decrease during acute stage of infection
Lymphocytes	25-40%	Increase in some viral and bacterial infection
Monocytes	3-7%	Increase during the recovery stage of acute infection

Red Blood Cells

Other things that the CBC measures and determines is the amount of oxygen carrying hemoglobin in each red blood cell (RBC), which is referred to as the MCH or the mean corpuscular hemoglobin, the amount or concentration of hemoglobin in relation to the size of the RBC, which is referred to as MCHC or mean corpuscular hemoglobin concentration, the average size of the red blood cells, which is referred to as the MCV or mean corpuscular volume, red cell distribution width (RDW) which measures the variations of the sizes of the red blood cells and the reticulocyte count which reflects the number or percentage of immature, young blood cells.

Elevated RBC counts and hematocrit can occur from a variety of causes such as smoking, dehydration, renal disease, lung disease and polycythemia vera. Polycythemia is defined as an excessive red blood cell count and secondary polycythemia is defined as an excessive red blood cell count that results from chronic hypoxemia as can occur with a congenial heart disorder and chronic obstructive pulmonary disease and other pulmonary or cardiac disorders. Clients with polycythemia are at risk for blood clotting and increased after load because the blood is thickened in the presence of polycythemia.

Low RBCs and hematocrit can result from anemia, hemorrhage, chronic renal disease, infections such as hepatitis, impaired bone marrow function as can occur secondary to radiation therapy, leukemia, multiple myeloma, some autoimmune disorders such as rheumatoid arthritis, red blood cell destruction which is referred to as hemolysis and inadequate nutrition that is lacking in iron, folate, vitamin B12 and/or vitamin B6.

Low hemoglobin can be secondary to hemorrhage and all types of anemia.

The normal red blood count for males is 4.7 to 6.1 million cells/mcL and, for females, the normal red blood count is 4.2 to 5.4 million cells/mcL.

The normal hematocrit for males is 40.7 to 50.3% and, for females, the normal hematocrit is 36.1 to 44.3%; the normal hemoglobin for males is 13.8 to 17.2 gm/dL and the normal hemoglobin for females is 12.1 to 15.1 gm/dL.

Other normal values related to the red blood cells include:

- *MCH: 27 to 31 pg/cell*
- *MCV: 80 to 95 femtoliter*
- *MCHC: 32 to 36 gm/dL*

Coagulation Studies

Coagulation studies can include direct measures such as those that measure the number of platelets, also referred to as thrombocytes, and indirect measures to see how effectively, or ineffectively, the platelets are functioning. These indirect measures are referred to as platelet function assays.

Platelets coagulate the blood and prevent bleeding by clumping together with other platelets, sticking to the site of the bleeding and by releasing substances that stimulate aggregation. They are produced by the bone marrow.

Some assays that measure platelet function are:

- *Closure time assays*

- *This test measures the closure time for the platelets to coagulate when exposed to an activating substance.*

- *Thromboelastometry or Viscoelastometry*

- *This test measures the strength of the blood clot has it is formed.*
- *Endpoint Bead or Endpoint Platelet Aggregation Assay*
- *This test measures the number of platelets that collect and aggregate after an activating substance is added to the blood sample.*
- *Bleeding Time*
- *This direct measurement of platelet functioning, although not done as often as it was in the past, reflects the amount of time that it takes for bleeding to stop.*
- *Platelet Aggregometry*
- *Platelet aggregometry consists of a number of different tests, all of which measure the aggregation of the platelets after an activating substance has been added to the sample.*
- *Flow Cytometry uses lasers to detect proteins on the surface of the platelet and how these proteins change when an activating agent is added.*

Clients with excessive and fast clotting are at risk for the formation of blood clots and emboli; clients with a slow or impaired clotting response are at risk for bleeding, therefore, all venipuncture and arterial puncture sites must have pressure applied to them to prevent bleeding.

Gram Staining

Some bacteria are classified as gram positive because they react to a Gram stain; these microbes have thick walls containing teichoic acid and peptidoglycan. Others are classified as gram negative because they do not react to a gram stain. These microbes, more common than gram positive bacteria, have thinner walls than gram positive bacteria; these walls are comprised of peptidoglycan and a lipid membrane which includes lipoproteins and lipopolysaccharides, which are endotoxins.

Some examples of gram positive bacteria include streptococcus pneumoniae (pneumococci), staphylococci, which can lead to respiratory and cardiac infections, such as endocarditis and pneumonia, and streptococci, which can cause pneumonia, bronchitis, pharyngitis, rheumatic fever and endocarditis.

Examples of gram positive bacteria associated with respiratory diseases include haemophilus influenzae, legionella pneumophilia and yersinia pseudotuberculosis.

Bacteria are also differentiated by their ability to resist color changes when subjected to a staining procedure in the laboratory. Acid fast bacteria resist decolorization when stained with a Ziehl-Neelsen or Kinyoun stain, for example.

Sputum specimens, including sputum cultures, are normally without any pathogenic organisms. When the sputum is cultured and the findings are abnormal, it can be an indication of a number of disorders and diseases such as a bacterial, viral or fungal infection, bronchitis, cystic fibrosis, chronic obstructive pulmonary disease, a lung abscess, pneumonia and tuberculosis.

Electrolytes

Electrolyte panels, alone or in combination with a metabolic panel, are used to both diagnose disorders and to monitor the outcomes of care for a particular disorder that can, or does, impact on the fluid, electrolyte, and acid base balances of the body. For example, a client with edema will have an electrolyte panel to diagnose their disorder and a client with chronic heart failure needs electrolyte panels to monitor this chronic disorder.

Electrolytes and fluids are transported through the body with both active and passive transport processes. Passive transport processes include diffusion, osmosis and filtration. The process of diffusion moves fluids and electrolytes from an area of higher concentration to an area of lower concentration; osmosis moves fluids through a selectively permeable membrane in the presence of at least one impermeable solute; and filtration moves fluids and small solute particles through a filtration membrane from an area of high pressure to area of low pressure. Active transport moves molecules across cell membranes from an area of lower concentration to an area of higher concentration as occurs with the movement of glucose and amino acids.

Electrolytes are ions that can have either a negative or positive charge when the number of electrons is either greater than or less than the number of protons. Cations have a positive charge; and anions have a negative charge.

The cations are:

- *Sodium (Na+)*
- *Potassium (K+)*
- *Calcium (Ca+)*
- *Magnesium (Mg++)*
- *The anions include:*
- *Chloride (Cl-)*
- *Bicarbonate (HCO3-)*
- *Sulfate (SO4-)*
- *Hydrogen phosphate (HPO4-)*

Although excesses and deficits of each of the electrolytes has specific signs and symptoms, the general symptoms that may occur with an electrolyte imbalance include fatigue, nausea, without vomiting, dizziness, trembling, constipation, dark urine, decreased urine output, muscle weakness, stiff or aching joints, dry skin, dry mouth, and bad breath. Serious symptoms are poor elasticity of the skin, tachycardia, sunken eyes, and a change in mental status, such as confusion, delirium, hallucinations or delusions.

The normal levels for some electrolytes and glucose are:

- *Potassium: 3.5 to 5.5 mEq/L*
- *Sodium: 135 to 145 mEq/L*
- *Chloride: 95 to 106 mEq/L*
- *Bicarbonate: 22 to 25 mEq/L*
- *Calcium: 4.5 to 5.5 mEq/L*
- *Glucose: 60 to 110 mg/100 mL*

Some of the specific signs and symptoms associated with deficiencies and excesses of the major electrolytes and glucose are in the table below.

Electrolyte	Excesses	Deficiencies
Potassium	Hyperkalemia Cardiac changes such as high T waves, widened QRS complex, depressed ST segment, bradycardia and flacid paralysis	Hypokalemia Cardiac changes such as depressed ST segment, inverted or flat T waves, premature ventricular contractions, ventricular fibrillation and cardiac arrest if left untreated, and muscular weakness
Sodium	Hypernatremia The signs and symptoms of dehydration	Hyponatremia Fluid overload
Chloride	Hyperchloremia The prolongation of the QT interval and the ST segment	Hypochloremia A wider or more rounded T wave and a shortened QT interval

Bicarbonate	Bicarbonate retention to compensate for respiratory acidosis that occurs as the result of an elevated carbon dioxide level	The excessive excretion of bicarbonate to compensate for respiratory alkalosis that occurs as the result of a decreased carbon dioxide level
Glucose	Hyperglycemia Fatigue, blurred vision, excessive thirst, headache, frequent urination, hyperosmolar syndrome, ketoacidosis and long term complications such as renal failure, nephropathy and diabetic retinopathy This is most typically the result of the poor management of diabetes.	Hypoglycemia Excessive hunger, sweating, anxiety, shakiness, heart palpitations, double or blurry vision, confusion, loss of consciousness, seizures, coma and death This is associated with diabetics who have taken too much insulin, too little food or have exercised excessively.

The treatment of electrolyte imbalances is dependent on what type of electrolyte is actually affected. For example, a patient with low potassium levels should be urged to watch their diet, take potassium supplements and given intravenous supplementation. If a patient's potassium levels are high, the client may be treated with diuretics.

In addition to the immediate treatment for the imbalance, it is vital that the cause for the imbalance is discovered and corrected. Possible causes include kidney disease, hormone/endocrine problems, stomach disorders, an improper diet, a loss of bodily fluids due to illness, and as the result of side effects of chemotherapy or medications. Some types of medications that can cause an electrolyte imbalance in the body are steroids, tricyclic antidepressants, birth control pills, diuretics, cough medicines, laxatives, steroids and excessive use of antacids.

Cultures and Sensitivity Testing

When a culture and sensitivity is indicated, as based on the client's clinical condition, the sample is microscopically examined, after which it is cultured in an appropriate medium such as a nutrient broth or agar. Cultures are useful for the identification of the microorganism, to determine whether the wound, for example, is colonized or infected and also to get a numeric values for the colony.

Sensitivity testing entails subjecting the culture to a number of different antibiotics in order to confirm whether or not the pathogen is treatable and sensitive to specific antibiotics or if it is resistant to the antibiotic, as is the case with methicillin-resistant Staphylococcus aureus (MRSA).

Specimens for microbiology, culture and sensitivity must be collected correctly and processed as soon as possible after collection because some microorganisms may not survive prolonged lengths of time before the laboratory processes them.

The use of antimicrobials for the treatment of infections is the most common therapeutic treatment. To the greatest extent possible, the selection of the antimicrobial and the dosage should be driven by the specific microorganism and the current physical condition of the host.

Antimicrobial prophylaxis can be a primary prevention or a secondary prevention measure. It is considered primary prevention when it prevents any infection; and it is considered secondary prevention when it treats and prevents the recurrence of an infection.

Antimicrobial prophylaxis is often, and perhaps too often, used to prevent the onset of an infectious disease. For example, preventive prophylactic antibiotics can be used for the prevention of urinary tract infections when a client has an indwelling urinary catheter, and to prevent other infections such as rheumatic fever which can lead to serious cardiac damage, herpes simplex recurring bouts of cellulitis, meningitis, endocarditis, as well as open wounds and open fracture infections.

Prophylactic antimicrobials, particularly antibacterials, are also used, and indicated, perioperatively for certain types of surgery, like gastrointestinal and total joint replacement surgical procedures, to prevent surgically related infections. For example, an intravenous antibiotic may be administered ½ hour to 1 hour prior to a surgical procedure.

Ideally, prophylactic antimicrobials should not be used, however, when it is necessary to use them they must be used judiciously. The ideal prophylactic antimicrobial should be limited in terms of the duration of use, inexpensive, nontoxic, target specific and bactericidal. Resistance remains a high public health concern.

The therapeutic use of antimicrobials should, under ideal circumstances be based on the components of the cycle of infection. For example, it should be based on the site of the infection, the host, and whenever possible, based on a definitive diagnosis of the infection and the offending pathogen. At times, when there is not yet a definitive diagnosis, the empiric use of antimicrobials is indicated.

The identification of the specific offending pathogen is extremely important especially when an infection can be life threatening, when the client is not responding to current therapeutic interventions and when the course of antimicrobial therapy is anticipated to be rather prolonged.

This accurate identification is dependent upon accurate and timely microbiological laboratory testing prior to the initiation of the therapy, whenever possible. In addition to laboratory testing, the client's past medical history, including an exposure history, and the presenting signs and symptoms also serve as considerations in terms of exactly which antimicrobial is the most effective and the most appropriate for the client.

The initiation of the antimicrobial therapy is based on a number of considerations including the condition of the client. For example, critically ill clients, like those with sepsis, should have an immediate initiation of antimicrobial therapy immediately after diagnostic specimens are obtained. When the client condition is stable, it is recommended that antimicrobial therapy be postponed until laboratory findings are complete.

The empiric use of antimicrobials is defined as the use of antimicrobial medications based on empiric signs and symptoms in the client's physical condition because microbiological results typically do not get done in less than 24 to 72 hours.

The antimicrobial agents that are used with empiric, rather than definitive, diagnoses are typically broad scope agents or a combination of agents until a definitive diagnosis is done.

Other commonly used blood laboratory tests used for infections includes the erythrocyte sedimentation rate (ESR), C-reactive protein (CRP) plasma viscosity (PV), all of which are sensitive to the increases in protein, which is a part of the inflammation process. The ESR, CRP and PV can be raised with primarily bacterial infections, abscesses and other disorders such as cancer, burns and a myocardial infarction. Some health problems like polycythemia, sickle cell anemia and heart failure can be signaled with a less than normal ESR. Additionally, urine testing and spinal fluid analysis can also be done.

The Erythrocyte Sedimentation Rate (ESR)

The erythrocyte sedimentation rate (ESR) measures the rate with which the red blood cells separate from the plasma and fall to the bottom of vertical tube of anticoagulated blood within a given period of time. A high erythrocyte sedimentation rate indicates the presence of infection because the proteins of infection cover the red blood cells thus causing them to fall more rapidly.

The normal erythrocyte sedimentation rate (ESR) for females is 0-20 millimeters per hour and the normal rate for males is 0-15 millimeters per hour. The normal sedimentation rate among elders can be slightly higher.

C Reactive Protein

C reactive protein, sometimes referred to as the acute phase of inflammation protein, can rise as high as 1000 times normal when infection and inflammation occur. The liver, in response to an inflammatory response, produces C-reactive protein, which is an acute-phase reactant. The inflammatory response causes neutrophils, granulocytes and macrophages to secret cytokines. It can also rise with burns, surgery and cancer.

C reactive protein is also a useful measure in terms of evaluating client responses to treatments. For example, the client's response to treatment for pyoderma gangrenosum ulcers can be measured and determined with the C reactive protein level throughout the course of treatment.

The normal C reactive protein is < 1.0 mg/dL or less than 10 mg/L. Some references cite the normal value as 2.6-7.6 mg/dL.

Plasma Viscosity

Simply stated, blood viscosity is the thickness of the blood. Some of the factors that impact on the viscosity of blood include plasma viscosity, or thickness, the hematocrit, the level of red blood cell aggregation and temperature. Higher temperatures lead to lower viscosity and lower temperatures lead to increase blood thickness and viscosity.

The normal viscosity of the blood, at 37 °C, is 3×10^{-3} to 4×10^{-3}.

Urine Tests

More than 100 different tests can be done on urine. A regular, or routine, urinalysis includes the color, clarity, odor, specific gravity, pH, proteins, glucose, ketones, nitrites, leukocyte esterase and microscopic evaluation.

Bacteria can make normally clear urine cloudy. Infections can also make urine odorous, In the presence of a urinary tract infection, nitrites will be present and the leukocyte esterase will show white blood cells, or leukocytes in the urine.

Microscopic analysis is done after the urine is centrifuged to render sediment for analysis. Some of the things that can be found in urine with microscopic analysis include the abnormal presence of red and/or white blood cells which indicates inflammation and infection, casts which can also indicate infection, crystals in the presence of stones, and bacteria, yeast, and/or parasites when an infection is present.

Spinal Taps

Spinal taps, also referred to as a lumbar puncture, is also done to determine if the cerebrospinal fluid is infected, as is the case with meningitis.

Normal values for cerebrospinal fluids are:

- *A pressure of 70 - 180 mm H20*
- *A colorless and clear appearance*
- *15 - 60 mg/100 mL of total protein*
- *3 - 12% of the total protein is gamma globulin*
- *50 - 80 mg/100 mL glucose*
- *0 - 5 mononuclear white blood cells*
- *No red blood cells*
- *110 - 125 mEq/L chloride*

Increased CSF pressure occurs as the result of increased intracranial pressure secondary to a head injury, for example. Protein can increase with an infection or any other inflammatory process; glucose can be decreased with infections like meningitis and tuberculosis; increased white blood cells can indicate an acute infection; and red blood cells indicate bleeding.

General Principles of Management

Select and Apply Topical Agents for Periwound Skin Protection

Topical Agents for PeriWound Skin Protection

There are a number of topical agents used for the protection of periwound skin, including the following:

- *Skin sealants*

    Skin sealants are made of a fast-drying solvent that are applied approximately every 14 days; they are manufactured as a transparent plasticized polymer which is left over the intact or irritated tissue. A non-alcohol choice of sealant is recommended If the skin is irritated. These sealants can help to protect the skin from urine, stool, exudate, chemicals, dirt, debris, and adhesive stripping. The sealant is applied with the ease of a spray, wand or wipe. Examples of some of these products include Skin Prep, Shield Skin, Bard Protective Barrier, Film Wipe, Allkare Convatec and Cavilon No Sting Barrier Film which does not contain alcohol.

- *Moisture barrier ointments*

    Moisture barrier ointments are zinc oxide based-products that are commercially packaged in small bottles or tubes; they are applied to the affected area to protect it from feces, urine, exudates and moisture. These products are popular with incontinent patients to help protect against incontinence dermatitis. This type of protection can be somewhat expensive; it must be reapplied after every dressing, brief change and any episode of incontinence. Some of these products include Caloseptine Ointment, Lantiseptic Skin Protectant, Proshield Plus Skin Protectant and Critic-Aid Clear Hydrophilic Ointment.

- *Moisture barrier pastes*

    Moisture barrier pastes are ointments that are mixed with a thickening powder to make them a thicker consistency. Although highly effective, these products are difficult to remove because of their thick consistency. Most of these paste products are transparent, which is a highly useful feature because it enables the nurse to clearly and continuously monitor the skin. Karaya is added to some of these pastes to make them adhere to the tissue better and better absorb exudates and protect the skin from drainage, urine, and feces. They are particularly useful for periwound tissues and peri-anal tissue. Barrier pastes include Critic-Aid Skin paste, Ilex Skin Protectant Paste and Remedy Calazime Protectant Paste.

- *Solid skin barriers*

    Solid skin barriers are solid waterproof moldable skin barriers made to protect the skin from feces, urine, exudates, and moisture.. Gelatine, karaya, pectin, hydrocolloids, carboxymenthyl cellulose or combinations of these substances are used for the contents of these barriers. They are usually in the form of rings, strips or wafers. They protect the skin from discharge and may be cut to fit snugly around the wound for protection. They are made to protect the wound and are they are more durable than ointments or pastes. Some examples of solid skin barriers include Hollister Flextend, Stomahesive, Eakin and Premium Skin Barrier.

- *Skin barrier Powders*

    Skin barrier powders are powders that can be sprinkled lightly on denuded skin to increase the sticking power of ointments, pastes and solid skin adhesive barriers. Once the skin heals the powder should be discontinued.

Cleaning Solutions and the Procedures Used to Minimize the Risk of Infection

The wound and the area surrounding the wound must be kept clean at all times. At every dressing change the wound and the area surrounding the wound should be carefully, completely and gently cleansed to remove any bacteria from the surface of the wound while being extremely gentle and careful in order to prevent any damage to the fragile tissue.

Drainage from the wound is removed and cleaned up with fresh gauze; it is important to note that a fresh piece of gauze is to be used for each wipe of the wound or the surrounding area to help prevent the spread of infection. The technique also includes moving from the cleanest to the dirtiest area.

Irrigation of the wound will help to clean it out and to encourage it to heal properly. All dressings, gauze, swabs, solutions, syringes and/or squeeze bottles used while the open area of a wound is exposed must be sterile at all times. Wound care is a sterile procedure.

Hand washing techniques must be adheres to before and after contact with a wound, even if gloves are used. It is important that all staff members adhere to the proper safety and infection control procedures set forth by the institution in order to minimize the risk of infection.

Identify the need for hydrotherapy or pulsed lavage

Hydrotherapy

For wounds that are a result of a burn, large in size, and/or have a significant amount of necrosis, the use of whirlpool hydrotherapy treatment is indicated to cleanse and debride the site of the wound or traumatic injury. The water temperature is maintained at 37 degrees C. In some instances antiseptics are added to the water, but this can at times irritate or stunt the healing process, therefore before adding anything to the water it is vital the treating physician is consulted.

The cross-contamination dangers associated with this kind of wound therapy because these tubs have multiple users have led to the fact that many facilities have chosen to forgo the use of whirlpools all together. When used, a through disinfection of all equipment is necessary before and after each patient use in order to avoid any possibility of cross contamination

Whirlpool therapy is contraindicated for some diabetic patients because they can be insensitive to the temperature of the water, therefore this therapy must be used with caution. Hydrotherapy is also contraindicated for venous ulcers because vasodilation can increase edema; and wounds secondary to arterial insufficiency typically do not benefit from hydrotherapy. Another disadvantage of hydrotherapy lies in the fact that other treatments include cleansing after treatment which reduces the amount of surface bacteria and whirlpool therapy does not.

Pulsed Lavage

Pulsatile high pressure lavage, more commonly referred to as pulsed lavage, is a way of irrigating a wound that is infected or necrotic by using an electrical power device that expels normal saline at a pressure of 8-15 psi. The amount of saline used as well as the amount of pressure can vary according to the size of the affected area, the amount of exudate originating from the wound and other wound characteristics.

The pulsed lavage treatment can be quite expensive because of the cost of the labor necessary, the costs of the unit and the costs of supplies. Pulsed lavage is usually performed one to two times a day, and, each time it is necessary to use a new hose and a new irrigating nozzle. The staff performing the treatment must wear protective equipment including eye wear gloves, a mask and an impervious gown because this treatment takes place in an enclosed space and the possibility of mists and droplets is high as the treatment is performed.

Types of Dressings

Dressings

There are a wide variety of different types of dressing that are used for all different types of wounds and stages of a wound; there is also a relatively large amount of options and alternatives that can be used for a particular wound.

The type of wound and the stage of the wound typically dictate which of the three main types of dressing is the most affective for the particular wound.

The three main types of dressings include:

- *The traditional dressing*

    This type of dressing includes gauze, tulle, etc, are primarily used to help cover the wound.

- *The interactive dressing*

    This include polymeric films, are usually transparent allowing for the continuous observation of the wound and permitting the wound to remain permeable to water vapor and oxygen. The interactive dressing also protects the wound from microorganisms. Examples of these dressings include hydrogels, hyaluronic acid and foam dressings.

- *The bioactive dressing*

    Bioactive dressings includes products that directly allow for the healing of wounds. Some examples of this type of dressing include chitosan, collagens, alginates and hydrocolloids.

Autolytic Debridement

With autolysis, the body uses its own enzymes, such as proteolytic, fibrinolytic, and collagenolytic enzymes, moisture, and white blood cells to debride a wound by rehydrating, softening and liquefying hard eschar and slough. The ideal environment and circumstances for good wound healing and autolysis include a warm moist environment and adequate vasculature to provide white blood cells and a neutrophil count of >500 mm3. Sepsis can occur when the neutrophils decrease.

Autolytic debridement is the most useful and effective when the client is affected with a stage III or IV uninfected wound that only has a light to moderate amount of exudate. Only necrotic tissue is liquefied with autolytic debridement and most patients feel little to no pain at all with this process.

Autolytic debridement can be done with an occlusive dressing, a semi-occlusive dressings, hydrocolloids, hydrogels and transparent films. Occlusive and semi-occlusive dressings maintain the contact of wound fluids and necrotic tissue.

As with most treatment options, there are a number of advantages and disadvantages to autolytic debridement.

The advantages include the following:

- *It is typically painless or only associated with very slight pain*
- *It is a relatively safe process. The cleaning of the wound of necrotic debris is done with the body's own defense mechanisms*
- *Surrounding skin will not be damaged*
- *It is effective and easy to perform*

The disadvantages include the following:

- *Monitoring of the wound must be done to make sure that an infection does not form.*
- *The process is not as rapid as surgical debridement is. It can take up to 72-96 hours before its effects begin.*
- *The proliferation of anaerobic can occur when an occlusive hydrocolloid is used for the treatment of the wound.*

The dressings most commonly used for autolytic debridement include:

- *Hydrocolloids*

    Hydrocolloids provide absorbency for wounds with small amounts of exudate but they may promote anaerobic infections if the dressing is occlusive.

- *Alginate dressings*

    Alginate dressings provide added absorbency for wounds with large amounts of exudate but they require a secondary dressing to secure it firmly in place.

- *Hydrogels*

    Hydrogels are particularly helpful when wounds are dry because they add the necessary moisture to promote rapid autolysis.

- *Transparent films*

    Transparent films promote autolysis for very small and shallow wounds. They are also used as a secondary dressing.

Odor and drainage increase as the wound debrides so the periwound tissue must be protected.

Enzymatic Chemical Debridement

Enzymatic debridement, which is a method of chemical debridement, can be used on any type of wound with a large enough amount of necrosis and eschar. This is especially beneficial with chronic wounds and burns.

Enzymes need a moist environment, therefore, if they are used to debride dry eschar, the eschar must be crosshatched through the upper layers of the wound with a scalpel. This step is necessary in order to allow the enzymes to adequately penetrate the eschar.

Chemical type enzymes are fast acting and they facilitate the sloughing of necrotic tissue. Some patients may have local irritation from the enzymes, but they do not damage viable tissue, as they are selective.

Enzymatic debridement is most effective and useful on any wounds that have a large amount of necrotic debris or eschar formation. With enzymatic debridement enzymes either directly digest the fibrin, bacteria, leukocytes, and other cell debris that comprises slough or dissolves the collagen that secures it to the wound.

The advantage of enzymatic debridement is that it is fast acting and, with proper application, there will be minimal or no damage to any healthy tissue. Unfortunately there are also disadvantages. Some of these disadvantages include the following:

- *A prescription is required*
- *It is costly*
- *The application must be performed carefully so it does not to harm any tissue that is not necrotic*
- *A specific secondary dressing may be required*
- *There is a chance of inflammation or discomfort to the client*

Any type of dressing can be used with enzymes but the dressings have to be changed at least once or twice a day, but when a moisture-retentive dressings is used it is found to increase the rate of wound healing.

Mechanical Debridement

Mechanical debridement, such as hydrotherapy, is a technique that allows the dressing to go from moist to wet after which the dressing is removed to facilitate and promote non-selective debridement.

Mechanical debridement is best when it is used on wounds with a moderate amount of necrotic debris. A primary advantage of mechanical debridement is that it is relatively inexpensive. The relatively inexpensive gauze is the only material that has to be purchased.

Some of the disadvantages that are associated with this type of debridement include the following:

- *Pain*
- *It is time consuming*
- *It can cause infection*
- *It is non-selective*
- *Healthy and healing tissue can be traumatized*

This type of debridement was a very popular choice for many years in the past, however, there are many reasons that it is not a popular choice now, although it is used in some cases.

Wet to dry debridement involves applying sterile saline moistened gauze to the wound, waiting for the gauze to dry out, and then removing the gauze. This time consuming disadvantage of this method is the primary reason that it is rarely used.

Surgical Debridement

Surgical debridement, such as laser debridement or sharp instrument surgical debridement, is the method of debridement that is the fastest when compared to other methods of debridement. It can be performed at the client's bedside, in a community outpatient wound center and in an operating room depending on the extent of the injury. Laser surgery, when compared to sharp instrument surgical debridement enables the removal of the necrotic tissue with a better chance of not injuring the adjacent healthy and healing this form of debridement is not only fast and, at times, the patient is under anesthesia, which in itself poses risks to the client.

Sharp Instrument Debridement

Sharp instrument debridement is a form of debridement in which a large portion of necrotic tissue can be removed with the use of a scalpel, forceps and scissors. Depending on the state of the wound, this form of debridement is the most aggressive form of debridement. It can be performed by the physician and, in some settings it can also be performed by a non-physician such as a nurse or physical therapist.

The speed of recovery and healing is faster than other debridement procedures.

Chemical Cauterization

This form of debridement is used for wounds and skin lesions in order to control hypergranulation tissue. For example, it is used for stomas or with warts.

Hypergranulation tissue is usually friable and it bleeds easily. When treating a wound with chemical cauterization, it is necessary to repeat the procedure at least twice daily for up to four days or more until the excess tissue sloughs off. These wounds treated in this manner are often associated with exudate production that interferes with wound healing and the production of a wound odor.

Selection of the Appropriate Topical Agents for Debridement

There are a variety of topical antibiotics that can be used with the different types of debridement. These antibiotics include the following:

- *Cadexomer Lodine (Iodosorb),*

    Effective against a broad range of bacteria including Staphylococcus aureus, MRSA, Streptococcus and Pseudomonas as well as viruses and fungi

- *Gentamicin sulphate*

    Effectively used against both primary and secondary skin infections which result from stasis as well as for other ulcers or skin lesions. It is an effective bacteriocidal agent that can be used to combat Staphylococcus aureus, Streptococcus, and Pseudomonas, but it does not have any antiviral or antifungal properties.

- *Metroidazole*

    Effectively used against MRSA infections

- *Mupirocin 2%,*

    Effectively used against Gram-positive bacteria and is it is used primarily for Staphylococcus, MRSA, and Streptococcus. It is also frequently used to treat nasal colonization of Staphylococcus because colonization is implicated and associated with subsequent wound infections among some clients.

- *Polymyxin B sulphate – Bacitrac in zinc neomycin, such as Neosporin*

    Effectively used to prevent infections in small cuts and lacerations, but it can also be used to treat infected wounds. This pharmacological agent is effective for the treatment of infections that result from Staphylococcus·aureus, Streptococcus and Pseudomonas.

- *Polymyxin B sulphate – Gramicidin,*

    This is similar to the above, but it is also effective with MRSA

- *Silver sulfadiazine,*

    Silver sulfadiazine is effectively used treating burns; it has a strong antimicrobial action against Staphylococcus aureus, MRSA, Streptococcus, and Pseudomonas.

- *Silver (ionized) in absorbent sheets*

    Are activated with sterile water. These sheets are used to effectively treat the same organisms as silver sulfadiazine. The moist environment increases reepithelialization.

Perform sharp instrument debridement

The actual procedure is performed as follows:

- *Antiseptic is used to clean the site and sterile equipment is used.*
- *The tissue is held with the forceps to allow the dissection area to be seen*
- *Dissection is performed avoiding vasculature*
- *Finalizing with saline irrigation of the wound and area surrounding it*

Perform chemical cauterization

Chemical cauterization destroys abnormal cells by using heat to burn or sear them. Then, for a short time, sliver nitrate sticks are activated by wetting them down with sterile water and rolled over the affected tissue to promote healing.

Identify indications for wound culture

Wound culture and sensitivities are done when there are signs of infection in a wound or no progress in healing has occurred with treatment over a two-week period of time. The wound culture identifies the specific offending pathogenic agent and the sensitivity identifies which antimicrobials are the most effective for the treatment of the infection.

The culture should be done prior to the administration of antibiotics because cultures done after the initiation of antimicrobial therapy may not be as accurate as those that are done prior to any antimicrobial treatments.

Sterile technique must be used in order to have a specimen that actually reflects what is contained in the wound rather than microorganisms on the surface of the skin or another contaminating microorganism. A culture is done by taking the sample from the wound itself rather than any exudate which, when done, can lead to an inaccurate laboratory test result.

There are three different methods of culturing:

1. *Swabbing*

   Swabbing is the most common method used but the sample is easily contaminated by surface flora.

2. *Needle aspiration*

   Needle aspiration of the fluid adjacent to and surrounding the wound is done with this method. It, however, may result in an underestimation of actual present microorganisms.

3. *Culturing by tissue biopsy*

   Culturing by tissue biopsy is the most effective method, but not all labs can process these samples and the process disrupts the wound and increases pain for the client.

Initiate pain control measures

A complete, timely and appropriate pain assessment must be done for wound care clients in order to initiate and maintain adequate pain management. At times, dressing changes can be very painful to the client, therefore, a number of considerations must be considered.

Some of these factors include the following:

- Frequent assessments of pain should be performed often and it should include the type and severity of pain, as well as the how the patient responds to any given analgesia. This information is helpful to manage the pain.

- Measuring increases in circulation to the wound, the oxygenation of the wound and assessing for signs of infection can be good indicators of the amount of pain that the client is experiencing..

- Improving the wound condition can be helpful in pain reduction

- Prior to a patient getting dressed they should be given any pain medication they are taking.

- Patient controlled analgesia, which is used for patients with severe pain, such as with severe burns, can help patients feel more independent. Another option to help patients feel more less anxious, which helps to rid some of their pain.

Adjuvant Pain Medications

Adjuvant medications have a potentiating effect when given with analgesic medications. The non-steroidal anti-inflammatory drugs (NSAIDs), corticosteroids, anticonvulsant medications and antidepressants are the most commonly used adjuvant medications.

According to the World Health Organization (WHO), pain should be treated in a step wise manner. The WHO has developed a Pain Ladder to describe these steps. The first step includes non-opioid medications, which is followed by mild opioids, such as codeine, and then strong opioids like morphine. Adjuvant medications help decrease the pain and they also are useful for decreasing anxiety associated with the pain or another cause.

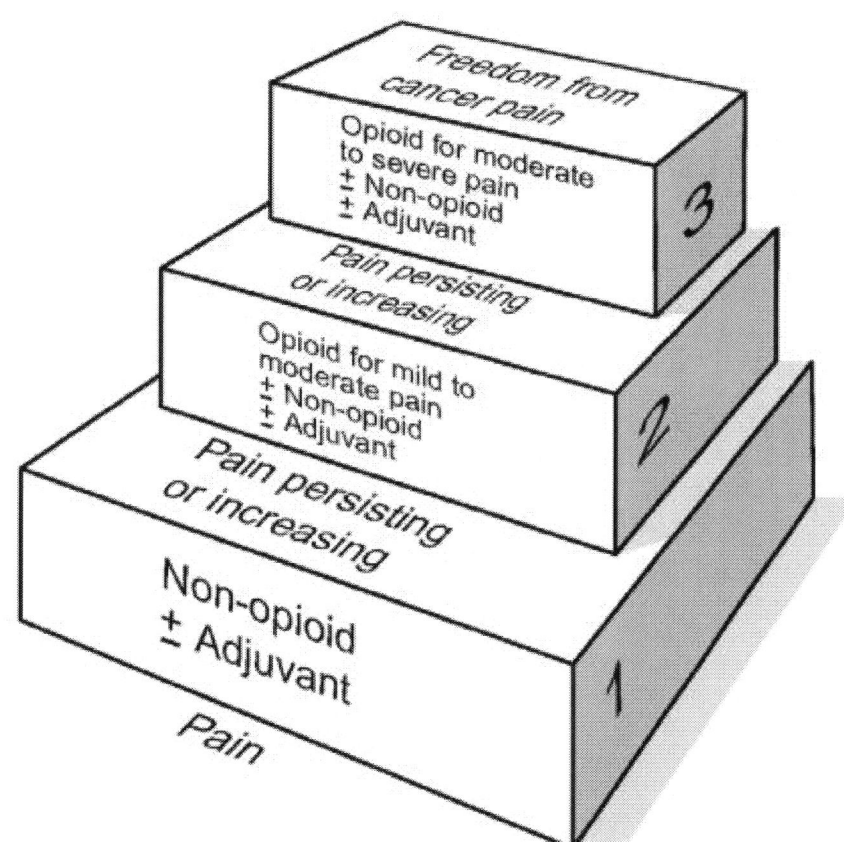

(World Health Organization (WHO))

http://www.who.int/cancer/palliative/painladder/en/

More detailed information about pain and pain management was previously presented.

Opioid Analgesics

DRUG	USUAL DOSAGE RANGE	Route	Indications
Codeine	30 mg q 4-6h	Oral	Mild to moderate pain
Fentanyl	50 mcg/hour (q 72h)	Oral, nasal, transdermal	Breakthrough pain
Hydrocodone	5-10 mg q 4-6h	Oral	Hydrocodone is available only in combination with other ingredients. Some hydrocodone products are used to relieve moderate to severe pain; other hydrocodone products are used to relieve cough.
Hydromorphone	2 mg 4-6h	Oral, injection, and rectal	Moderate to severe pain.

Methadone	2.5-5 mg BID-TID	Oral	Moderate to severe pain not relieved by non-narcotic pain relievers
Morphine	Immediate release 10 mg q 4h Sustained release 15 mg q 12h	Oral, rectal and injection	Moderate to severe pain
Oxycodone	Immediate release 5 mg q 4-6h Sustained release 10 mg q 12h	Oral	Moderate to severe pain
Oxymorphone	Immediate release 5-10 mg q 4-6h Sustained release 10 mg q 12h	Oral	Moderate to severe pain

Nonsteroidal Anti-Inflammatory Drugs (NASIDS)

DRUG	USUAL DOSAGE RANGE	Route	Indications
Naproxen	250-500 mg q 12h	Oral, rectal	Pain related to inflammatory conditions and chronic inflammatory conditions
Naproxen Na	275-550 mg q 12h	Oral	Pain and inflammation from muscular injuries
Oxaprozin	600-1200 mg q 24 h	Oral	Pain, stiffness and inflammation associated with rheumatoid and osteoarthritis
Aspirin	650-1000 mg q 4-6h	Oral	Pain, fever, and inflammation
Diflunisal	250-500 mg q 8-12h	Oral	Mild to moderate pain and inflammation
Salsalate	750-2000 mg q 12h	Oral	Pain, tenderness, swelling, and stiffness

Meclofenamate	50-100 mg q 6-8h	Oral	Mild to moderate pain, tenderness, swelling, and stiffness
Mefenamic acid	250 mg q 6h	Oral	Mild to moderate pain relief
Ketorolac (Toradol)	15-30 mg IV or IM q 6h or 20 followed by 10 mg q 4-6h	Oral, IM, IV and IV	Short-term management (up to 5 days) of moderately severe acute pain that otherwise would require narcotics
Diclofenac	50-100 mg, followed by 50 mg q 8h	Oral	Mild to moderate pain, fever and inflammation
Etodolac	200-400 mg q 6-8h	Oral	Inflammation and pain relief
Indomethacin	25-50 mg q 6-8h	Oral and rectal	Fever, pain and inflammation
Sulindac	150-200 mg q 12h	Oral	It is used for treating pain, fever, and inflammation.

Piroxicam	20-40 mg q 24h	Oral	Fever, pain, and inflammation
Acetaminophen	650-1000 mg q 6-8h	Oral	Acetaminophen relieves pain by elevating the pain threshold and it is also an antipyretic
Fenoprofen	200-600 mg q 6h	Oral	Mild to moderate pain, tenderness, swelling, and stiffness
Flurbiprofen	50-200 mg q 12h	Oral	Pain, tenderness, swelling, and stiffness relief
Ibuprofen	400mg q 4h to 800 mg q6h	Oral	Prescription strength and over the counter preparations are available. It relieves pain, tenderness, swelling, stiffness and fever
Ketoprofen	25-50 mg q 6-8h	Oral	Prescription strength and over the counter preparations are available. It is used to relieve

			pain, tenderness, swelling, stiffness, minor aches and pains from headaches, menstrual periods, toothaches, and backaches as well as an antipyretic
Celecoxib	100-200 mg q 12h	Oral	Pain, tenderness, swelling and stiffness

Anticonvulsants

Drug Name	Usual Dosage and Route	Indications for Pain Management
Carbamazepine	Oral dose two to four times a day Extended release tablet twice a day	Chronic low back pain, cancer pain, and restless leg syndrome
Gabapentin	Oral once every 12 hours Extended release once a day	Chronic low back pain, cancer pain, and restless leg syndrome
Phenytoin	Oral two or three times a	Chronic low back pain, and

	day Extended release capsules 1 to 3 times a day	cancer pain
Pregabalin	Oral capsule once daily	Chronic low back pain, cancer pain, and neuropathic pain
Topiramate	Oral twice a day (same time each day preferably morning and evening)	Chronic low back pain, cancer pain and prevention of migraine headaches
Carbamazepine	Oral two to four times a day and extended release tablet twice a day, and extended-release capsule twice a day	Cancer pain and facial nerve pain
Levetiracetam	Oral twice a day at the same time each day preferably in the morning and evening	Cancer pain
Oxcarbazepine	Oral twice a day at the same time each day preferably in the morning and evening	Cancer pain
Zonisamide	Oral capsule once or twice a day at the same	Cancer pain

	time each day	
Valproic acid	Oral once a day	Restless leg syndrome

Tricyclic Antidepressants

Drug Name	Usual Dosage and Route	Indications for Pain Management
Amitriptyline	Oral one to four times a day	Neck pain, low back pain, chronic pelvic pain and chronic pain syndrome
Doxepin	Topical and oral capsule one to three times a day	Neck pain, low back pain, chronic pelvic pain, and chronic pain syndrome
Imipramine	Oral	Neck pain, low back pain, chronic pelvic pain, and chronic pain syndrome
Desipramine	Oral	Low back pain, and chronic pain syndrome

Nortriptyline	Oral	Low back pain, and chronic pain syndrome
Maprotiline	Oral	Low back pain
Trazodone	Oral	Chronic pelvic pain

Patient Education Including Risk Factors and Care and Prevention Strategies

An important part of wound management relates to the patients and care givers knowing, or being taught risk factors and prevention strategies. Clients and family members should be taught about modifiable and non-modifiable risk factors, as well as preventive strategies. For example, clients and families should be educated about the fact that age and genetics cannot be modified, but a poor nutritional state can be changed and modified to decrease risk.

The risk factors associated with wounds and wound infections include biological risk factors, socioeconomic risk factors, psychological risk factors, intellectual risk factors and occupational risk factors.

Biological Risk Factors

Genetics, poor nutrition, the lack of regular exercise, age, obesity, poor lifestyle choices, risky behaviors, such as illicit drugs, disability and the presence of an illness or infection are examples of physical or biological risk factors.

Social and Economic Risk Factors

Some social and economic risk factors include a lack of relationships with others, a lack of social support, poverty, homelessness, and the lack of access to available and affordable healthcare resources.

Emotional and Psychological Risk Factors

Stress, ineffective coping skills, depression, the lack of insight, emotional distress, physiological defense mechanisms like denial, and one's lack of acceptance of one's own limitations are examples of emotional and psychological risk factors that can impact on the client.

Intellectual Risk Factors

Cognitive limitations, decreased levels of consciousness, literacy, and level of education impact on the occurrence disorders. For example, some clients do not utilize preventive care services and treatment options because they do not understand the benefits of it.

Occupational Risk Factors

Some occupations are filled with risk and others are not. For example, people who cut trees, roofers, miners, heavy equipment operators, and those exposed to environmental toxins, such as asbestos and chemicals are at greater risk for illness, accidents and disease because of the very nature of their job or occupation. People with office jobs are at least risk. Avocations, or hobbies, like sky diving and mountain climbing can also increase the client's risk of wounds, trauma and infections.

Some of the concepts relating to risk include:

- *Susceptibility*
- *Exposure potential*
- *Relative risk ratios*

Risk can be defined as the likelihood, or probability, that an event, such as a wound or trauma, will occur. Risk and risk factors indicate that an individual or group is more susceptible to an event than others. For example, an immobile individual may be at risk for a pressure ulcer, and much more susceptible than others, because they are not mobile and ambulatory.

Some populations are more at risk than others because they have an increased exposure potential. For example, diabetic clients are at greater risk for impaired microcirculation than others because they have the diabetes.

Relative risk ratios are statistical methods used in cohort and case series studies to determine risk cohort or case-series studies. Populations at risk, referred to as target groups, are targeted for intervention since they are at risk.

Some of the preventive strategies that clients and family members should be instructed about include the following:

- *Impaired circulation*

    Depending on the cause of the impaired circulation, clients can be instructed about daily exercise, positioning in a way to increase circulation, the elimination of restrictive clothing and the use of supportive hose.

- *Contamination with feces and urine*

    Adult diapers with assistance in hygiene and skin barriers, control of incontinence through medical and dietary instructions, and voiding schedules

- *Malnutrition*

    Depending on the source and cause of the nutritional need, Meals on Wheels, a culturally sensitive planned diet and/or dietary supplements can be recommended.

- *Cognitive impairment*

    Safety measures must be emphasized, turning and positioning cues as well as assistance with hygiene and elimination practices are sometimes helpful when the client has a cognitive impairment or a decreased level of consciousness.

- *Limited Mobility*

Proper physical and/or occupational therapy may be indicated and some patients may need the assistance of healthcare providers to turn and position in order to prevent a pressure ulcer, for example.

- *Diabetes*

    Foot care, continuous foot assessment, proper footwear and glucose monitoring and control are essential.

Management of the Systematic Factors Affecting Wound Healing

Perfusion

Perfusion and wound perfusion can be improved in many different ways. Examples of measures that can improve overall perfusion is the correction of low blood pressure and the elimination of pressure points when the client is lying down or sitting up.

Some wound perfusion interventions include surgical revascularization to replace damaged vessels and reducing the possibility of clot formation with preventive aspirin therapy. Diet, other measures to control high blood pressure, the management of highly glucose levels, dietary changes, smoking cessation, hyperbaric oxygen therapy to increase the oxygenation by 10 to 20% and medications to reduce the lipid levels are often also helpful.

As a result of the 10 to 20 time increase through hyperbaric oxygen therapy, the blood that is saturated will increase the perfusion of the tissues. This is indicated for diabetic ulcers, peripheral artery disease and comprised skin from grafts.

Other examples of improving wound perfusion are topical hyperbaric oxygen therapy which increases the circulation directly to the wound bed instead of systematically, circular boot therapy, which is used for end-diastolic compression and is useful for the treatment of lower extremity ulcers. It is also approved by the FDA to help treat deficient arterial blood flow.

Nutrition

Nutrition, as previously discussed, is individualized and based on the unique needs of the individual, but when a wound is involved some essential increases are required for good wound healing. For example the amount of protein to increases to 1.25 to 2.0 g per kilogram, iron needs increase to 20 to 30 mg, vitamin B vitamins increase by 200% of the RDA recommendation, vitamin C increases to from 100 to 1000 mg, and vitamin A needs range from 1600-2000 retinal equivalents.

Glucose Control

Diabetes has to be controlled carefully at all times including during wound healing. This control includes maintaining an HbA1C level of 6.5% or lower, keeping glycemic levels normal during healing, maintaining exercise, controlling the diet including sugar intake, smoking cessation and making any and all lifestyle changes that can affect both the diabetes as well as the wound care and healing.

Immune Compromise (i.e., immunosuppression)

Conditions, such as AIDS, medications such as steroids and chemotherapy can result in significant immunosuppression among our clients. This unfortunately can effect wound healing as well as increase infection risks.

Immunocompromised clients should work closely with the medical team and be closely monitored to see if medications and other interventions are needed or they need to be adjusted, changed or discontinued,

Maintaining a clean, safe and protective environment is essential in order to prevent infections including opportunistic infections, such as candidiasis.

Other systemic factors

A group of hemolytic blood disorders, known as sickle cell diseases, are inherited and result in the destruction of hemoglobin. Misshaped cells tend to cluster together, which occludes vessels and causes the patient to suffer severe pain. These misshapen cells are "sickle-shaped", which contributes to the name, sickle cell disease. Patients often suffer from an ulceration(s) on the malleolus, which is the bony protuberance on either side of the ankle, at the lower end of the fibula or of the tibula. They can have one to several of these lesions, they can vary in size, and they are usually a result of edema and slow healing.

Another important systemic factor to be aware of and properly managed is the management of skin lesions. Sickle cell diseases are one example. It is an inherited blood disorder in which lesions can occur usually on the lower extremities.

Treatments include:

- *Infection monitoring*
- *Debridement as needed*
- *Dressings that are moisture retentive to promote the healing process*
- *Medications or transfusions to control the disease*
- *Edema reduction through elevation, compression and bed rest*

Another inherited disease includes thalassemia. This disease is known to cause abnormal hemoglobin as well as microcytic anemia. This disorder is commonly associated among populations with a mediterranean descent. Patient's suffering from this are also more susceptible to trauma and tissue damage, due to the decrease of iron in their hemoglobin, as well.

Treatment includes:
- *Wound protection to decrease the risk of further trauma*
- *Blood transfusions and iron-chelation therapy to control the disease*
- *The prevention of wound hypothermia*
- *Using moisture-retentive dressing*

Recommend:
Hyperbaric Oxygenation

As mentioned earlier in this review book, hyperbaric oxygenation treatments (HBOT) increase available oxygen to tissues by 10 to 20 times. This treatment is given in a high pressure chamber while the client is inhaling 100% oxygen. The type of wound being treated dictates the exact treatment course, but it is important to note that a maximum of ninety minutes of treatment not be exceeded to avoid oxygen toxicity.

This treatment increases the perfusion of the tissues of blood as they are saturated with this high level of oxygen in combination with the pressure. Those who have ulcerations of a lower extremity are less likely to need an amputation when this treatment is rendered. This therapy is used for a variety of different conditions but hypoxic wounds such as those that are associated with peripheral arterial insufficiency, compromised skin from grafts and diabetic ulcers benefit the most.

Hyperbaric oxygenation treatments hyperoxygenate tissues and blood and they also increase the antibiotic effectiveness of medications, such as amphotericin B, aminoglyocsides, and fluoroquinolone, because these medications need active transport across cell walls and hyperbaric oxygenation treatments reduce capillary leakage with vasoconstriction.

Growth Factor Treatment

Growth factors are proteins that are necessary for the growth and migration of cells and, as such, they are highly critical elements in the healing of wounds. Growth factors may be isolated from tumor cells, platelets, macrophages, ovarian follicles and the placenta but recombinant DNA techniques have allowed us to more effectively and cost effectively produce synthetic growth factor from other sources such as from bacterial cultures and human cells with the growth factor genes. When growth factors are used for the treatment of wounds they are applied topically to the affected area(s).

Growth factor treatments include:

- *Connective Tissue Growth Factor (CTGF) is being studied for use to combat fibrosis.*
- *Epidermal Growth Factor (EGF) is used for burns and venous ulcers.*
- *Fibroblast Growth Factor (FGF) is used for burns and pressure ulcers.*
- *Insulin-Like Growth Factor (IGF) is being studied as a means to reduce HbAIC in diabetes.*
- *Platelet-Derived Growth Factor (PDGF) is used for pressure and diabetic ulcers.*
- *Transforming Growth Factor-Beta (TGF) is used with chronic skin ulcers*

Negative Pressure Wound Therapy

Negative pressure wound therapy is used on wounds that are difficult to heal such as those that have only healed <30% over a period of four weeks. When negative pressure wound healing is indicated, the wound must be debrided of necrotic tissue prior to it.

Negative pressure wound therapy consists of negative or subatmoshheric pressure that is exerted by using a suction unit and a semi-occlusion vapor-permeable dressing. The therapy results in a reduction of the periwound and interstitial edema, thus promoting successful wound healing. This treatment stimulates the production of new cells and it also increases the rate of granulation and re-epithelialization which both speed up the healing process.

There are some situations, however, some conditions and situations that contraindicate the use of negative pressure wound therapy. For example, negative pressure wound therapy is contraindicated when the client is affected with a wound malignancy, untreated osteomyelitis, exposed blood vessels, exposed organs, as well as nonenteric and unexplored fistulas.

Communication Relevant to Coordinating Patient Care and Discharge Planning

All client care should be multidisciplinary or interdisciplinary. For this reason all nurses, including wound care nurses, must actively and continuously communicate with and collaborate with other members of the healthcare team in terms of coordinating care, planning care and discharge planning. Some of the other members of the healthcare team who are intimately involved in the care and treatment of clients with wounds include the physician, the dietitian, the pharmacist, and perhaps a physical therapist to help the client with mobility problems.

The planning process consists of establishing priorities, developing expected outcomes, or patient goals, and deciding on implementation strategies at the appropriate level of care, that are consistent with the need, and other considerations, such as evidence based practice.

When planned interventions are deemed consistent with the client's goals, the client is then linked to the available resources that best address their needs both within the healthcare facility itself or in the community as often occurs with discharge when the client is discharged to the home or another facility with an appropriate level of care for the unique client. For example, the wound care nurse may recommend that the client be discharged to a different level of care in a subacute care facility after discharge from an acute care facility or they may recommend follow up care in a community based wound care center.

Pressure Ulcers

Pressure sores are also referred to as decubitus ulcers, trophic ulcers, stasis ulcers, ischemic ulcers and bedsores. These ulcers occur as the result of external forces such as pressure over a bony prominence of the body, moisture (incontinence), and shearing and friction when a client is pulled up and/or repositioned in the bed. Most pressure ulcers can be prevented.

Some of the intrinsic factors that place clients at risk for pressure ulcers are poor nutritional status, a thin person body type, a condition that prohibits a client's free movement (paralysis), some diseases like diabetes, vascular deficiencies, and incontinence.

Pressure

The tissues of the body become more distorted the greater the pressure on the skin is. The blood flow can be interrupted due to distortion of the blood vessels that can occur from pressure on the skin over the bony prominences. Cell damage can also occur from the accumulation of toxic substances due to the pressure on and occlusion of the lymphatic vessels.

The most common area of pressure sores are over the areas of the body where a thin layer of tissue is all that covers bony prominences, although areas that are subjected to prolonged or excessive pressure in other areas of the body can also develop pressure sores.

Clients who are immobilized are at risk for pressure ulcers because they are often unable to move themselves about in the bed and reposition themselves like those who are not immobilized can. Normally, people unconsciously turn every ten minutes during sleep or rest periods. This movement is essential to the circulation of blood, the stimulation of the organs in the body, as well as preventing pressure ulcers.

Friction and Shearing

Friction and shearing also distort soft tissue when the layers of the skin move over one another due to pressure being applied at an angle. Tissue necrosis and the development of pressure sores occur when the dermal capillaries are distorted and occluded.

These forces jeopardize the client's skin integrity when they are not moved up and around the bed or chair in the proper manner. Friction and shearing can be reduced by eliciting the client's cooperation with movements in the bed when possible, using draw or pull sheets, using a mechanical lift and getting the support of additional staff when turning a client. These extrinsic factors can be exacerbated when other risk factors are also present.

Intrinsic factors are those factors that are characteristics specific to the client's condition. Intrinsic factors that place the client at risk for pressure ulcers include:

- *Nutritional Status*

    Poor and inefficient cellular growth and repair occurs as a result of inadequate nutrition; poor nutrition also causes the bodily tissue to become more vulnerable to damage and it typically also leads to the client's having less prevention protection over their bony prominences and, therefore, more vulnerable to the adverse effects of prolonged pressure on a body part.

- *Body Type*

    A thin person is more at risk because the bony prominences are more bony, but an obese client is also at risk, particularly when the obese person's body and its excessive weight is subjected to shearing and friction forces.

- *Mobility*

    A client who has a limited amount of mobility and is unable to move in order to redistribute their weight on pressure areas is also at risk.

- *Neurological Factors*

    Certain disease states, such as spinal cord injury, paralysis, multiple sclerosis and diabetes mellitus, can cause reduced sensitivity to pain and/or pressure. In these situations there may be an impairment of the transmission of the impulses from the receptors in either the skin or muscles to the brain which makes the body move to avoid and respond to pressure.

- *Vascular Factors*

    Certain disease states, such as arteriosclerosis, cardiac failure or diabetes mellitus can result in reduced local tissue perfusion which places clients at risk for pressure ulcers. Poor local tissue oxygenation and a poor nutritional status are the primary causes of pressure sores.

- *Incontinence*

    Skin excoriation or maceration can result from urinary and fecal incontinence and the moisture that it produces.

Signs and Symptoms

There are four stages, based on severity, in which pressure ulcers fall. These stages are defined by The National Pressure Ulcer Advisory Panel, and are as follows:

1. *Stage I*

   The skin is intact; it may appear as a red spot on people with a lighter skin color and it may be present when the skin color does not return to the normal color but remains blanched after digital pressure is applied and released.

   Among people with darker skin, there may be no change in the color of the skin and the skin may not blanch when touched or, in some cases, the skin may appear ashen, bluish or purple.

   All clients with all skin colors may also experience tenderness and/or burning of the skin in addition to edema, a firm skin feeling, a soft skin feeling and feelings of either coolness or heat at the affected area.

2. *Stage II*

   The stage II ulcer is an open wound; the outer layer of skin (epidermis) and part of the underlying layer of skin (dermis) is damaged or lost.

   The pressure ulcer may appear as a shallow, pinkish-red, basin-like wound or as an intact or ruptured fluid-filled blister. There may also be some peeling and/or cracking of the skin

3. *Stage III*

   The ulcer is a deep wound at this stage of pressure ulcer development. This stage occurs when the full thickness of the skin and the subcutaneous tissue is damaged. A serous bloodstained discharge is commonly evident at this stage. Slough, which is composed of dead tissue, forms and it appears as a black necrotic area and, at this stage, there is an invasion of rapid multiplying microorganisms as well.

   The loss of skin usually exposes some amount of fat. The ulcer has a crater-like appearance. The bottom of the wound may have some yellowish dead tissue (slough).

   The damage may extend beyond the primary wound below the layers of healthy skin.

4. *Stage IV*

   A stage IV pressure ulcer involves damage to the full thickness of skin and subcutaneous tissue. A deep ulcer is formed. There is exposure and possible damage to structures, such as fascia, muscle, connective tissue and bone underlying the ulcer.

A stage IV ulcer exhibits large-scale loss of tissue. The wound may expose muscle, bone and tendons. The bottom of the wound likely contains slough or dark, crusty dead tissue referred to as eschar.

The damage often extends beyond the primary wound below layers of healthy skin.

The prevention of pressure sores requires repositioning, skin care, regular skin inspections and good nutrition. Frequent repositioning is essential. Those in a wheelchair should be moved and reposition every fifteen minutes and the use of extra cushioning with a gel pad can also help. Those on complete bed rest require repositioning at least every two hours and they can also benefit from repositioning devices, special supportive mattresses, slight head of the bed elevation and the protection of their bony areas.

There are also a number of complications associated with pressure ulcers including sepsis, cellulitis, osteomyelitis and squamous cell carcinoma.

The Treatment of Pressure Ulcers

With conservative care of the wound, stage I and II pressure sores will heal within several weeks to months. Pressure sores that are stage III and IV are more difficult to treat. If the patient also has a terminal illness the treatment may focus more on pain relief as opposed to treating the sore itself.

When treating a pressure sore, there are different options, and sometimes a patient requires a combination of the options. Treatments available include pressure relief, which includes repositioning and support services, removal of the damaged tissue which includes surgical debridement, mechanical debridement, autolytic debridement and enzymatic debridement, cleaning and dressing the wounds, pain management, antibiotics, a healthy diet and surgical repair.

Lower Extremity Ulcers

Assessment

Assessment of perfusion is performed by not only checking venous filling time and capillary refill, but also checking the skin temperature between the limbs, checking for bruits, monitoring pulses and monitoring the ankle-brachial index and toe-brachial index.

Lower extremity fine motor function is assessed by having the client place each of their heels on the opposite shin, as close to the knee as possible, and then run the heel down the leg, while in a supine position.

Skin and Toenails

A complete and thorough assessment of the skin and toe nails entails the assessment of the color, changes in the color which can be described as pallor or rubber for example, warmth and differences in these characteristics when the skin on the extremities, for example, are compared on the right and the left extremity. Other assessments, in addition to those described in the physical assessment section above include the presence of hairlessness, shiny skin and pale skin, all of which can indicate peripheral artery disease.

Sensorimotor Status Monofilament

The ability to feel pain, temperature and touch are included in sensory function. The nylon monofilament test, which is a simple test, is used to test for neuropathy. This test's supplies are commercially prepared in kits and it is administered by evaluating how many, out of the 10 tested sites, are sensed and detected by the patient with the #10 monofilament. If the client tests with only the detection of four or less sites, the client is at risk for lower extremity ulcers and wounds as the result of a sensorimotor impairment.

Range of Motion

Assessment of the range of motion of the ankle is important to see if it can flex past 90 degrees. This range of motion is necessary for unimpaired walking and venous return to the calf.

Pulses

At first the pulse should be taken on the patient in the supine position, followed by the pulse being taken with the patient's legs dependent. Checking the lower extremity pulses entails comparing the pulses bilaterally and moving from the proximal pulses to the distal pulses. Pulses should be equally intense bilateral.

Pulses should be taken and evaluated for rhythm, rate and intensity at both the posterior tibialis and the dorsalis pedis pedal pulse sites. The grading scale for pulses is typically noted according to a 0 to 4 scale; a 0 is an absent pulse; 1 is a weak pulse and one that is difficult to palpate; 2 is a normal pulse; 3 is a full pulse and 4 is strong and bounding pulse.

Peripheral arterial disease typically presents with an absent pulse using both palpation and a Doppler probe; on some occasions, however, pulses can be palpable with peripheral artery disease.

Capillary Refill

Checking venous filling and capillary refill are observed as a part of the assessment of perfusion. Capillary refill consists of applying the thumb and index finger around the toe bed and applying several seconds of pressure until blanching occurs. Once the blanching occurs, the toe nail bed is released and a count of how long in seconds is necessary for the bed to regain the normal coloring. If it takes more than 2 to 3 seconds to recover, arterial occlusion is suggested. This capillary refill test is done on both feet.

Venous refill time is performed by having the patient lay in the supine position for a few minutes and then having them sit up with their feet on the floor. At this time, the nurse observes the veins on the dorsum of the foot to determine how many seconds it takes to refill. Venous occlusion is suggested if and when the refill time is greater than 20 seconds.

Assess and Monitor Severity of Edema

Edema is checked and monitored by pressing the tissue on the top of each foot with the index finger. The spot which is pressed is located behind the medial malleolus and over the shin starting distally and then moving proximally to the highest level of edema. Present edema is assessed and recorded bilaterally.

A four point scale is used to assess and document the client's level of edema. This rating scale is as follows:

> *1-There is slight pitting to approximately 2 mm which is present for about 10 to 15 seconds.*
>
> *2- There is moderate pitting to approximately 4 mm which is present for 10 to 15 seconds.*
>
> *3- There is moderately severe pitting to approximately 6 mm which persists for more than a minute*
>
> *4- There is severe pitting to 8 mm or more which persists for a period of 2 to or more minutes.*

Ankle-Brachial Index (ABI)

Another method to evaluate and assess peripheral arterial disease is by performing the ankle-brachial index examination. This examination is performed with a blood pressure cuff, a Doppler device and a stethoscope. It is performed on both arms and both ankles, and, in some cases the readings are taken before and after five minutes of walking on a treadmill.

Upon completion of the ankle-brachial index examination, the person performing the assessment mathematically divides the ankle systolic pressure by the brachial systolic pressure. The normal finding is to have the ankle systolic pressure equal to or just slightly higher than the brachial systolic pressure.

This calculation is easily preformed. For example, when the ankle systolic pressure is 80 and the brachial systolic pressure is 110, it is calculated as:

80 divided by 110 = 0.73

The score of this examination indicates the degree and extent of the peripheral artery the disease. The following table shows this scoring:

Score	Degree of the Peripheral Artery Disease
>1.3	Abnormally high
	It may indicate the calcification of vessel wall
1 – 1.1	Normal reading
	The client is typically asymptomatic
<0.95:	This finding indicates the narrowing of one or more leg blood vessels
<0.8:	Moderate disease
	This is often associated with intermittent claudication during exercise
< 0.6-0.8:	Borderline perfusion

0.5-0.75:	Severe disease
	Ischemia is present
<0.5:	Pain is present even at rest
	The limb is threatened
0.25:	Critical limb-threatening condition

Toe-Brachial Index (TBI)

This is yet another testing method. The procedure is as follows:

1. Blood pressure cuff is applied to one arm, brachial pulse is palpated and conductivity gel is placed over the artery

2. The Doppler device tip is placed at a 45 degree angle into the gel at the brachial artery and the pulse is listened for

3. The cuff is then inflated until the pulse sound ceases. The cuff is then inflated 20mm Hg above that point

4. Air is then to begin being released until such time that the sound of the pulse returns, and this is the brachial systolic pressure

5. The procedure is then repeated on the other arm, and the higher reading is used for the calculations

6. The same procedure is repeated on the great or second toe. The cuff is applied around the base of the toes and the gel over the pulse to obtain the toe systolic pressure

7. The toe systolic pressure is then divided by the brachial systolic pressure to obtain the TBI

The normal values are >0.6

Transcutaneous Oxygen Pressure (Tcpo2)

The non-invasive test, known as the transcutaneous oxygen pressure test, is used to measure the effectiveness of the dermal oxygen in the skin and tissues. The test is used for several different reasons including determining the appropriate amputation site for a client with hypoxic limbs, determining the amount of hypoxia present with venous diseases, finding the degree of oxygenation and peripheral disease and for determining if there is the proper amount of oxygen transport available for effective hyperbaric oxygen therapy treatments.

This test is performed by placing electrodes in specific locations on the body and then heating the body to help increase the flow of blood. The test is given in two or three different sites. Contact gel and electrodes are applied to the lower extremities to determine variations in oxygen tension.

The test results are as follows:

- *40 mm Hg: This indicates that there is an adequate amount of oxygenation for healing*
- *20 – 40 mm Hg: This indicates that an increase in oxygenation is needed for healing, but it is not so low that marked ischemia is present*
- *<20 mm Hg: This indicates that there is marked ischemia which will adversely affect healing*

Venous Insufficiency

Venous insufficiency is when the veins, which lack the musculature that arteries have, are not able to effectively send blood from the limbs back to the heart; this causes blood to pool in the legs. Chronic venous insufficiency results in edema of one's lower extremities. This causes an increased risk of ulcers, as well as discomfort.

Treatments include the following:

- *Compression therapy*
- *Leg elevation*

If these options do not provide the necessary relief and care then surgery may be indicated. These options can include ligation and stripping, which removes a vein or section of a vein that is damaged, or deep vein reconstruction.

Physical therapy and weight control are essential, and medications can be used to treat symptoms, but they are not a cure.

Dermatitis

Dermatitis is a broad term that describes an inflammation of the skin. It can occur in many forms and has a number of different causes, but it almost always appears as an itchy rash on swollen, red skin.

Venous or stasis dermatitis is an inflammation of the epidermis and the dermis that causes scaly, erythematous, weepy, crusty, itchy skin, which is usually located in the lower leg, such as the ankle and tibia. Redness and itching appear prior to other possible symptoms, and it is progressive.

Atopic dermatitis or eczema appears as an itchy, red rash most commonly seen in the folds of the skin like behind knees and in the elbow fold. If scratched, the fluid can leak and crust over. Contact dermatitis appears on the area of skin that is touched with an allergen or irritant like poison ivy and poison oak. Blisters can appear and the rash can cause stinging, burning or itching.

Seborrheic dermatitis is a condition that causes a red rash which is accompanied with yellowish oily scales. It is commonly seen on the scalp and face, especially around the ears, nose and mouth. It often causes dandruff and, among infants, this dermatological disorder is referred to as cradle cap.

Common treatments include corticosteroid creams, applying wet compresses, avoiding allergens or irritants, and in some cases, exposing the skin to controlled amounts of natural and artificial light.

Lichen simplex chronicus

Lichen simplex chronicus, also referred to as neurodermatitis, is a skin condition that causes the patient to itch and to scratch the patch of skin that is affected. Itchy skin in a single limited area, leathery or scaly skin to the touch, and raised, rough patches that appear either red or a color darker than the rest of the patient's skin can occur.

In order to control the itching, corticosteroids, antihistamines and anti-anxiety medications may be prescribed. Antibiotics may be indicated if a bacterial infection occurs.

Lichen planus

Lichen planus is an inflammatory condition of the skin and mucous membranes that occurs as a result the patient's immune system attacking their own skin and/or mucous membrane cells.

Common signs and symptoms include itching, nail damage or loss, hair loss, scalp discoloration, painful oral or vaginal ulcerations, white spots which appear in the mouth, inside the cheeks, or on the gums, lip or tongue, blisters that can break to form crusts or scabs, and also bumps on the inner forearm, wrist or ankle and sometimes on the external genitals that appear flat topped and purple in color.

For itchiness, medications such as corticosteroids, retinoids, non-steroidal ointments or creams and antihistamines can be prescribed. Phototherapy can also be helpful in the treatment of lichen planus.

Psoriasis

Psoriasis is a common, persistent and chronic disease that affects the life cycle of cells. On the surface of the skin the cells build up rapidly and they form silvery scales and itchy, dry, red patches, which in some cases are painful as well.

There are three main types of treatment for psoriasis, including topical treatments with corticosteroids, vitamin D analogues, anthralin, retinoids, calcineurin inhibitors, salicylic acid, coal tar, and moisturizers, light therapy using sunlight, UVB phototherapy, narrowband UVB therapy, Goeckermantherapy, photochemotherapy or psoralen plus ultraviolet A (PUVA), excimer laser, pulsed dye laser, and combination light therapy, and, lastly, systemic medications such as retinoids, methotrexate, cyclosporine, hydroxyurea, biologics, and thiguanine.

Erythema multiforme

Erythema multiforme, also referred to as Stevens-Johnson syndrome, is a type of skin disorder that results from an infection, some medications or an allergic reaction. Medications that can cause erythema multiforme include barbiturates, penicillin, phenytoin, and sulfonamides; and infections that can cause this are herpes simplex and mycoplasma.

The ultimate aims of treatment are to prevent infection, control the causal illness and relieving the symptoms. If the cause is a certain medication, ceasing to take the medication is important, but, because some medications cannot be abruptly stopped, it may be necessary to wean the patient off some medications slowly. Mild symptoms, such as itching, can be treated with antihistamines and moist compresses. If fever is present, administering acetaminophen can be helpful to reduce the fever and discomfort. An antiviral can be used for herpes simplex; and, if the patient has mouth sores, topical anesthetics can be used to help ease the discomfort associated with these sores.

The treatment of severe symptoms includes antibiotics if a skin infection is present, corticosteroids to control the inflammation and IV immunoglobulins to stop the disease process. Severe cases, such as Stevens-Johnson syndrome and toxic epidermal necrolysis, are treated in an intensive care or burn center unit.

Venous dermatitis presents on the ankles and lower legs, and it can cause severe pain and itching in the area affected. This type of dermatitis can also deteriorate the skin and cause ulcers to form.

Edema

Edema of the lower extremities is a painful result of chronic venous insufficiency. An increased risk of ulcers occurs when edema is present.

The treatment options are as follows:

- *Compression therapy*
- *Elevation of the affected limb above the level of the heart for a minimum of 1 to 2 hours a day*
- *Weight control and weight loss when indicated. At times surgical interventions may be necessary.*
- *Physical therapy to prevent atrophy, to enhance and maintain mobility and to keep the range of motion full and active*
- *Medications to ease symptoms*

Surgical interventions are used as a last resort when all other conservative treatment options have failed. Some of the surgical interventions can include ligation and stripping to remove and ligate a vein and deep vein reconstruction.

Recommend and apply:

Dynamic Compression Therapy (E.G., Pumps)

Intermittent pneumatic compression therapy, also referred to as dynamic compression therapy, is indicated for those who are immobile, and for those who have failed with static compression therapy.

The device has a garment and a pneumatic pump used to inflate the garment.

This device is placed on the patient's lower leg or plantar area of the foot. There is usually a double lined stocking that is put on the leg; the inner lining contains an air bladder which allows for air filling in different areas up the leg to increases venous return, which is protected under the outer lining. The blood flow is stimulated when the patient uses the foot pump with a pumping motion. This treatment is performed 1 to 2 times a day for a period of 1-2 hours to decrease edema and to facilitate the healing of peripheral ulcers.

Static Compression Therapy

Static compression therapy is used to increase venous flow, while supporting the calf muscle, ankle and knee. Static compression applies external graduated pressure to the lower extremity. This therapy is used as a preventative measure and also as a therapeutic treatment to decrease and eliminate edema, but it is not curative. The underlying cause of the edema should be treated whenever possible.

Static compression therapy is a very effective form of therapy but it is contraindicated in patients with peripheral arterial disease and heart failure. It should also not be used if the patient's ankle brachial index is <0.5.

There are different types of static compression therapy devices depending on the need of the patient. These options are explained below.

Bandages (Wraps)

- *Layered wraps* are a specific type of static compression therapy. Layered wraps contain 2 to 4 layers elastic and non-elastic materials with layers inside to help to protect bony prominences and absorb drainage. The skin underneath is lubricated in order to prevent drying from occurring. This type of dressing is applied only by a professional and it is changed 1 to 2 times a week. Both ambulatory and non-ambulatory patients are able to benefit from this dressing.

- A long reusable elastic wrap, known as *single layer wrap*, can be helpful when used upon early diagnosis. They are fairly inexpensive and most caregivers in the home can apply them after they are educated about the application techniques.

- Another wrap is known as *Unna's boot*. This is a gauze wrap that is not suitable for non-ambulatory patients but they can be used for those with peripheral artery disease. Care must be used while applying these boots properly.

- Another bandage available is a *short-stretch or stretch wrap*. It is reusable and can be used for those who are ambulatory and with ankle brachial index of >0.5 and <0.8. This type of wrap can be used initially and caregivers can apply in most cases when instructed how to do so. A disadvantage is that they tend to slip off.

Therapeutic Support Stockings

Therapeutic support stockings are used for patients to prevent ulceration among those who have an existing ulcer when the edema has somewhat receded, for those with varicose veins and stable venous insufficiency after edema is controlled. They are available in many sizes and they can be used for both ambulatory and non-ambulatory patients

Therapeutic support stockings are contraindicated among clients who are affected with lipodermatosclerosis, because of the difficulty associated with proper and accurate stocking fitting. Proper fitting is essential so that the correct level of compression is applied. The following table illustrates this:

Class		
Class 1	20 -30 mm Hg	Varicose Veins
Class 2	30 -40 mm Hg	Venous ulcers and prevention

| Class 3 | 40 – 40 mm Hg | Refractory venous ulcers and lymphedema |
| Class 4 | 50 – 60 mm Hg | Lymphedema |

Orthotic Devices

An orthotic device, known as CircAid Thera-Boot, is made to cover the foot and ankle with Velcro straps; it is thin enough to fit in a shoe and it provides the patient with the necessary continuous compressions and it supports the calf muscle pump function.

Although this boot is used to treat venous ulcers, it cannot be used until any present edema has sufficiently subsided. Patients can use this as an initial treatment and they can also use it for continuous care.

Arterial Insufficiency

Assess for Subtle Indications of Infection

Arterial insufficiency due to the lack of arterial circulation is often accompanied with the typical and classical signs of inflammation without any visible or noticeable signs of infection. It is, therefore, vital to observe for the subtle signs of infection because an infection, if not detected, can lead to cellulitis, osteomyelitis and/or the necessity of an amputation.

All wounds should be observed carefully and dry necrotic wounds need a 10% providone-iodine applied to them after which they should be dressed and covered with dry sterile gauze.

The early detection and identification of infections is essential to early treatment and positive client outcomes. The following signs must be continuously monitored for:

- *Erythema about the perimeter of the wound*
- *Increased pain in the ischemic limb or an ulcer and/or increased edema.*
- *Increased size of the necrotic area of an ulcer*
- *Periwound tissue has fluctuance which is a soft texture upon palpation*

Recommend:

Lifestyle Changes to Maximize Perfusion

There are a variety of lifestyle changes that can help to avoid serious complications and/or amputation among clients with arterial insufficiency. These changes include:

- *Managing pain to prevent further vasoconstriction*
- *Refraining from wearing cold and constrictive clothing*
- *Smoking cessation because nicotine has vasoconstrictive properties*

- *Daily foot and nail care*
- *Wearing shoes that are fitted properly*
- *Refrain from walking with bare feet*
- *Avoid the use of antiseptics or chemicals except as prescribed*
- *Report even small injuries or changes in skin promptly.*
- *Keep feet warm in cold weather by wearing warm socks*
- *Do careful skin inspection and skin care, drying skin, using emollients and lamb's wool or foam between toes*
- *Maintain adequate hydration to decrease blood viscosity, but avoid caffeine which is vasoconstrictive*

Pharmacologic Measures to Maximize Perfusion

Reduction of the risk of thrombosis is the primary focus of the pharmacologic measures used to maximize perfusion.

To maximize perfusion the primary pharmacologic measures used are as follows:

- *Anticoagulants*, such as heparin, Coumadin and Lovenox, which are used to prevent blood clots from forming.

  Anticoagulants prevent clot formation; they are used for the treatment and prevention of deep vein thrombosis, coronary thrombosis, cerebrovascular accidents and pulmonary embolism. These medications do not dissolve clots, however, they do prevent their formation and growth.

  Coumadin is absorbed from the gastrointestinal tract; heparin is poorly absorbed from the gastrointestinal tract, therefore it is administered subcutaneously or intravenously. Low molecular weight heparin, a new category of anticoagulants, is a safer form of anticoagulation that is accompanied with fewer side effects.

  Heparin, via the intravenous route, has immediate onset, and an almost immediate peak, but it has a short duration. The clotting time will typically return to the baseline within 2 to 4 hours. Coumadin, on the other hand, has a longer onset, peak and duration. The half life of heparin is dose related and typically about 1 to 2 hours; the half life of warfarin is 0.5 to 3 days.

  Low molecular weight heparin is administered subcutaneously; and the dosage is based on the client's weight and anti-factor Xa.

- *Vasodilators*, such as Pietal dilates arteries and decreases clotting; it is used for the control of intermittent claudication.

  Vasodilators can be used to treat heart failure, as it decreases venous blood return to the heart and it results in a decrease in cardiac filling, ventricular stretching or preload, and oxygen demand on the heart. The arteriolar dilators act in the following three ways.

1. Reducing cardiac afterload which increases cardiac output
2. Dilates the arterioles of the kidneys which improves renal perfusion and increases fluid loss
3. Improves circulation to the skeletal muscles

- *Hemorrheologics*, such as Trental, reduces fibrinogen, reduces blood viscosity and decreases the rigidity of erythrocytes; however, clinical studies show limited benefit. It may be used for intermittent claudication.

- *Antilipemic*, such as Zocor and Questran, slow the progression of atherosclerosis.

    Antilipemics are used to lower lipoproteins, which include the following four major categories:

    1. *High-density lipoprotein (HDL) (good lipoprotein)*, which contains more protein and less fat than the other types. The function of HDL is to remove cholesterol from the blood stream and deliver it to the liver for excretion in bile.
    2. *Low-density lipoprotein (LDL) (bd lipoprotein)*, which contains 50-60 percent of cholesterol in the bloodstream. There is a greater risk of developing atherosclerotic plaques and heart disease when there is an elevated LDL level.
    3. *Very low lipoprotein (VLDL)*, carries mostly triglycerides and less cholesterol.
    4. *Chylomicrons*, are large particles that transport fatty acids and cholesterol to the liver. These are composed primarily of triglycerides.

- *Antiplatelet agents* such as aspirin, Ticlid, and Plavix, interfere with the function of the plasma membrane and clotting. These agents are ineffective for the treatment and dissolution of clots but they do not prevent clot formation.

    Heparin, Coumadin and low molecular weight are used for the prevention of venous thrombosis, whereas, antiplatelet medications are used for the prevention of arterial thrombosis because they suppress platelet aggregation.

    These medications, such as clopidogrel, highly bind to protein and they are rapidly absorbed; the half life is 8 hours and it is excreted with urine and feces.

    The onset of action is 1 to 2 hours; it peaks in 2 to 3 hours.

- *Analgesics* may be necessary to improve quality of life. Opioids may be needed in some cases. Analgesics including narcotics and NSAIDs were fully discussed above.

- *Thrombolytics* may be injected into a blocked artery under angiography to dissolve clots.

    Within four hours after an acute myocardial infarction, the thrombus or blood clot disintegrates when a thrombolytic drug is administered. Prevention or minimization of necrosis occurs as a result from the blocked artery.

    These drugs should also be used within three hours of a thrombolic stroke. Other uses for these medications include deep vein thrombosis, pulmonary embolism, and non-coronary artery occlusion resulting from acute thromboembolism.

    Five common thrombolytics are as follows:

    1. *Alteplase*
    2. *Reteplase*
    3. *Tenecteplase*
    4. *Streptokinase*
    5. *Urokinase*

Evaluation for Surgical/Vascular Intervention

The ultimate goal of managing arterial insufficiency and ulcers are to save the limb and improve perfusion. Unfortunately in some cases lifestyle changes and medications are not enough and surgical interventions are indicated. The following are a number of reasons for which surgical interventions may be indicated:

- *Condition that is limb-threatening*

    These can include severe ischemia that causes increased pain when at rest, an infection, which can cause rapid wound deterioration, and/or gangrene

- *Pain that is intolerable*

    This can include rest pain, and intermittent claudation, which causes the patient to be unable to perform their normal daily activities, such as working, or as simple as dressing and grooming

- *Healing prognosis that is poor*

    This can include patients whose perfusion is severely compromised

- *Non-response to conservative treatment*

    This can include pharmacology treatments and lifestyle changes

Surgical intervention is indicated only for patients with whom radiologic imaging procedures show patent distal vessels.

There are three different types of surgical/vascular procedures that are used for treating severe arterial insufficiency. They include the following:

1. *Bypass grafts*

   Damaged arteries bypassed by harvesting a section of the saphenous vein or upper extremity vein, which are reversed or stripped of their valves before attaching, to supply blood to the distal vessels. Synthetic grafts have a much higher failure rate, so they are less commonly used.

2. *Angioplasty*

   Angioplasty can only be used if the disease is not that extensive, and the patient's arteries must be large enough to allow for the procedure to be performed successfully. Anticoagulants used improves the success rate, which is less positive in the long-term.

3. *Amputation*

   This is the obvious last choice, but if ischemia is irreversible or severe necrosis is present and there is a life-threatening infection, it may be required.

Neuropathic Ulcers:

Assess for Foot Deformity

Charcot Changes

A direct result of neuropathy that weakens the muscles of the foot and reduces sensations is known as charcot changes. The muscles supporting the bones are weakened as a result of the neuropathy, and therefore, they may fracture easily. The patient suffering from the loss of sensation may be unaware of the fracture and continue to walk and use the affected area and cause further damage.

As time passes inflammation and temperature rise in the area, despite the fact that the client may not be experiencing any pain.

Treatment includes the following:

- *Compression bandages are worn for 2-3 weeks to reduce edema and inflammation.*
- *Total contact or non-weight-bearing cast applied for up to 9 months.*
- *Gradual weight bearing after skin has resumed normal temperature.*
- *Electrostimulation of the bone may improve healing.*
- *Medications, such as Fosamax and Aredia may be used to decrease bone destruction.*

Hammer Toes

Hammer toes are a condition in which the affective toe is bent downward. In some cases it is congenital, but it is most likely to occur as the result of wearing shoes that are too tight or restrictive in the toe area. Very rare cases can result from nerve damage or spinal cord problems.

The toe often starts to appear almost as a claw because the middle joint becomes bent. Over time it may become progressively more difficult and more painful to move. The patient can develop a callous as a result of the toe's irregular shape, which can either rub against another toe and/or it can rub against their shoe.

Treatments for children include splinting, possible physical therapy, planned exercises and manipulation of the toe. Changes in shoe type and size and wearing insoles or padding can be helpful. There are stores including medical supply stores and in podiatrists' offices that offer different types of devices and shoes that can be proven helpful.

In severe cases surgery may be indicated. Surgery can involve cutting, moving tendons or ligaments and, in some cases, the bones may have to be fused together.

Recommend:

Measures for Off-Loading

Upon getting an orthotic device, such as an ankle or foot orthotic device, the client is able to offload a diabetic ulcer; it is important that this device does not redistribute the pressure to any other area that has the potential to develop a new ulcer on another part of the foot. These devices are made and custom fitted in such a manner in order prevent further injury and to promote healthy healing at the same time.

Patient Referral for Orthotics and Shoes

Patients may need a prescription for orthotics and, in some cases, they also need a prescription for shoe inserts.

Recommend and Refer for Management of Lymphedema

Lymphedema is the abnormal swelling of the arm(s) and/or leg(s) that results from a blockage in the lymphatic system that normally drains the lymphatic fluid.

The signs and symptoms of lymphedema are restricted range of motion and swelling in the arm or leg, aching or discomfort, hardening and thickening of the skin, a feeling of heaviness and recurring infections in the affected limb.

The treatment focuses on making the client more comfortable, which can include ice to reduce inflammation and to help numb the pain. Other treatments include light exercise that can help the fluid move out of the client's limb and back into the circulatory system, wrapping the affected area in ace bandages, massage, which is known as manual lymph drainage, pneumatic compression and compression garments that apply pressure on the fluid to drain it from the affected area and other forms of decongestive therapy.

Other Types of Wounds

Recommend Topical Therapy Surgical Wounds

Topical therapy is generally a conservative option for surgical wounds. It is usually not indicated to use antimicrobials and antiseptics, due to the danger of resistance and the cytoxic properties of some of these agent which may delay healing.

The choice to use a topical therapy for surgical wounds depends on a number of different considerations including how the wound is healing and if an infection is developing. This type of therapy includes a lightly applied dressing to absorb any exudate and to apply light compression on the wound for a total of 48 – 72 hours in order to allow sealing of the wound to begin.

If there is any sign of infection a topical antimicrobial, for example Neosporin, should be used in addition to an antiseptic such as iodine. Once the initial healing begins, the dressing can be removed in some situations, but it does depend on the specific wound and its level of healing.

Traumatic Wounds

Insects/Parasites

Lice

Lice are tiny, parasitic insects that feed on blood. Lice can be found on the head, the body, and the pubic area, which are referred to commonly as "crabs".

Signs and Symptoms

Signs and symptoms include intense itching and small, red bumps on the scalp, neck and shoulders. Adult lice are about the size of a sesame seed and the nits resemble dandruff.

Treatment

Treatment for head lice includes a special over-the-counter shampoo, malathion, benzyl alcohol lotion or lindane.

Scabies

An itchy skin condition caused by Sarcoptes scabiei, a tiny burrowing mite, is known as scabies. This condition is contagious and can it can spread quickly.

Signs and Symptoms

The signs and symptoms include itchiness, often worse at night, thin, irregular burrow tracks made up of tiny blisters or bumps on the skin. In adults it is mostly found between fingers, in armpits, on the inner elbow, soles of the feet, around breasts, around male genital area, along the insides of wrists, and around the waist. In children, it is commonly seen on the scalp, face, neck, palms of the hands and soles of the feet.

Treatment

Treatment includes medications, such as permethrin 5 percent, lindane, and crotamiton. In some cases the oral medication ivermectin is used for those who do not respond to the prescription lotions and creams.

Bee Stings

Insect stings involve some amount of injected poisons that produce local and systemic reactions.

Signs and Symptoms

Local signs and symptoms include pain, erythema, edema, and itching at the site; systemic reactions can be severe to life-threatening if the person has an anaphylactic reaction which is characterized with unconsciousness, laryngeal edema, and cardiovascular collapse. Epinephrine and a bronchodilator are the drugs of choice for anaphylaxis.

Treatment

Removing the stinger can be done by pulling it from the skin without squeezing because this may cause additional venom to be injected. Ice packs to the area and elevation of the extremity is done if there is a large edematous local reaction. Oral antihistamines should be given and the site cleansed with soap and water. A tetanus vaccination may also be appropriate.

Wound care starts after the patient has been assessed for shock and treated for possible shock and poisoning by venom. By shaving the surrounding area allows for better visualization of the area, and for the effective adhesion of dressings to the skin. The wound should be gently irrigated with copious amounts of isotonic sterile saline or sterile water to remove debris. A catheter-tip syringe (an irrigation/bulb syringe) may be used. If the wound is grossly contaminated, the physician may need to anesthetize the wound before proceeding. Then, a surgical scrub with antiseptic is followed by copious amounts of sterile solution. Removal of tissue that has been devascularized or is impeding the healing process will promote healthy re-growth of granulation tissue. If the wound is intended to be closed, it is called primary closure, and performed with sutures, staples, or skin adhesives/tape.

Wound dressing consist of three layers, a non-adherent layer against the surface of the wound, an absorbent layer, and a cover layer that keeps the dressing in place; the cover may consist of a gauze wrap or pad. Infection potential of an open wound is always a concern. Antibiotic ointment can be used for minor wounds while IV antibiotics may be needed for major wounds to prevent infectious complications. Elevation of the affected extremity for the first 48 hours will assist the healing process by reducing the amount of edema; and the client should be instructed to sleep with the head of the bed elevated if facial wounds are present.

Snake Bites

Rattlesnakes, copperhead snakes, and coral snakes are the poisonous snakes indigenous to this country.

Signs and Symptoms

In addition to a puncture wound, the client may show the signs of severe cardiac and respiratory

compromise.

Treatment

Assess the airway, breathing, and circulation and be prepared for resuscitation. Watch for signs of local reactions such as burning, itching, swelling at the site, blisters and extremity edema and discoloration; and assess for systemic reactions including nausea, diaphoresis, light headedness, euphoria followed by drowsiness, difficulty swallowing, dyspnea, and muscle paralysis. The affected area should be kept below the level of the heart.

Other treatments include the use of a Sawyer pump suctioning, and the administration of antivenom.

Fractures

Fractures result from a traumatic impact or some undue pressure on the bone that cannot be sustained without damage to the bone itself. Risk factors associated with fractures include age, bone size, bone density, neoplastic disease, a poor physical condition, and hazardous occupations and avocations. Many fractures occur as the result of an accident or trauma; however, some may also occur as bone stressors, as occurs among athletes.

Fractures are classified in many ways, such as following:

- *An incomplete fracture where only a part of the bone is affected*
- *A complete fracture where the entire cross section of the bone is fractured*
- *A pathological fracture which results from weakened bones as a complication of a disease process rather than trauma or stress*
- *Unstable fractures which are displaced and require reduction*
- *Stable fractures which are not displaced so reduction is not necessary*
- *Open fractures, or compound fractures, break through the skin and soft tissue in the surrounding area*
- *Closed fractures also referred to as a simple fractures, do not penetrate the skin. The skin remains intact*

Fractures are also described in terms of their pattern. The patterns associated with skeletal fractures are transverse fractures that go straight across the bone, a spiral fracture that twists and turns around the bone, an oblique fracture that cuts across the bone at an angle, comminuted fractures which involve bone splinters and fragments, an impacted fracture that leads to a part of the bone being impacted or wedged into another bone, compression fractures which are characterized with the collapse of the bone, a greenstick fracture which only affects one side of the bone, an avulsion fracture that entails a bone fragment that has pulled off the bone at the tendon or ligament, and lastly, a depressed fracture which occurs when bone fragments are driven inward as occurs with a depressed skull fractures.

Some examples of the signs and symptoms of fractures are deformity, bruising at the site, swelling and tenderness, pain at the site, loss of function, a possible grating sensation and paresthesia. Altered neurovascular status is signaled with progressive, uncontrollable pain, diminished capillary refill, paresthesia, loss of active motion, and diminished distal pulses with pallor

All skeletal injuries can lead to serious neurological and vascular changes because of the fact that bones are proximate to, and surrounded by, circulatory vessels, peripheral sensory nerves and motor nerves.

Healing and the prevention of deformity are the goals of treatment. Fractures are immobilized with a splint in order to prevent further injury. Open wounds related to a compound open fracture and/or another traumatic injury are protected with a moist sterile dressing. Proper bodily alignment is insured throughout care and treatment.

Plaster casts, traction and other forms of immobilization, when indicated, must be applied with care and caution. Pain is managed with immobilization, elevation of the affect limb, the application of cool packs and analgesic medications.

Burns

A first degree burn is superficial that typically heals in a couple of days without scarring but they are painful. A second degree burn is a partial thickness injury consisting of the epidermis and the upper dermis. A third degree burn injury involves all layers of the skin and the underlying tissue including the bones, muscles, nerves. Virtually every organ of the body is affected by a major burn.

A burn is considered major if it the burn covers more than 25% of the total body surface area. The rule of nines is used as a quick estimate for burn size until a more thorough assessment is done. The anterior and posterior portion of each leg is considered 9% and all other areas are areas in multiples of 9%. For example, the anterior and posterior of each arm is 4.5%. The anterior and posterior chest is 18% and the anterior and posterior of the face/skull is 4.5%.

Respiratory alterations include hyperventilation, increased oxygen demand, pulmonary edema, initial respiratory alkalosis from the hyperventilation which is often followed with respiratory acidosis associated with pulmonary insufficiency.

Hemodynamic changes include less circulating blood volume resulting in lower cardiac output and tachycardia, decreased stroke volume, hyponatremia, increased blood viscosity, vasoconstriction, initial hyperkalemia followed by hypokalemia as the potassium is depleted by fluid shifts, and inadequate tissue perfusion which can lead to acidosis, renal failure and irreversible "burn shock".

Metabolic changes are the release of catecholamines in response to burn injury, hyperglycemia because insulin levels decrease early in the burn response, a need for 3,000-5,000 calories to reverse the negative nitrogen balance and to promote a positive nitrogen balance necessary for healing and increased metabolic needs.

Fluid changes include fluid shifts out of the vascular compartment, the hematocrit rises, blood flow is impaired in the micro-circulation, compensatory mechanisms for plasma volume losses include vasoconstriction, capillary permeability increases and hypovolemic shock can occur.

Renal changes can include a decrease in renal blood flow, high output failure or oliguric renal failure, decreased creatinine clearance, decreased glomerular filtration and the release of hemoglobin and myoglobin into the urine which could result in tubular necrosis unless increased fluids are given.

Hematological changes are thrombocytopenia, impaired platelet function, decreased fibrinogen levels, diminished fibrinolysis, the inhibition of plasma clotting factors and the destruction of red blood cells which can lead to anemia.

Gastrointestinal effects include decreased peristalsis, gastric ulcers and duodenal ulcers and gastrointestinal hemorrhage.

The client may have immunological changes including decreased imunoglobulins, serum albumin, cellular immunity, lymphocytopenia and signs of the inflammatory response.

The treatments, depending on the severity and the stage of the burn, include fluids like Lactated Ringer's, silvadene skin ointment, cool compresses and hydrocortisone cream for pain and perhaps a nonsteroidal anti-inflammatory drug (NSAID). The life threatening complications of major burns include infection and shock.

Abrasions, Avulsions And Lacerations

Injury	Description	Signs and Symptoms	Treatment
Abrasions	A skin friction wound that involves one or more layers of the epidermis to be removed	Pain, redness and minor bleeding	Wound irrigation and debridement. Abrasions are kept moist to aid healing A nonadherent, sterile dressing is placed over the wound.
Avulsions	Avulsions are the traumatic tearing away and loss of the epidermis and dermis	Pain, bleeding and skin integrity alterations	Wound irrigation and debridement Approximation of wound edges is not possible Severe injuries may require skin grafting

Injury	Description	Signs and Symptoms	Treatment
Lacerations	The skin is torn or cut and separated without other tissue loss	Pain and bleeding	Irrigation and debridement Sutures may be necessary for deep lacerations and those over moving joints; wound closure strips can be used for superficial lacerations For 48 hours after closure a non-adherent dressing should be applied until epithelial bridging has taken place

Puncture wounds

A puncture wound is caused by something sharp and pointed object or projectile, such as a nail, that penetrates the skin and underlying structures and tissues. These wounds are typified with a small skin opening and very little bleeding. Despite the lack of dramatic signs and symptoms, however, puncture wounds are highly susceptible to infection.

Treatment includes stopping the bleeding, a tetanus vaccine, prophylactic antibiotics, cleaning and applying a clean bandage for minor wounds; and, additionally, surgical interventions may be necessary for more severe puncture wounds.

Degloving

Degloving injuries are traumatic avulsion skin traumas that include the tearing away of the dermis and the epidermis.

The treatment of degloving injuries includes wound irrigation which may be followed with debridement. Management includes copious wound irrigation and debridement. These wounds are typically left to heal by secondary intention and just covered with a sterile dressing. Large areas of involvement may necessitate skin grafting.

Autoimmune Wounds

Pemphigus Vulgaris

A dangerous and potentially deadly autoimmune disease is known as pemphigus vulgaris (PV).

Approximately fifty to seventy percent of patients present with symptoms including blisters of both the skin and the mucous membranes. These burn-like wounds that often start in the patient's mouth and/or their genital areas. These wounds heal slowly and some do not heal at all.

If treatment is not received, the blisters on the skin can rupture which can then cause ulcerations, hypergranulation and crusting.

Treatment includes careful observation for possible secondary infections, wearing protective clothing and minimize trauma to skin, keeping up with good oral hygiene with a soft toothbrush and talcum powder applied to sheets if lesions are present on the back and other bodily areas that may touch the client's sheets.

Other treatments include the following:

- *Potassium permanganate lotion bath (1:10000) and chlorhexidine tulle gauze dressing of the denuded areas*
- *Plasmapheresis with plasma removed to reduce antibodies*
- *Donated plasma infused*
- *Nutritional assessment, which involves focusing on vitamin D and calcium. Supplemental vitamins and calcium are usually recommended.*
- *Corticosteroid medications, such as prednisone, and an immunosuppressive medication such as Imuron*
- *Rituxan, which is a drug successfully used for patients with lymphoma and leukemia to go into remission when mix with other drugs*

Neoplastic Wounds

Fungating neoplastic wounds occur in up to 10% of those with metastasis particularly among clients who are affected with oral cancer or breast cancer.

Fungating wounds are ulcerating wounds with necrosis and slough. They may have a foul odor and small to copious amounts of drainage. Infection is common and the periwound tissue may become inflamed, macerated and tender.

The prognosis is very poor and treatment may be primarily palliative depending upon the condition of the patient. The treatments can include:

- *The control of bleeding*

    These ulcers will bleed as the vasculature of the ulcer erodes. It may be necessary to use a hemostatic dressing, such as Gel foam, alignates and silver nitrate. Cauterization may be necessary. Non adherent dressings and long term dressings should be used to prevent further damage and trauma to the wound.

- *Exudate management*

    The use of foam, alginate, hydrofiber dressings or wound pouches may be indicated.

- *Odor control*

    Using chloromycetin solution or charcoal dressings

- *Wound cleansing*

    Cleansing with an ionic cleaner and/or antiseptics

- *Protection of the periwound tissue*

- Barrier ointments, skin sealants and hydrocolloids

- *Pain control*

    Analgesics should be given as necessary

Atypical Wounds/Ulcerations

Pyoderma Granulosum

Pyoderma granulosum is a condition which is often associated with an underlying systemic disease, such as inflammatory bowel disease, and dysregulation of immunity involving the neutrophils. This ulcerative condition can be quite painful.

There are two types of pyoderma granulosum:

1. *Classical pyoderma granulosum*

    Classical pyoderma granulosum consists of deep ulcerations with an overhanging wound bed border. They are most commonly seen on the legs, but they are also seen on stomas.

2. *Atypical pyoderma granulosum*

    Atypical pyoderma granulosum consists of vesicopustular draining lesions that are usually on located on the top of the hands, the forearms, or on the face.

The treatment of pyoderma granulosum is somewhat dependant on the type and the extent of the wounds. It is typical to provide local wound care and dressings, which can include moisture-retentive non-adhesive dressings, topical antibiotics to control infection, and possible treatment of an underlying systemic cause. For example, an intervention to treat an underlying cause can include a colectomy for when the client is adversely affected with ulcerative colitis. Other treatments that may be necessary include topical and systemic corticosteroids and systemic immunosuppressive drugs. Autolytic is the only debridement method that is indicated because of the risks of worsening the disease and its lesions with other forms of debridement. The surgical treatment of lesions is usually avoided.

Vasculitis

Vasculitis is a large number of disorders that result in the inflammation of veins, arteries and capillaries. This inflammation results in changes to the vessel walls.

There are a wide variety of different signs and symptoms that can accompany these disorders, but the most frequently experienced ones include fever, general malaise, myalgia, loss of appetite and skin lesions. Skin lesions may range from macular rashes to large necrotic ulcerations. Vasculitis is also accompanied with hemorrhagic rashes or ulcerations. Lesions are commonly on the lower extremities and may be confused with venous lesions. Vasculitis

There are a number of disorders that can cause vasculitis including Behcet's syndrome, Henoch-Schonlein purpura, rheumatoid vasculitis, systemic lupus erythematosus, polyarteritis nodosa, and Wegener's granulomatosis.

The treatment of vasculitis includes the medical control of underlying disease process, debridement of all necrosis present, systemic corticosteroids, antihistamines and immunosuppressants. Moisture protective retentive dressings with absorptive material may be needed for exudates; and skin sealant or barriers are used to protect periwound tissue from exudates whenever needed.

The patient's nutritional status must be monitored; supplements are provided when needed. The client must be observed for any signs of infection and, if an infection occurs, the client is treated with topical or systemic antibiotics as needed.

Epidermolysis Bullosa (EB)

Epidermolysis bullosa (EB) is a group of inherited and non-inherited bullous or blistering disorders. These disorders have a variety of damage levels to the epithelial tissue; even mild mechanical trauma can result in blistering.

The signs and symptoms of epidermolysis bullosa vary greatly. They can range from slight seasonal blistering to erosions of the skin that can be life threatening. The internal epithelial tissue in mucous membranes and the organs may also be adversely affected as well as the external dermal layers of the client's skin.

There are four different categories of EB, which include:

1. *Simplex epidermolysis bullosa*

    Simplex epidermolysis are intraepidermal lesions

2. *Junctional epidermolysis bullosa*

    Junctional epidermolysis bullosa are blistering at lamina lucida or the space between the epidermis and basement membrane

3. *Recessive dystrophic epidermolysis bullosa,* which are separation at basement membrane; slight mechanical trauma that causes excessive scarring and blistering; leading to hemorrhage and ulceration; predisposes patient to squamous cell carcinoma.

4. *Dominant dystrophic epidermolysis bullosa,* which are below basement membrane blisters with scarring; Not as severe as RDBE.

Epidermolysis bullosa treatment includes routine nutritional assessments with supplements as necessary, topical antibiotics or silver-impregnated dressings for infections, trauma avoidance protection and non-adhesive dressings over the affected area.

It is important to note that Fenestrated non-adherent dressings secured with stockinet, roll gauze, or tubular gauze is recommended.

Calciphylaxis

Calciphylaxis, which is usually caused by sepsis, is a rare fatal disease related to end-stage renal disease and uremia. Calciphylaxis can lead to the vascular calcification of cutaneous blood vessels and necrotic lesions with typical violet discoloration. Mortality rates range from 60-80%.

Patients present with painful discolored lesions that progress to nodules and ulcerations that, later, can become infected and gangrenous. Lesions are most common in areas with an accumulation of fatty tissue. Blood flow distal to the ulcerations is usually intact. The etiology is unclear, but it is associated with hypercalcemia, hyperphosphatemia and hyperparathyroidism.

Treatment is often palliative and there is no successful standardized approach. This disorder frequently results in amputation of the affected limb.

Some of the treatment options include:

- *Control of calcium and phosphorus levels*
- *Intravenous sodium thiosulfate to reduce calcium deposits*
- *Surgical or medical treatment of hyperparathyroidism*
- *Antibiotics as indicated for wound infections*
- *Aggressive debridement with absorbent moisture-retentive dressings.*
- *Analgesia as indicated.*

Toxic epidermal Necrolysis

Toxic epidermal necrolysis is a rare life-threatening condition of the epidermis which is most often caused by these types of drugs:

- *Antibiotics (sulfonamides, allopurinol, and ampicillin),*
- *Anticonvulsants (phenytoin, carbamazepine, and phenobarbital),*
- *Analgesics (acetaminophen and NSAIDS).*

An initial maculopapular rash gives way to erythema and painful skin that sloughs off even with the slightest pressure. At times, it can leave the client's body with >10% of the body denuded of its epidermis. The skin, mucous membranes, eyes, and respiratory tract may be involved. The mortality rate is 30-40%.

Some of the treatments for toxic epidermal necrolysis include:

- *Surgical debridement of sloughing skin with a saline-moistened cloth*
- *Porcine xenografts stapled into place*
- *Patient placement in air-fluidized bed in burn unit*
- *Fluid and electrolytes monitored and replaced*
- *Nasogastric tube feedings*
- *Systemic antibiotics*
- *The cessation of any corticosteroids*
- *Pain control with opioids*
- *Pulmonary and ophthalmic care.*
- *Grafts trimmed as they desiccate and wounds heal.*

Graft-versus-host disease is caused by a severe host reaction to bone marrow transplantation. Acute Graft-versus-host disease typically occurs within 100 days after surgery; and chronic graft-versus-host disease usually occurs after 100 days post transplantation.

The condition affects the following organs:

- *The skin*
- *The liver which can cause jaundice and pruritis*
- *The large and small intestines which can lead to bleeding and diarrhea*

A maculopapular (red to violet) rash usually begins on the hands, plantar area of foot, face or upper trunk, after which it spreads and becomes more diffuse. This then may result in desquamation and formation of bullae. The disease is staged from 1to 4 depending on severity of the disease.

The treatment includes:

- *Colony-stimulating factor (CSF) for 6 months in addition to other appropriate immunosuppressive therapy*
- *Topical corticosteroids*
- *Careful observation for signs of infection*
- *Cleansing of skin*
- *Severe denudement requires debridement and transfer to the burn unit for treatment to prevent further deterioration.*
- *Adhesive occlusive dressings should be avoided.*

Mechanical Trauma

A mechanical trauma is a trauma that occurs in which there is stripping of the epidermis and in some cases the dermis as well. This type of trauma can be a laceration, due to the removal of tape from the skin or a blunt trauma, which can occur as a result of bumping into a solid object or being struck with one.

The Payne-Martin Classification System is used to categorize skin tears from 1 to 3. This scoring is as follows:

1. *Skin tear leaves avulsed skin adequate to cover wound. Tears may be linear or flap-type.*

2. *Skin tear with loss of partial thickness involving either scant (<25% of epidermal flap over tear is lost) to moderate-large (> 25% of dermis in tear is lost).*

3. *Skin tear with complete loss of tissue involving a partial-thickness wound with no epidermal flap.*

The treatment includes many prevention and protective interventions such as applying adhesives correctly, avoiding adhesives all together and recognizing fragile skin. Other treatment options include applying emollients, skin sealants and skin barriers prior to applying adhesives or using steristrips or another type of non-adhesive products.

Bacterial and Fungal Skin Infections

Bacterial Skin infections

Folliculitis

Folliculitis is a bacterial infection that, in most cases, affects the hair follicles of the face.

The infection results in pustules, erythema and crusts that can cause a great deal of pain for the patient; the client can also be affected with itchiness and pruritis.

There has been a recent outbreak in cases of community-acquired methicillin-resistant Staphylococcus - aureus folliculitis infections. Chronic nasal colonizations of MRSA can be the cause.

Folliculitis can be a primary or secondary infection.

Treatment options include topical or oral antibiotics and antibiotic soap.

Impetigo

Impetigo is a contagious bacterial infection of the skin that can be transmitted with Streptococcus or Staphylococcus.

This itchy bacterial infection, which is seen most commonly in children, generally appears on the face or hands, and causes clusters of blisters or sores. Group A Streptococcus is mostly seen as small blisters that crust over, whereas the Staphylococcus aureus usually causes larger blisters that can be bullous and with lesions from 2-3 cm in terms of size and persist for months.

The treatment includes gentle cleansing of the affected area with a gentle soap and water; topical Bactroban3 is applied three times a day and itching should be treated to avoid the client's scratching which can lead to further damage and infection.

Erysipelas

Erysipelas is a superficial bacterial infection that invades the skin in areas where a trauma has occurred. This infection usually affects the face or legs and it involves the cutaneous lymphatic system. It is seen most often among children and the elderly.

A Streptococcus infection, following a nasopharyngeal infection, is usually the cause of facial erysipelas and infections that appear on the legs are more often related to non-group A Streptococcus.

The infection is fast spreading and it is accompanied with streaking, erythema and cellulitis.

Lymphedema can occur as the result of the local lymph nodes becoming inflamed and possibly damaged.

Analgesics are used to control the pain, bed rest with the elevation of the affected wound and ice packs to improve circulation are typical interventions. In severe cases oral antibiotics, such as penicillin G and penicillin VK, may be indicated, and hospitalization may be indicated among those who are severely affected and those who are very young, elderly and/or immunocompromised.

Fungal Skin Infections

Candidiasis Infections

Oral candidiasis

Oral candidiasis or oral thrush is a yeast infection of the oral cavity, in which the fungus candida albicans accumulates on the lining of the mouth. It is seen most commonly among clients with diabetes, denture wearers, drug users, people getting chemotherapy, those on antibiotics, pregnant women or those on birth control pills, people with poor nutrition, those with an immune deficiency, such as HIV, and people who use inhaled steroids used for certain lung conditions.

Oral candidiasis can appear as white or pale yellow spots on the inner surfaces of the mouth and throat, the tongue and the lips. It can be difficult to scrape off the membranes, therefore attempts to do this often leads to bleeding sores. A burning feeling in the mouth or throat can also occur.

The first line of treatment is to practice meticulous oral hygiene. Killing the overgrown yeast with anti-fungal medications, such as nystatin, amphotericin B suspension, clotrimazole lozenges and fluconazole may be indicated.

Candidiasis

Candidiasis is a fungal infection (myosis) of any species that comes from the yeast genus Candida. The most common type seen in humans is candida albicans. Oral candida albicans, or thrush, is fully discussed above. Most cases of candida albicans involve the skin, pharynx or esophagus, the gastrointestinal tract, the urinary bladder, the fingernails or toenails, or the genitals.

The symptoms of candidiasis depend on the location affected. In most cases the symptoms include itchiness and discomfort as well as redness. If the infection affects the vagina, symptoms can include severe itching, burning, soreness, irritation and a whitish-gray cottage cheese-like vaginal discharge.

If the infection affects the male genitalia, the symptoms can include redness or itchiness around the head of the penis, swelling, irritation, soreness, a thick, lumpy discharge under the foreskin, phimosis, an unpleasant odor and pain while urinating or engaging in sex.

Perianal candidiasis can present with pruritis ani and/or lesions that can be erythematous, papular or ulcerative; it is not considered a sexually transmitted disease. Symptoms can include dysphagia, or in rare cases odynophagia, when this fungus affects the esophagus.

Treatment options, in most cases, include antimycotics; and these antifungal drugs include topical ketoconazole, fluconazole, topical nystatin, and topical clotrimazole.

Toxic shock syndrome (TSS)

Toxic shock syndrome (TSS) is most frequently caused by the Staphylococcus aureus and streptococcal pathogens. Prior to the changes in the manufacturing of tampons, toxic shock syndrome was primarily due to tampon use, now, however it is associated with a number of other conditions such as burns, surgery, childbirth and trauma.

The original causative agent was Staphylococcus aureus and infections were related to use of tampons, but the infection can occur also with wounds or surgical sites where the bacteria can find entry. There are now two forms of toxic shock syndrome, namely, Staphylococcus aureus (TSS) and Streptococcal toxic shock syndrome (STSS). STSS occurs secondary to an infection in the body, often an infected wound, causing severe hypotension, dyspnea, tachycardia, liver and kidney failure, and a splotchy rash that may peel.

The signs and symptoms of toxic shock syndrome include hypotension, a high fever, myalgia, scaling and desquamation of the hands and palms of the hands, a diffuse erythematous rash, and multiple system dysfunction and shutdown which can be life threatening.

The renal system effects are signaled with an elevated urea nitrogen and creatinine; and the neurological system can be affected with changes in the level of consciousness. Other signs and symptoms include the signs of infection, nausea, vomiting and diarrhea.

Hospitalization, and even critical care, is typically indicated so that the client can be treated and monitored in order to reduce the risk of complications and mortality. The patient is given antibiotics and fluids as they are monitored for hemodynamic stability. At times, airway management and drugs to treat refractory hypotension are needed. Topical non-adhesive, non-occlusive dressings with absorbent materials are also used as indicated.

The antimicrobial drugs of choice are a first generation cephalosporin and penicillin. Vancomycin or clindamycin are used when the client is allergic to penicillin. Surgical intervention may be necessary to address the cause of the infection, such as an abscess.

Ostomy Care

In this part of the review book the general principles of assessment, such as the patient's environment, social and other factors impact on their cultural diversity will be discussed . Management and teaching of the patients will also be explored. Colostomy, ileostomy, urostomy will all be discussed in full, as will the continent fecal and urinary diversions and fistulas and percutaneous tubes and drains.

General Principles of Assessment

Assess environmental, social, and other factors that impact patients' adaptation

The Assessment of the Client's Adaptation to a Colostomy

Psychological Factors That Impact on Clients' Coping

Some of the most commonly occurring psychological and emotional alterations include anger, anxiety, denial, grief and loss, fear, guilt, depression, alterations of bodily image, loss of control, poor coping, and intimacy/relationship issues.

Anger and Hostility

Many clients experience anger and hostility. Client's family members and significant others may also experience these same feelings. Anger is a common psychological response to these conditions, as described below in the Stages of Grieving model Kubler-Ross.

Simply defined, anger is a psychological or emotional state that is related to displeasure. It is often accompanied with feelings of guilt because it is not socially acceptable to be angry and to express these feelings. Outward expressions of anger can include hostility towards others, destructiveness, aggression and even violence.

At times, anger and hostility can be directed toward the precipitating event and at times it can be displaced toward others when the person employs the psychological defense mechanism of displacement. For example, a client who becomes angry about their loss of a normal body image as a result of their illness and surgery and directs this anger towards their spouse, family members, nurse and other members of the healthcare team, is using displacement.

Nurses can intervene in terms of anger and hostility by accepting the fact that the client has the right to be angry and attempt to understand the meaning and the source of the anger. The nurse should also encourage the client to openly ventilate their anger.

Anxiety

Anxiety can be categorized as mild, moderate, severe and at panic level.

The signs and symptoms of anxiety include affective ones (increased helplessness, irritability, fright and worry), behavioral ones (insomnia and vigilance), sympathetic ones (anorexia, increased pulse, blood pressure and pulse), physiological ones (diaphoresis and trembling), parasympathetic effects (fatigue, urinary changes, weakness and faintness) and cognitive changes (poor problem solving skills and a lack of an adequate attention span).

The nurse should assess the level of anxiety for both the client and the significant other. As based on this assessment, some of the treatments can include empathy when the anxiety is rationale, encouraging the person to ventilate their feelings and perceptions, explaining all procedures, and using some techniques like cognitive/behavioral therapy, relaxation techniques, positive self talk, massage and therapeutic touch.

Denial

Denial is a psychological defense mechanism. Psychological defense mechanisms, also referred to as ego defense mechanisms, are unconscious mechanisms that protect the client from stress and anxiety that can arise from inner tensions and conflicts. They are the precursor to coping in a cognitive, conscious manner.

Denial occurs when the client refuses to acknowledge any facts or realities that are threatening to them. It protects the person from being adversely affected with a traumatic event or reality until they are ready to do so.

Some other psychological defense mechanisms, their purposes and some examples are below.

- *Defense Mechanism: Reaction formation*

    Mechanism: The person acts out in a manner that is the opposite of what their true feelings are.

    Protective Purpose: Allows the person to act out their feelings in a more appropriate manner.

    Example: A spouse who resents their husband may support all of their ideas and suggestions in a cooperative and polite manner.

- *Defense Mechanism: Sublimation*

    Mechanism: A socially unacceptable sexual or aggressive urge is replaced with a socially acceptable activity that substitutes for this urge.

    Protective Purpose: This defense mechanism protects the person from acting in a socially unacceptable, impulsive manner.

Example: A person with incestuous feelings may become active in a church.

- *Defense Mechanism: Undoing*

    Mechanism: Undoing allows the client to feel as though they have made up for, and atoned, for wrongdoing.

    Protective Purpose: This allows the person to rid themselves of guilt by atonement for one's wrongdoings.

    Example: An abusive husband brings flowers home to his wife.

- *Defense Mechanism: Compensation*

    Mechanism: Personal weakness is covered up with overachievement in another area.

    Protective Purpose: This ego defense mechanism allows the person to protect their ego and level of self-esteem by excelling in another area to make up for their weakness.

    Example: A young child, who cannot excel in school like his older sibling, may choose to play a piano, and excel in it, to make up for his scholastic weaknesses.

- *Defense Mechanism: Displacement*

    Mechanism: Displacement moves hostility from one person, or object, to another person, or object.

    Protective Purpose: The purpose of this defense mechanism is to allow the affected individual to express their feelings, but in a manner that is less harmful and dangerous to other people, or objects.

    Example: A man who has been fired from work may come home and punch a hole in the wall, rather than punching the boss in the face.

- *Defense Mechanism: Projection*

    Mechanism: Others and the environment are the factors that have lead to the client's weaknesses, shortcomings, and failures.

    Protective Purpose: This defense mechanism helps the client to protect their own self image and self-esteem by placing blame on other people or the environment.

    Example: A college student who fails out of college blames the college and the professors rather than self.

- *Defense Mechanism: Repression*

    Mechanism: Repression helps the person to keep threatening thoughts, desires and feelings deep down so they do not erupt into consciousness.

    Protective Purpose: This ego defense mechanism protects the person from trauma until they are ready to cope and deal with it.

    Example: A client may experience repressive amnesia after a traumatic automobile accident which does not allow them to remember any events surrounding and after the accident.

- *Defense Mechanism: Regression*

    Mechanism: Regression helps the person to a less demanding and threatening stage of development.

    Protective Purpose: This ego defense mechanism allows the person to move back to a previous stage of development when they were cared for and dependent upon, others.

    Example: An ill hospitalized 8-year-old child may regress to thumb sucking and bed-wetting.

- *Defense Mechanism: Identification*

    Mechanism: The affected client imitates the behaviors of a person that they fear.

    Protective Purpose: This defense mechanism helps the client to preserve the value of self and to prevent personal devaluation.

    Example: A child imitates the father that she fears.

- *Defense Mechanism: Minimization*

    Mechanism: The affected client minimizes the significance of a problem.

    Protective Purpose: This mechanism allows the person to avoid taking responsibility and accountability for their own actions.

    Example: A diabetic client with severe leg ulcerations may state that it is "no big deal".

- *Defense Mechanism: Rationalization*

    Mechanism: Attaching socially acceptable motives and faulty logic to actions and behaviors.

    Protective Purpose: This helps the person to cope with their inability to meet standards and goals.

    Example: A husband who pushes his wife rationalizes it by stating that his wife was not hurt.

- *Defense Mechanism: Introjection*

    Mechanism: A person accepts the norms, values and beliefs as one's own despite the fact that they are not consistent with, and often contrary to, those that the person previously held.

    Protective Purpose: This ego defense mechanism prevents the person from being ostracized by society.

    Example: A person may suddenly embark upon a healthy lifestyle and personal responsibility when, in the past, they did not.

- *Defense Mechanism: Intellectualization*

    Mechanism: Forced rational thinking is used to decrease the significance of a threatening and traumatic event.

    Protective Purpose: Identification protects the person from psychological trauma and pain.

    Example: The spouse of a diabetic who has died may state that her husband did not want to live any longer with his complications of diabetes.

The nurse should not strip these psychological defense mechanisms away from the client. The nurse should simply acknowledge the person and their feelings but NOT argue with the client about their lack of insight or better coping mechanisms. These mechanisms are beneficial to the client; they protect the person from psychological distress and other psychological problems.

Depression

Depression, of varying degrees, often affects the client and those close to the client when the person is affected with a serious, terminal illness like cancer. Depression leads to physical, emotional and cognitive changes.

The signs and symptoms of depression include feelings of hopelessness, helplessness, sadness, dejection, despair, sleep loss, listlessness, headache, weight loss, anorexia, social withdrawal, lack of sexual desire, crying, poor levels of concentration, poor decision making and problem solving skills, diminished performance, personality changes, and a lack of self worth and self esteem.

The care and treatment for a depressed client is multifaceted. The client needs social support, perhaps spiritual support, cognitive behavioral therapy, and often medications such as antidepressants, and non-pharmacological approaches such as stress reduction and relaxation techniques.

Fear

Fear is a feeling of dread and apprehension relating to some impending danger or threat. It can result from a real or unreal thereat, but, nonetheless, the client is adversely affected with it. Although fear and anxiety are highly similar and often occur simultaneously, they are also different. Fear is typically related to a current threat and anxiety is most often related to a future, anticipated threat. Lastly, anxiety is vaguer than fear; anxiety often arises from emotional conflict and fear is most often associated with a specific physical or psychological threat like having a colostomy.

Some of the signs and symptoms include apprehension, muscular tension, feelings of dread, panic, terror, jitteriness, diminished cognition and problem solving skills, dyspnea, dry mouth, fatigue, rapid pulse and respirations, increased systolic blood pressure, nausea, vomiting, pallor, pupil dilation, increased alertness with a narrowed focus on the source of the fear, avoidance and/or aggression.

Interventions, after assessment, can include confronting the fear, verbalizing the fearful feeling, assisting the client to distinguish between real and imagined treats, and psychological support measures such as cognitive behavior therapy, relaxation techniques and massage.

Distress

Distress can be described as troubling feelings that can range from mild to severe and even disabling. Its intensity can vary and become more severe as the client's disease or disorder progresses. It can negatively impact on the client's coping.

Distress can be seen with a variety of different physical, emotional, mental and behavioral symptoms, including back pain, neck pain, tension headaches, migraine headaches, muscle tension, dry mouth, enlarged pupils, diarrhea, constipation, moodiness, depression, anxiety, nightmares, forgetfulness, difficulty concentrating, racing thoughts, frustration, irritability, mumbled or fast speech, defensiveness, and nervous habits, such as biting nails, foot tapping, and an inability to sit still.

The treatment for distress can include relaxation techniques, counseling, and the support of family, friends and healthcare personnel to overcome their feelings. Some of the symptoms can be treated with medications such as antidepressants, benzodiazepines, and pain medications, as indicated.

Grief and Loss

Loss, often associated with grief, is multidimensional. Loss can be actual, perceived, or anticipated. It occurs when a person has a significant change that causes the loss of something of value, when the person anticipates a loss and when the person has a perceived the loss of something of value.

Grieving is a normal response that includes physical, emotional, spiritual, social and intellectual responses. Sources of loss can originate from many things including an intrapersonal loss of self and one's bodily image and extrapersonal losses like the loss of savings with the costs of medical care. All losses impact on the client.

Perceived losses are those losses that are not verifiable by others. This perception, although faulty, still impacts on and affects the person. People have anticipatory grief and loss before an actual or perceived loss actually occurs. For example, a son may undergo severe anticipatory loss and grief soon after his mother has been diagnosed with terminal cancer. Similarly, a woman may have anticipatory loss relating to her their loss of sexuality after a colostomy.

Clients and significant others are affected with grief and loss.

Theories and Conceptual Frameworks Relating to Grief and Loss

Kubler Ross's Stages of Grieving

Similar to the other theories of loss, grieving and death, Kubler Ross's stages of grieving includes:

- *Denial*
- *Anger*
- *Bargaining*
- *Depression*
- *Acceptance*

Bargaining is a unique phase of this theory. During the bargaining stage, the client negotiates and bargains to avoid the loss. Spiritual support is often helpful during this stage.

Engel's Stages of Grieving

According to Engel, the stages of grieving are as below:

- *Shock and disbelief*
- *Developing awareness*
- *Restitution*
- *Resolving the loss*
- *Idealization*
- *Outcome*

During shock and disbelief the client denies the loss and refuses to accept it. Later the client consciously acknowledges the loss and may even express anger towards others including family members and healthcare professionals.

During the resolution stage, the client contemplates the loss and may accept a dependent role in terms of their support network. Clients' family members may deify and idealize the lost loved one and may, also, experience guilt and ambivalence. During the outcome phase of Engel's model, the person adjusts to the loss as based on the characteristics of the loss, as discussed above.

Sander's Phases of Bereavement

The phases of bereavement, according to Sander's theory, are:

- *Shock*
- *Awareness of the loss*
- *Conservation and withdrawal*
- *Healing or the turning point*
- *Renewal*

These phases are quite similar to those of Engel with some variations. For example, during the conservation and withdrawal phase, the person will withdraw from others and attempt to restore their physical and emotional wellbeing; and during the healing stage, the person will move from emotional distress to the point where they are able to learn how to live without the loved one. During the renewal phase, the person is able to independently live without the loved one.

The defining characteristics of grief can include sleep disturbances, altered immune responses, anger, blame, withdrawal, pain, panic, distress, suffering and alterations with neuroendocrine functioning.

Nurses can assist the client with the grieving process by encouraging the person to ventilate their feelings, by encouraging effective coping strategies, by involving the family and significant others in the care of the client, and, when needed, refer the client and significant others to sources of psychosocial and spiritual support.

Guilt

Like all of the other psychosocial issues, the family and significant others are often affected with feelings of guilt and ambivalence. For example, the client may experience feelings of guilt for the effect that their colon cancer is having on the family unit after years of the family's attempts to get the client to change their diet. A client may also feel guilty about leaving their family in poor financial status because of the medical expenses associated with the illness. Families may also experience feelings of guilt because they may have not cared for the person enough or they are no longer able to care for the client in the home.

The purpose of guilt, when grounded in fact, is to alert the person that they have done some wrong. This feeling of guilt then encourages the person to change behavior so they no longer violate social and moral standards.

Some of the signs and symptoms associated with guilt can include physical, psychological and spiritual distress and despair.

Nurses can teach the client about the purpose of guilt in terms of learning and changing behavior, encouraging the client to make amends, facilitating the client's acceptance of the fact that they did something wrong but there is a need to move on and grow, and to understand that humans are not perfect and that forgiveness is possible.

Clients and family members may need psychological, spiritual and religious support to resolve feelings of guilt.

Intimacy and Relationship Issues

The physical and psychological effects of illness can lead to several sexual changes in the client. These changes in sexuality vary according to the client, their illness and any treatments that they are taking. For example, a woman with breast cancer who is being treated with chemotherapy may have a decrease in libido, and a man with a colostomy can experience no changes in libido, or sexual desire.

The National Cancer Institute (NCI) states that the loss of sexual desire, depression, anxiety, early menopause and body image alterations can adversely affect patients and their sexuality. The National Cancer Institute recommends that couples discuss all their concerns and feelings about the current state of their sexual life and try to work together to find ways with which they can remain in a close and loving relationship, as they cope with, and adjust to, changes in sexuality.

Physical/Biological Factors That Impact on Clients' Coping

Some of the physical/biological factors that impact on client's coping and self-care include:

- *Level of disease and illness*
- *Functional abilities*
- *Level of pain*

Psychological/Cognitive Factors That Impact on Clients' Coping

Some of the psychological/cognitive factors that impact on client's coping and self-care include:

- *Fear and anxiety*
- *Decreased level of consciousness*
- *Confusion*
- *Lack of motivation*

Socioeconomic Factors That Impact on Clients' Coping

Nurses, and other members of the healthcare team, including case managers and social workers, assess the client's socioeconomic status upon admission and determine if there are any socioeconomic issues that have to be addressed.

Clients are affected by socioeconomic forces that can impact on their coping with illness, surgery and bodily alterations such as an ostomy. Some of the factors include financial ones and others are related to their level of support by others and tapping into the resources in the community, including social support and peer support groups.

Healthcare and healthcare systems as well as individuals are impacted with economic forces including those that result of increased healthcare costs, those that affect access to health care services and those that result from poverty.

Some of the economic concerns, in addition to those relating to loss of work and limited income, include the lack of adequate healthcare insurance to pay medical expenses. Some healthcare insurance programs are discussed below.

Medicare and Medicaid

The United State's Medicare administered program and the states' administered Medicaid programs are two primary governmental reimbursement programs. Medicare, under the U.S. Social Security Act, reimburses for the health care of adults who are 65 years of age and older, and some younger permanently disabled people and their dependents. Medicaid, on the other hand, provides healthcare reimbursement for low income individuals, families and chronically ill children.

Medicare Part A, as stated, covers hospital, skilled nursing, and hospice care. Part B medical insurance includes physician and nursing services, renal dialysis, laboratory and other diagnostic tests, blood transfusions, chemotherapy, immunosuppressive drugs for organ transplant clients, prosthetic devices, oxygen, and durable medical equipment like canes, walkers, and wheelchairs.

Clients and family members should be educated and informed about Medicare, Medicaid and how to access necessary supplies, services and durable medical equipment.

Third Party Insurance Companies

The benefits, admission criteria, coverage limitations and reimbursement methods, however, may vary somewhat so if you are managing reimbursements for your clients, check with the individual's specific insurance company for their specific requirements and benefits.

It is necessary that the nurse collaborate with the client and significant others to identify all of the available community resources that may be of benefit to them. Some of these community resources can include social support and counseling agencies, community service agencies, volunteers, home care nursing agencies, and peer support groups or self-help groups.

Family systems and family dynamics are assessed and responded to by the nurse. Some of the most commonly occurring family dynamics issues for clients include some factors, and the interrelationships of factors, like family strife, interpersonal conflicts, role disintegration, geographic distance, and patterns of coping and expressing grief.

Environmental Factors That Impact on Clients' Coping

Nurses also assess the environmental factors and forces that can impact on the client's coping and adaptation. For example, the client may not be able to access medical care and basic needs like groceries because of the lack of available public transportation and geographic distance they are from these resources.

Geography also impacts health. People who live in rural and remote geographic areas have less access to care than those in urban and heavily populated areas. Access to care is also negatively impacted with homelessness, the lack of transportation and the lack of health insurance. These barriers to care affect the affordability and accessibility of healthcare services.

Nurse and other members of the healthcare team will seek out resources like Meals on Wheels, volunteer transportation services and other resources in the community.

Identify:

Indications for Urinary or Fecal Diversion Surgery

Urinary diversion surgery is indicated when the bladder is unable to function safely and/or properly for the containment of urine. Some examples of disorders that may have to be corrected with urinary diversion surgery include ureter blockage due to kidney stones or a tumor, cancer, bladder extrophy, neurogenic bladder and interstitial cystitis

Fecal diversion surgery is also indicated for a variety of different disorders including colorectal cancer, certain traumatic injuries, intestinal obstruction, diverticulitis, Chron's disease, incontinence and constipation.

Postoperative

During recovery the patient has to learn how to contain and control their feces or urine and minimize odors in order to maintain their self-esteem and dignity.

Postoperative complications from urinary diversion surgery include the following:

- *Nocturnal enuresis*
- *Distended bladders*
- *Clinical kidney infections*
- *Hypercontinence*
- Intraperitoneal *rupture of catheterizable bladders*
- *Urinary tract infection*
- *Urinary stone formation*
- *Vitamin B12 deficiency*
- *Bowel habit changes*
- *Changes in pH*
- *Skin rashes and/or infections*

Postoperative complications from fecal diversion surgery include the following:

- *Wound infection*
- *Wound dehiscence*
- *Bowel obstruction*
- *Ureterocutaneous fistula*
- *Ischemic ileostomy*
- *Peristomal hernia*

Pouching and Containment Strategies

Clients should be instructed about and able to perform self-care pouching and containment strategies.

As previously discussed Dorothea Orem's Self Care Theory This theory is based on fact that most clients want to and can care for themselves as much as possible. This self-care allows clients to recover more holistically and rapidly than those who do not perform self-care. Self-care also promotes independence, self-esteem, dignity and a better quality of life.

Nurses must assess and consider barriers to self-care. Some of these barriers are psychological, some are physical, and still more can be cognitive barriers to self-care. When one or more barriers to self-care are identified, the nurse must then plan interventions to facilitate self-care by overcoming and accommodating for these barriers.

Complications can range greatly in terms of severity. Some complications can lead to other complications; some complications can appear immediately or shortly after surgery and other can appear later, therefore, it is important that the patient and caregiver are instructed and competent in knowing what to look for in terms of complications and what they should do when these complications arise.

Complications include stenosis, retraction, prolapsed, necrosis, mucocitaneous separation, stoma trauma and parastomal hernias. Each of these is described below:

Stomal Stenosis

Stomal stenosis is a condition in which the stoma or its lumen is narrowed and constricted; it can occur at the fascial level or at the skin. It can be caused as a result of a variety of different things, such as hyperkeratosis, surgical technique, local inflammation, hyperplasia, sepsis, adhesions and from radiation given prior to the surgery. With ostomies, both urinary and gastrointestinal the effulent output may reduced and changed as the result of stomal stenosis.

Signs and Symptoms

Bowel obstruction is common with gastrointestinal stoma stenosis; flatus in an initial symptom. Other symptoms of gastrointestinal stoma stenosis are as follows:

- *Abdominal cramps*
- *Explosive stool*
- *Diarrhea*
- *Urinary stoma stenosis is accompanied by the follow symptoms:*
- *Frequent urinary tract infections*
- *Flank pain*
- *Decrease in urine output*
- *Urine output forceful*
- *High residual urine in conduit*

Treatment

Surgical intervention is required for partial or complete bowel obstruction and stoma stenosis at the fascial level. Conservative treatment includes a change in diet to a low-residue diet and using stool softeners or laxatives. In most cases, complications associated with stomas are attributed to poor placement, therefore, most clients will then require surgery for the correction of this complication with a stomal replacement.

Stoma Retraction

In the ideal situation, the stoma is properly placed with the lumen located at the top center or apex of the stoma which allows the stoma to protrude approximately 2.5 cm; this permits the guiding of the effluent to be able to flow freely into the pouch.

A stoma retraction recedes below the skin and up to approximately 0.5 cm. There are some different causes of this but, if it occurs during the immediate postoperative period of time, it usually relates to stenosis, poor nutrition, obesity, the premature removal of the loop stomal supporting device, poor blood flow and stoma placement in a deep skin fold and/or abdominal walls that are thick.

If it occurs later in the postoperative period of time, it can be the result of adhesions or weight gain. Stoma retractions are most commonly seen among those who have had an illeostomy rather than other ostomies.

Signs and Symptoms

Retracted stomas tend to appear as a bowl type shape that is concave. Peristomal skin complications are common because retractions cause a poor pouching surface.

Treatment

Stoma retraction treatment includes care of the pouch seal, a different pouching system and a stoma belt.

Stoma Prolapse

Stoma prolapsed occurs when the stoma moves or is somehow displaced from its original position. The proximal segment of the bowel intussuscepts and slides through the orifice of the stoma. It is seen most commonly with a loop transverse colostomy.

Stoma prolapsed can result from poor muscle tone, pregnancy, obesity, increased pressure on the abdomen, large openings in the abdominal wall, and an unsuccessful or improper bowel fixation to the abdominal wall. This type of stoma increases in both size and length.

Signs and Symptoms

Some patients can experience the symptoms of bowel obstruction, pain, and signs of circulatory problems; others do not experience any symptoms at all.

Treatment

Treatment is usually conservative. The patient is instructed to sit in a supine position. Once the prolapsed reduces, the following options can be helpful:

- *Hernia support binder*
- *Stoma shield*
- *A larger stoma pouch*
- *Cold compresses*

In some cases regular table sugar can induce osmotic therapy which promotes a fluid shift across the stoma mucosa which can then reduce any edema that is present.

Stoma Necrosis

Stoma necrosis is a result of a decrease in blood flow to the area; this impaired blood flow can occur from venous and/or arterial blood compromise. At some times, this complication can occur as the result of excessive trimming of the mesentery and/or the vascular system during the surgical procedure which results in tension and the impairment of blood flow to the intestine. Other possible causes of vascular compromise and resulting stomal necrosis include things like excessive edema, embolus and hypovolemia.

Signs and Symptoms

The signs and symptoms include the following:

- *Discolored stoma which can appear as cyanotic, black, dark res, brown or dusty blue-purpley.*
- *The normal color should be red, moist and shiny.*
- *Mucosa that is hard, dry or flaccid*
- *Stoma with a bad odor*

Treatment

In most cases the healing may occur on its own and spontaneously; superficial necrosis, for example, can spontaneously resolve when necrotic tissue simply sloughing away. In other cases, surgery is necessary because the tissue below the ficial level is involved. A two piece pouching system that is transparent is often suggested so that the stoma can be observed often; additionally the pouch itself may need frequent resizing.

Mucocutaneous Separation

If the stoma and the skin, where it was placed, separate, it is known as mucocutaneous separation. This can be superficial in nature or it can be deep. Some of the causes of this complication include tension or tautness of sutures and conditions that are associated with poor wound healing capacity, such as diabetes, malnutrition, infection, etc.

Signs and Symptoms

Separation of the wound and drainage may be seen.

Treatment

Initially, the wound drainage has to be absorbed and then covered with a dressing that is appropriate for the wound. A two piece pouch system is another option, but it depends on the wound especially if an infection is present.

Stoma Trauma

Stoma trauma can occur from a variety of different causes, although lacerations are the most commonly occurring cause. It can also occur from clothing, or injury. Lacerations are most commonly seen in the small opening in the flange or a misaligned pouch opening. Other possible causes can include stomal prolapsed and parastomal prolapse with the possibility of edema or enlargement of the stoma.

Signs and Symptoms

Symptoms include a visibly cut, bright red blood/bleeding and discoloration of the stoma that is yellowish-white.

Treatment

Treatment may not be necessary because, sometimes, the laceration of the stoma will heal itself, however, if the cause is from the pouching system it is vital that anything in the system does not come in contact with the stoma. Direct pressure should be placed on any area that is actively bleeding until the bleeding ceases; if this pressure is not successful further treatment is indicated.

Parastomal Hernia

With this type of ostomy complication, the stoma exits the abdominal area and the intestine or bowel actually extends beyond the abdominal cavity and muscles. The area around the stoma looks swollen.

Parastomal hernias most often occur within two years postoperatively but it is possible that this complication can occur at any time.

Signs and Symptoms

Distention around the stoma is usually the initial symptom; this initial symptom is usually followed by pain and an overall feeling of discomfort as the hernia progressively enlarges. Pouching problems may also occur as a result of this complication, therefore this must be carefully observed because this problem can lead to peristomal skin problems.

Treatment

Initially pouching system changes are made including the size of the pouches. Other treatment choices include a hernia binder and/or a pouch support belt.

Peristomal Skin Complications

As mentioned above some people have difficulties with the pouch seal. This can result in leaking. The patient can experience recurrent peristomal skin problems from the leakage and, when the problem persists, it may be necessary to perform a stoma revision.

The incontinence management guideline goals include prevention of perineal dermatitis, prevention of incontinence related skin breakdown and early treatment of incontinence compromised skin. It is vital to remove stool and urine from skin contact as soon as possible to prevent maceration and contact damage to the skin. Protection of the skin once cleaned can be performed by using perineal care washcloths with 3% dimethicone.

Goals of Rehabilitation

The purposes of rehabilitation include the following:

- An interdisciplinary approach to managed care including medical consults to manage any underlying disease processes
- Engaging the patient and promoting their participation when possible to promote physical and psychological comfort
- Manage pain locally first, then systemically if required
- Cleanse wound with normal saline or sterile water depending on pain tolerance to salt
- Promote gentle autolytic debridement with absorptive dressings
- Manage exudate with absorptive dressings while maintaining a moist wound bed

- Manage infection—local wound management using antimicrobial absorptive dressings
- Minimize frequency of dressing changes in response to exudate volume and pain tolerance
- Remove ostomy system and dressing gently/slowly to minimize pain and further trauma
- Identify and minimize/avoid trauma to affected area
- Replace a convex skin barrier with a more flexible pouching system to prevent pressure to the peristomal skin
- Secure a non-adherent pouching system with an ostomy belt to prevent traumatic removal of the skin barrier and minimize pressure to the affected area

General Principles of Management and Patient Teaching

Management and Patient Teaching

Patient and family education is highly important to achieve optimal client outcomes. Some components of this teaching include pouching and/or containment strategies, resuming an optimal life style, the surgical procedure and recovery process postoperatively, informed consents, guardianship and advance directives.

Implement Pouching and/or Containment Strategies

The components of pouching and containment strategies and client and family educational activities include:

- *Incontinent pads and briefs*
- *Indwelling urinary catheter*
- *Linens*
- *External pouching, which is only appropriate for application to intact peri-anal tissue*
- *Internal containment system, which is used for patients who produce liquid stool 500cc or greater within 24 hours*
- *Self-adhesive skin barrier attached to a drainable pouch*

Provide Sexual Counseling

Interventions regarding sexual disorders and/or difficulties are discussed in length, later in this review. Sexuality and impairments of sexuality vary according to the client, their illness and any treatments that they are taking. Patients who experience difficulties regarding their sexuality are encouraged to seek help from the nurse, and/or other professionals like a sex therapist or psychologist.

Facilitate Understanding of Surgical Procedures

The Surgical Procedure and the Postoperative Recovery

Clients and family members must be educated about all phases of the perisurgical process. Prior to surgery they must be informed fully about the procedure, what to expect during the immediate postoperative period of time and things that they should know about the postoperative period. For example, the client must be knowledgeable and competent to perform deep breathing, coughing, splinting, out of bed transfers and leg exercises prior to the procedure.

Informed Consent

All clients have the legal right to accept or reject all treatments and interventions. Patients must be fully informed and knowledgeable about the risks, benefits, and alternatives for all interventions and aspects of care. The client will then consent to, or reject, the treatment. A parent will consent for their minor child; a legally appointed guardian or health care proxy will consent when the client is not competent to do so.

Guardianship and Health Care Proxy

Guardianship, also referred to as a conservatorship, refers to the legal process with which another person makes decisions for a person who is not competent to make sound decisions on their own.

Alternatives to guardianship include durable powers of attorney, health care surrogacy and the appointment of a health care proxy.

Legally appointed guardians have legal decision-making power in terms of accepting/rejecting treatment(s) and end of life decisions. Legal guardians can be family members or another person who takes the person's interests, desires and well-being into mind when making decisions.

Advance Directives and Living Wills

Advanced directives and living wills contain the wishes of the client in terms of treatments and interventions that they do and do not want to be carried out when they are no longer able to competently provide these consents and rejections of treatment. For example, a young male person with no history of disease may elect to NOT have CPR or a ventilator in the event of sudden death. Another client with cancer may choose to have tube feedings but no IVs in their advanced directive.

Customize Teaching Based on Developmental Stage, Readiness to Learn, Knowledge Level, Cultural Background, and Learning Style

The phases of the teaching/learning process are the same as the phases of the nursing process- assessment, diagnosis, planning, implementation and evaluation.

Assessment

The purpose of assessment is to determine the client's learning needs, their level of motivation and readiness, personal, ethnical and cultural aspects, age specific characteristics and needs, barriers to learning, including cognitive impairments, language, level of comprehension or reading level and physical as well as psychological barriers to learning. Simply stated, a learning need = what should be known minus what is actually known.

Diagnosis

The diagnosis phase includes the generation of a learning diagnosis that is based on the analyzed assessment data. These diagnoses can include things like "A lack of knowledge about...", and "A knowledge deficit related to...".

Planning and Establishing Learning Goals or Objectives

The purpose of planning is to ensure that the patient and family teaching is consistent with identified learning needs, and that it can be evaluated in terms of effectiveness (outcome evaluation).

Planning consists of generating objective and specific learning goals, among other things. Learning objectives are specific, measurable, behavioral, learner centered, consistent with assessed need and congruent with the domain of learning. Examples of well-worded learning objectives are the "Patient will be able to list basic food groups" (cognitive domain) and the "Patient will demonstrate the correct use of a blood glucose monitor" (psychomotor).

Implementation

The implementation phase consists of conducting the education activity in an environment that is conducive to learning, which includes a physically comfortable environment as well as one that is trusting, open, respectful and accepting. Appropriate educational materials, including reading materials are used, as based on the learning needs and the characteristics of the learner, such as sensory impairments and learning styles.

Evaluation

There are two types of evaluation in the teaching/learning process. They are referred to as formative and summative evaluation.

1. *Formative evaluation* is the continuous assessment of the effectiveness of the teaching while the teaching is being conducted. This allows the teacher to modify the plan, as indicated.

2. *Summative evaluation* at the end of the learning activity allows the educator to determine whether or not the education has achieved the established learning objectives for the individual or group.

The Domains of Learning

There are three domains of learning that are the basis of all education, including patient and family education. These domains are:

- *The Cognitive Domain*

    This domain consists of both knowledge and understanding. An example of a cognitive domain patient outcome is, "The patient verbalized knowledge of all of their medications and side effects".

    The six levels of the cognitive domain from the basic to the most complex are knowledge, comprehension, application, analysis, synthesis and evaluation. Some of the teaching/learning strategies for this domain include online/computer based learning, peer group discussions, reading material and a discussion or lecture.

- *The Psychomotor Domain*

    The psychomotor domain consists of "hands on skills" like taking a blood pressure and using a blood glucose monitor correctly.

The seven levels of this domain are perception, set, guided response, mechanism, complex overt response, adaptation and origination. Some of the teaching/learning strategies for this domain include demonstration, return demonstration and a video with a step-by-step demonstration of the psychomotor skill.

- *The Affective Domain*

    The affective domain includes the development of attitudes, beliefs, values and opinions. An example of affective domain competency is developing a belief that exercise is a valuable part of wellness.

    There are five levels, which are receiving, responding, valuing, organization and characterization by a value or a value complex. The teaching/learning strategies for this domain include role-playing and values clarification exercises. The affective domain is rarely used for patient teaching.

Adult and Childhood Learning

Pedagogy is childhood learning and androgogy is adult learning. Unlike pedagogy, adult learning has immediate usefulness in terms of solving problems; it involves active learner involvement and participation; and the curriculum and content are based on the learner's needs and desires.

Below is a table that compares and contrasts pedagogy and androgogy.

	PEDAGOGY	**ANDROGOGY**
CURRICULUM	The state and the teacher develop and design the teaching, based on what they decide is important.	The learner, in collaboration with the nurse develops and designs the teaching, based on learner needs and other characteristics, such as their preferred learning style.
LEVEL OF INPUT	The child is a somewhat passive learner. The learner has a low level of involvement in all the phases of the teaching process.	The adult is a highly active learner. The learner has a high level of involvement in all the phases of the teaching process.

TEACHING METHODS	Homework & Teacher Lecture	Active learner participation The adult learner has a large amount of knowledge and experiences to share with others and to relate to the learning activity.
THE PURPOSE OF LEARNING	Childhood learning has little immediate application. This learning prepares the child for the future and their future needs.	Adult learning should have immediate application and usefulness. The learning aims to solve problems.

Barriers to Learning and Overcoming These Barriers

Some of the barriers to learning are discussed below.

- *Literacy*

    Sadly, many people in our nation are not able to read at all. Some may only be able to read and comprehend material at a low-grade level. It is sometimes recommended that patient education material be authored at or below 6th grade reading level to accommodate for these comprehension and literacy needs.

    The nurse must assess the client's literacy level and provide learning materials that are appropriate to the client in terms of their reading level so that the person is able to benefit from them.

- *Health Literacy*

    Patients are considered "health literate" when they are able to understand information and use it to make appropriate health care decisions. Almost 50% of patients are NOT health literate.

    Nurses and other healthcare professionals, must modify their communication and teaching to accommodate for this weakness and to insure comprehension. For example, simple anatomy and physiology information relating to their disorder is preferred over complex, biochemical explanations that the client cannot understand. Additionally, the use of medical jargon and terminology should be avoided.

- *Motivation and Readiness*

    Clients will not learn unless they are motivated and ready to do so. Nurses can motivate learners by involving them in the entire teaching/learning process, by focusing the learning on solving immediate and pressing concerns, and by explaining the benefits of learning in terms of problem resolution, while maintaining an environment that is supportive of an open, honest and highly respectful learning environment.

    Motivation to learn and motivation to change are assessed as part of the assessment phase of the teaching process. Motivation will be further discussed below.

- *Learning Styles and Preferences*

    Whenever possible, individual learning styles and preferences should be accommodated for. Some learn best by listening, some by watching, some by reading and some by doing. Some like to read, or watch a video, or use a computer; others do not. Learning styles and preferences will be discussed below.

- *Cultural Aspects*

    Communication patterns, vocabulary, slang and/or terminology, are differences that can separate the members of the group, or culture, from those who are not members. Nurses must become culturally competent about the cultures, norms and gestures of others and also modify their terminology and behavior according to what is acceptable and understandable to the learner of a different culture.

- *Age Specific Characteristics*

    Some examples of teaching modifications based on age are simple concrete and brief explanations for the toddler, simple and brief explanations for the pre-school child, the encouragement of questions and more detailed explanations for the school age child, and adult like teaching for the adolescent.

- *Language Barriers*

    Communicating with, and teaching, those who speak a language unlike our own is challenging indeed. However, these barriers can be overcome to a great extent with some relatively simple techniques, such as speaking slowly, clarifying, reclarifying, using pictures and diagrams, and eliciting the help of an interpreter.

- *Health Beliefs*

    Health beliefs can also be a barrier to learning and changes in behavior. Clients who place a high value on health, health promotion and wellness will be more highly motivated to learn than those clients who do not place priority value on health, health promotion and wellness.

    Nurses can overcome this barrier to learning by facilitating the client's understanding of the importance of these values in terms of their disorder and ways that the person can enhance their health, health promotion and wellness, despite the presence of the medical issue. These concepts will be further discussed below.

- *Religious and Spiritual Beliefs*

    Religious and spiritual beliefs can include the use of symbols, dreams, spiritual practices and beliefs, including those that are metaphysical in nature.

    For example, maintaining health may involve the use of proper clothing and proper diet (physical facet), the support of others including family members (psychological facet) and things like meditation, prayer and formalized religious practices (spiritual facet).

    Similarly, health protection can be facilitated with symbolic clothing and special spiritual foods (physical facet), the avoidance of people and things that can lead to disease (psychological facet), and the use of religious customs, superstition, and amulets like the "Evil Eye" to ward off evil and harm (spiritual facet).

    Lastly, the restoration of health is enabled with alternative healing methods, such as massage, herbs, homeopathic remedies and special foods (physical facet), exorcism, the use of culturally traditional healers, like medicine men and curanderos (spiritual facet), relaxation techniques (psychological facet) and religious rituals, special prayers.

- *Family Dynamics and Other Social Forces*

    Many diabetic clients have social support systems and family supports; however many lack these supports. For example, the newly diagnosed diabetic client may be widowed, single, geographically separated from family and friends, and/or may not have family or friends that support them and their need for education and behavior changes.

    The nurse can increase social support systems by utilizing available community resources such as diabetic support groups, Meals on Wheels and transportation to and from healthcare related services, as indicated.

- *Psychological Factors*

    Nurses and other healthcare professionals have to assess and accommodate for any actual or potential cognitive, sensory and psychological/emotional barriers to learning. For example, cognitive limitations can be overcome with slow, brief, simple and understandable explanations.

    Psychological barriers can be minimized with establishing trust, reinforcing learning with positive feedback, and minimizing stress. Moderate stress is a motivator; extreme stress and pain prevent learning. For this reason, extreme stress and pain should be addressed before the educational activity.

- *Physical Capabilities and Limitations*

    Sensory barriers can be accommodated for with large print materials and Braille for the visually impaired, louder discussions with clients affected with a hearing loss, and the use of assistive devices like magnifiers, eyeglasses and hearing aids.

Readiness to Change Behavior

Motivation

Clients will not learn unless they are motivated and ready to do so. Nurses can motivate learners by involving them in the entire teaching/learning process, by focusing the learning on solving immediate and pressing concerns, by explain the benefits of learning in terms of problem resolution, and with the maintaining of an environment supportive of an open, honest and highly respectful learning environment.

Motivation to learn and motivation to change are assessed as part of the assessment phase of the teaching process.

Models and Theories That Are Related to Motivation, Readiness to Learn and Behavior Changes

There are a wide variety of theories and models that can be highly useful to the Nurse in terms of their clients' needs, their readiness to change behavior, their level of motivation, their confidence in their ability to change, and the value of change, etc.

Adaptation Models

Adaptation models and theories address health as a function of how successfully the client is able to flexibly cope and adapt when they are confronted with a health related problem. Disease occurs with maladaptation; and health is facilitated with successful coping skills and healthy adaptation.

Education about the specific disorder allows the person to cope with and adapt to this chronic disorder. The client will be motivated to learn when they believe that they can cope with, and manage, their disorder.

The Health-Illness Continuum: Ryan and Travis

This model describes health and illness as ever changing states along a continuum with a high level wellness at one end of the continuum and a high level of illness, and death, at the opposite end of this continuum. The center of the continuum is a "neutral zone" which represents neither health nor illness.

Clients move along the continuum from illness toward health when they are successfully treated. Conversely, they can also move from a high level of wellness through the "neutral zone" to all degrees of illness when they are affected with an acute or chronic disorder, disease or health threat.

Clients can move along the continuum from illness toward health when they are successfully controlling their disorder as the result of patient education.

Holistic Models of Health and Wellness

Holistic approaches of health and wellness facilitate the Nurse's fuller understanding of the client's physical, psychological, social, and spiritual status and all the simultaneous interrelationships of these dimensions within an ever-changing environment.

Changes in the client lead to simultaneous changes in the environment as well as among the various other dimensions of the client. The client and the environment are both open systems with dynamic interactions and interrelationships of the parts.

The Dimensions Model

This model is particularly useful to guide a complete and thorough assessment and the identification of needs based on all of these dimensions.

The six dimensions of health are:

1. *Biophysical*: Genetic composition, physical risk factors, and diseases
2. *Psychological*: Coping and mental health
3. *Behavioral*: Lifestyle choices like exercise and good nutrition
4. *The physical environment*: Air pollution and contaminated water supplies
5. *Socio-cultural*: Societal norms and beliefs
6. *Health systems*: Accessibility, availability and affordability of health care services.

This model is particularly useful to nurse in terms of identifying and assessing the total client and all of the factors that impact on the client and their needs.

The Agent – Host – Environment Model: Clark and Leavell

Disease occurs as the result of the interrelationships among the agent, the host and the environment.

The agent is any environmental factor or stressor that, with or without, their presence, can lead to disease. Some of these environmental factors can include biological, physical, chemical, mechanical, and psychosocial forces or stressors. For example, the genetic makeup of a client can lead to a variety of hereditary diseases/disorders; and the existence of healthy life style choices, like exercise and nutrition, facilitate wellness and the control of ostomies, for example.

The host is the client, or patient. The host may or may not be at risk for an illness or disease. Some hosts are more susceptible and vulnerable than others. For example, factors like age and diet can positively or negatively impact on the host's vulnerability and susceptibility to complications with certain types of ostomies, for example.

The environment consists of all factors that are external, or extrinsic, to the client. Some elements of the environment can place a person at risk for a disease or illness; other environmental factors predispose the person to wellness. For example, a social stressor, such as the loss of a loved one, can increase blood glucose levels.

The High – Level Wellness Model: Halbert Dunn

This model consists of two axes (the horizontal health axis and the vertical environment axis) and four quadrants, which are called high-level wellness in a very favorable environment, emergent high-level wellness in an unfavorable environment, protected poor health in a favorable environment, and poor health in an unfavorable environment.

An example of high-level wellness in a very favorable environment is when a client maintains a healthy lifestyle and actively participates in primary, preventive care and they have the financial ability to do so.

An example of emergent high-level wellness in an unfavorable environment is the client's lack of ability to maintain a healthy lifestyle as the result of job and family responsibilities that prohibit a favorable environment.

Protected poor health in a favorable environment occurs when a client with a disease or illness, is ill but they have access to health care services that address these needs. Access to health care services, including Nurses, is a favorable environment that can facilitate wellness.

Poor health in an unfavorable environment is the most challenging of all of Dunn's grids. Poor health in an unfavorable environment is present when an ill person is in an unhealthy environment. For example, uncontrolled diabetic clients with poor nutrition who live in a community without fresh fruits and vegetables are an example of poor health in an unfavorable environment.

The Seven Components of Wellness: Anspaugh, Hamrick and Rosato

The seven components of wellness are the physical, social, emotional, intellectual, spiritual, occupational and environmental components of health.

The physical dimension consists of things like overall functioning, fitness, and physical health; the social dimension includes things like the initiation and maintenance of relationships, including social and intimate relationships; the emotional or psychological dimension includes health and illness variables like personal insight, emotional stability, and realistic views of one's strengths, weakness and limitations; the intellectual dimension is reflected with lifelong learning, personal growth and effective coping skills; the spiritual dimension, which is not necessarily religious, is manifested when the client has purpose and meaning in life; the occupational dimension includes the client's ability to get and maintain a job and balancing their work life with their personal and social lives; and lastly, the environmental dimension includes environmental factors that protect and promote health, such as the provision of basic safety, clean water and clean air.

The Nurse must assess and address all of these seven components, or dimensions, because they all impact on the individual's state of wellness, health and illness.

The HEALTH Traditions Model

The HEALTH Traditions Model is highly useful for meeting the cultural, ethnic, and spiritual, or religious needs of clients. According to the HEALTH model, the physical, mental or emotional, and spiritual aspects of health can be fulfilled in terms of maintaining health, protecting health, and restoring health.

Some facets, or aspects, of health and some examples of each are listed below.

- *Mental and Emotional Aspects*
    - *Mental or Emotional Health Maintenance: Social support networks and relaxation techniques.*
    - *Mental or Emotional Health Protection: The avoidance of negative people and influences.*
    - *Mental or Emotional Health Restoration: Cultural healers, medicine men and other practices like exorcism.*
- *Physical and Biological Aspects*
    - *Physical Health Maintenance: Exercise, diet, and healthy lifestyle choices.*
    - *Physical Health Protection: Special ethnical or cultural foods and symbolic attire.*
    - *Physical Health Restoration: Acupuncture, massage and homeopathic treatments.*
- *Spiritual Aspects*
    - *Spiritual Health Maintenance: Prayer, meditation and formal religious ceremonies.*
    - *Spiritual Health Protection: Wearing a cross to protect against evil spirits.*
    - *Spiritual Health Restoration: Religious and spiritual rituals and ceremonies.*

Health – Belief Model: Rosenstock and Becker

This model addresses the relationships among the client's perceptions, behaviors and health. This model can predict whether or not a person will engage in things like screening tests and patient education, such as those based on their personal and/or cultural perceptions and beliefs. The factors that impact on health beliefs include personal perceptions, modifying factors and the likelihood of action.

Some of the personal perceptions that impact on health are perceived seriousness, perceived susceptibility and perceived threat. Clients who perceive a health threat as serious, and one that they are susceptible to, will most likely be motivated to act in order to avoid the serious threat.

Factors that modify the client's perceptions include things like structural barriers (the lack of accessible and affordable healthcare and the lack of culturally competent care within the system), demographics (gender, age, culture, race and ethnicity), psychosocial forces (peer pressure, the lack of support for healthy habits), and cues to action. These cues can be external like the illness of another family member, and also internal or innate. Some of the internal cues to action are discomfort and fear.

Client motivation and readiness to learn are enhanced when the client perceives their disorder as serious; they will most likely be motivated to act in order to avoid this serious threat. Patient education gives the client the knowledge, skills and abilities to act in the appropriate manner to control this threat.

Pender's Health Promotion Model

Health is the actualization of inherent and acquired human potential through goal directed behavior, according to this model. Human potential is maximized with goal directed behavior that is motivated by the client's commitment to action.

The client's level of motivation and commitment are impacted by many factors including emotions, affect, behavior specific cognitions, the client's prior experiences, personal characteristics, such as cultural characteristics, feelings of self-efficacy and the support of others.

Whenever possible, the Nurse should maximize the above impacting factors to change behavior.

The Self-Care Deficit Theory: Dorothea Orem

This theory is based on the premise that clients can, and want to, care for themselves as much as possible. This self-care allows clients to recover more holistically and rapidly than those who do not perform self-care. The three types of systems that Orem identifies are the supportive-educative (developmental), partly compensatory, and the wholly compensatory systems.

The supportive-educative (developmental) system aims to provide clients with the support, assistance and care that they need to continue their independent self-care. The supportive-educative system includes client education relating to the patient's disorder and treatment options.

The wholly compensatory system meets the self- care needs of those clients who can perform some, but not all, self- care functions. For example, a conscious client who has had a stroke can usually perform some, but not all, of their self-care activities.

Lastly, the wholly compensatory system provides all care to the client because the client is not able to perform any self-care. Infants, very young children and clients in a coma, are examples of clients who need wholly compensatory care.

Self-care requisites, according to Orem, fall into one of three categories. These categories are:

1. *Universal self-care requisites*: These needs are inherent to and universal for all people. The need for food, air and water, are examples of some universal self-care requisites.

2. *Developmental self-care requisites*: These self-care requisites are maturational and situational in nature. For example, the maturation needs vary across the age groups and they vary when a traumatic event or another situation.

3. *Health deviation self-care requisites*: These requisites, or needs, occur as the result of a disease, disorder, illness and disability

The Interpersonal Relations Model: Hildegard Peplau

A Nurse will enter into a personal and therapeutic relationship with a patient when a need arises. The educator assumes multiple roles in this relationship including the roles of surrogate, counselor, leader, teacher, and resource person in this relationship.

The four phases of Interpersonal Relations Model that the Nurse-patient therapeutic relationship moves through are as follows:

1. *Orientation*

    The Nurse assesses the client's needs and explains these needs and problems to the client. The client then asks the Nurse for help and support.

2. *Identification*

    The Nurse understands the patient's perspective and their interpretation of their problems. The client acts dependently, independently or interdependently with the nurses (relatedness).

3. *Exploitation*

    The client is now able to use services and get benefit and value from these educational services, as based on the patient's interests and needs.

4. *Resolution*

    The patient is able to progress to new and higher level goals as they discard older resolved needs and fulfilled goals.

The Goal Attainment Theory: Imogene King

This theory focuses on the processes that the client uses to meet and achieve their goal(s). The Nurse and the client collaboratively establish goals, they communicate information to each other and then this dyad (Nurse and client) takes the necessary actions to achieve those goals. It includes fifteen concepts including things like self, stress, roles, communication and power, for example.

The patient, according to King, is a social being who has three fundamental needs. These needs are as follows:

1. *The need for care when the patient is unable to care for themselves*
2. *The need for health information*
3. *The need for care to prevent illness*

The ultimate goal of the Nurse-patient relationship is to help the patient achieve their goals in terms of attaining and maintaining health. By using Imogene King's Theory of Goal Attainment, a nurse can more effectively work and motivate their clients to achieve these goals.

The Adaptation Model of Nursing: Sister Callista Roy

The client is a biopsychosocial human with interrelated systems (biological, psychological and social). Even though there is no absolute level of balance, the patient strives to attain and maintain an optimal balance between and among these interrelated systems and the outside world (environment).

Roy's four modes of an adaptation, which are relatively easy to understand, are:

1. *The Physiologic-Physical Mode*
2. *The Self-Concept- Group Identity Mode*
3. *The Role Function Mode*
4. *The Interdependence Mode*

The Human Caring Theory: Jean Watson

Caring consists of the following 10 interventions, which were formally referred to as carative factors:

1. *Developing a helping-trust relationship*
2. *Promoting transpersonal teaching-learning*
3. *Assisting with the gratification of biophysical and psychosocial human needs*
4. *Forming a humanistic-altruistic value system*
5. *Instilling faith-hope*
6. *Cultivating a sensitivity to self and others*

7. Promoting expressions of positive and negative feelings

8. Using problem-solving for decision-making

9. Providing and maintaining a supportive, protective, and/or corrective mental, physical, societal, and spiritual environment

10. Allowing for existential-phenomenological-spiritual forces.

Lewin's Forced Field Theory of Change

Lewin's Forced Field Theory of Change is perhaps the most popular of all change theories. Lewin's change theory consists of unfreezing, freezing and refreezing, the three phases of change. Lewin also describes barriers to change and facilitators to change.

In order for change to occur the force of the facilitators to change must be greater in strength than the barriers to change. In other words, the pluses must outweigh the minuses for change to occur.

This theory, as well as other change theories, helps the nurse to understand how they can impact on behavior changes and positive choices for the client, most often as the result of patient and family education. It also assists the nurse to understand and facilitate change in the organization within which they work.

- *The Unfreezing Stage of Change*

    During the unfreezing stage of change, there is awareness that there is a problem, need, or an opportunity that has to be addressed with some action. For example, the nurse may observe that the current outcomes of care do not currently meet expectations, established benchmarks and/or evidence based practices. The nurse is aware that there is a problem, and that there is a need, or opportunity, for improvement.

    This unfreezing process is challenging because many people, and groups, resist change and prefer the status quo. Resistance, nonetheless, can be overcome with things like motivational techniques, individual/group involvement and participation, and good communication. Humans are most apt to accept change when they understand, and know, that real benefits can result from the change.

- *The Freezing Stage of Change*

    The planned change is implemented during the freezing stage. Those affected with the change may experience feelings such as fear, uncertainty and resistance. These barriers, too, can be overcome with effective strategies like communication, education, and ongoing reinforcement of the fact that benefits will be realized with positive change and the control of one's illness or disorder.

- *The Refreezing Stage of Change*

    During the refreezing stage, the affected person has fully accepted and implemented the change. It becomes somewhat routine for them. Some of the factors that can positively impact on this stage, in order to promote long lasting and sustained change, include support, continued positive reinforcement and the stabilization of the change. The nurse also plays a highly critical role in the refreezing stage of change.

Havelock's Six Phases of Planned Change

The six phases of Havelock's Six Phases of Planned Change are developing relationships, diagnosing the existing problem, collecting available resources, choosing a solution, garnering acceptance and stabilizing the change.

Lippitt, Watson and Westley's Seven Phases of Change

The seven phases of change in Lippitt, Watson and Westley's Seven Phases of Change are client awareness of the need for change, the development of a change agent/client relationship, which includes the nurse-client relationship, the problem is defined, the goals are established, the plan for change is implemented, the change is accepted, and the change agent/client relationship changes.

Roger's Innovation-Decision Process

The nurse, as change agent, provides the client with knowledge and information about the benefits of change during the five stages of Roger's Innovation-Decision Process, which are knowledge, persuasion, decision, implementation and confirmation.

Chaos Theory

This change theory addresses the constantly changing environment that impacts on the client as an open system. Nurses have to always expect the unexpected and never assume that predicted outcomes will occur automatically.

Factors that Impact on Motivation and Readiness

Some of the factors that impact on motivation and readiness to learn are:

- *Level of pain*
- *Level of stress*
- *Developmental level*
- *Perceived learning needs*
- *Attitudes*

Level of Pain

Clients who are in severe pain cannot learn. They are not motivated to learn, because they have unmet physical needs and they are also not capable of active participation in learning activities. When at all possible, the level of pain should be decreased prior to a teaching activity.

Level of Stress

Contrary to popular belief, stress is essential to the maintenance of basic life functions and it is also essential and necessary for the motivation to learn. We do not breathe unless our body becomes stressed with increased levels of carbon dioxide; and we would not learn unless we are affected with stress and anxiety.

Moderate levels of stress and anxiety motivate learners to learn. However, high-level anxiety and stress is not conductive to learning. High stress interferes with the learner's ability to focus and concentrate on the issue at hand.

Developmental Level

Some of the variables that are assessed and addressed in the developmental dimension of the teaching/learning process include communication techniques, motivational techniques, and teaching strategies, in addition to the principles of pedagogy and androgogy, which were discussed above.

Some examples of teaching modifications, as based on age, are simple concrete and brief explanations for the toddler, simple and brief explanations for the pre-school child, the encouragement of questions and more detailed explanations for the school age child, and adult-like teaching for the adolescent.

Further information about growth and development are included below.

- *Perceived Learning Needs*

    As described above, many theories and models support the fact that motivation can be positively and negatively impacted by the client's perceptions in terms of their overall needs and the benefits that they perceive can be derived from educational activities.

- *Attitudes*

    Some clients have an external locus of control and others have an internal locus of control. Some clients with an external locus of control view their problems, such as diabetes, as something that occurs, because of external forces and something that they have no control over. Other clients with an internal locus of control are motivated with an internal locus of control, which is demonstrated with the client who believes that they can control their diabetes and they will act accordingly in terms of necessary behavioral changes.

The locus of control can be moved from an external locus of control to an internal locus of control when the educator is able to convince the diabetic patient that they can, like so many other diabetic clients, successfully control and cope with their diabetes. The client can then develop a "can do" attitude.

- *Strategies to Enhance Motivation and Readiness*

Motivation and learning readiness are critical to the teaching-learning process. People will not learn unless they are motivated and ready to do so. Clients and family members can be motivated to learn when the nurse utilizes the following strategies:

- *The learning should be made an extremely active and participative process.*

An explanation of the benefits of the learning to the client and family members is highly motivating because the learner believes that the teaching can help them to solve problems. and the prevention of complications. Clients are motivated to learn when they believe they can solve problems as the result of the learning activity.

- *Relate the new knowledge to the client's past knowledge and experiences, so the learner can comfortably fit this newly gained knowledge, skills and abilities into their life and life style.*

Involvement of the learners in the entire teaching-learning process encourages, and motivates, the learner to learn. The learner must have input into ALL the aspects of the learning plan, needs assessment, the teaching session and the evaluation of the outcome.

Focus the teaching/learning on the immediate problems and the concerns of the learner and family members. The nurse should explain how the learning can be applied immediately to their life situation and their healthcare problem relating to their disorder and the control of it.

- *Maintain an open, honest and highly respectful learning environment.*

Encourage the learner to debate, share and exchange their knowledge, ideas and past experiences with the nurse and others. Small group teaching activities provide learners with these opportunities.

Learning Styles And Preferences

People have unique learning styles and learning preferences that can facilitate learning and also impede learning. For example, auditory learners prefer and do well with patient education discussions; but visual learners do not get the same benefits from discussions, they prefer visual information using pictures and diagrams.

Some of the learning styles and preferences include:

- *Active and reflective learners*
- *Sensing and intuitive learners*
- *Verbal, auditory and tactile learners*
- *Sequential and global learners*

All of these learning styles differ in terms of the learners' strengths and weakness and in terms of their preferred form of learning. Most people, however, have a mix, or combination, of more than one learning style. For example, a reflective learner can also have the characteristics of a verbal and/or sequential learner.

Active and Reflective Learners

Active Learner Preferences: Active learners prefer to learn with active engagement, doing, discussions, and group projects. Lectures without physical activity are more difficult for active learners when compared to reflective learners.

Tips for Active Learners: Use group discussion and study groups.

Reflective Learner Preferences: Reflective learners prefer to learn by thinking about the learning and content material first. They prefer solitary work rather than group work.

Tips for Reflective Learners: Encourage the learner to reflect on readings, contemplate applications and summarize material rather than the memorization of facts.

Sensing and Intuitive Learners

Sensing Learner Preferences: Sensing learners prefer memorizing facts, detail oriented learning, and practical, real world oriented learning, rather than abstraction; they use reliable methods of problem solving and they do not expect unanticipated results.

Tips for Sensing Learners: Seek out procedures and concepts that can transform abstract concepts in concrete and practical solutions.

Intuitive Learners: Intuitive learners consider relationships among various pieces of information. They prefer novel and innovative ideas rather than learning by routine. They are tolerant, and welcoming, of abstractions, including mathematics, and a more rapid pace than sensors.

Tips for Intuitive Learners: Encourage the learner to employ careful thought before answering a question and solving a problem. Encourage the learner to connect theoretical and abstract thinking to facts.

Visual, Verbal and Tactile Learners

- *Visual Learners*

Visual learners prefer, and learn best, when they see things. These learners benefit from flow charts, demonstrations, diagrams, medical models, and videos. Discussions are not the strategy of choice for visual learners. They benefit greatly from pictorial handouts and other visual strategies.

- *Verbal Learners*

Verbal learners, on the other hand, benefit from the spoken and written word. Discussions and lectures are preferred over demonstration and the use of pictures.

Whenever possible, the nurse should employ strategies that meet the individual learning style preferences and, when group learning is being used, the nurse should employ both strategies to accommodate the needs and preferences of both the visual and verbal learners.

- *Tactile Learners*

Tactile learners tend to remember things by doing, rather than listening or reading. This type of learner tends to learn best from hands on experimentation. This type of learner tends to excel in areas such as dance, athletics or other mobility or movement based activities.

Tactile learners learn through imitation and practice. There is a tendency to have difficulties with reading and comprehension.

Sequential and Global Learners

Sequential learners learn best when the material is presented with logical, orderly and linear steps; global learners, on the other hand, move the content and material all around in a seemingly illogical and disorder manner until the learner makes connections among the pieces of information and then understands it.

Sequential learners follow logical steps to find a solution and to master the material. They are also able to explain how they solved a problem. Global learners have difficulty explaining why and how the problem was solved but, nonetheless, global learners tend to have the ability to rapidly solve complex problems.

Whenever possible, the nurse should employ strategies that meet the individual learning style preferences and, when, group learning is being used, the nurse should employ both strategies to accommodate the needs and preferences of both the visual and verbal learners.

Assessing Developmental Status

Age and developmental stages are assessed not only to determine if the client is at the expected level of development but also to modify all aspects of care, and communication, according to the client's specific needs. Erik Erickson's developmental tasks and Piaget's stages of cognitive development are most often used for the framework of this assessment and data analysis, although there are a couple of other theories and frameworks that can be useful.

Erik Erikson

Erik Erickson proposed eight major stages of development and expected tasks along the life span from infancy to old age. People who are able to resolve their age related tasks are successfully able to progress to the next task; however, barriers to personal development and unresolved issues occur when a person is unable to achieve their age related task.

Nurses must consider the major developmental challenges facing their clients and modify their care accordingly. These stages, developmental tasks and signs of unsuccessful resolution are listed below.

Age Group: Infant

Task: Trust

Effects of the Lack of Resolution of the Task: Mistrust and a failure to thrive

Age Group: Toddler

Task: Autonomy, self control & will power

Effects of the Lack of Resolution of the Task: Shame, doubt and a low tolerance for frustration

Age Group: Preschool

Task: Initiative, confidence, purpose and direction

Effects of the Lack of Resolution of the Task: Guilt and fear of punishment

Age Group: School Age Child

Task: Industry, self-confidence and competency

Effects of the Lack of Resolution of the Task: Fears about meeting the expectations of others and feelings of inferiority

Age Group: Adolescent

Task: Identity formation, sense of self

Effects of the Lack of Resolution of the Task: Role confusion and poor self-concept and self-esteem

Age Group: Young Adult

Task: Intimacy, affection and love

Effects of the Lack of Resolution of the Task: Isolation and the avoidance of relationships

Age Group: Middle Aged Adult

Task: Generativity, productivity, and concern about others

Effects of the Lack of Resolution of the Task: Stagnation, self-absorption and a lack of concern about others

Age Group: Older Adults

Task: Ego integrity, wisdom and views life with satisfaction

Effects of the Lack of Resolution of the Task: Despair and feelings that life is meaningless

Jean Piaget

Jean Piaget's levels of cognitive development from birth until 12 years of age are used as a guideline for assessing infants and children in terms of their growth and development.

These levels and characteristics are described below:

- *Up to 2 Years of Age: Sensorimotor thought*

    This consists of six substages and it includes the development of the skills and abilities to manipulate concrete objects.

- *From 2 to 7 Years of Age: Preoperational and symbolic functioning*

    The development of language

- *From 7 to 11 Years of Age: Concrete operations*

    Logical reasoning and the ability to solve concrete problems

- *12 Years of Age and Older: Formal operations*

    Cognitive functioning is completely developed. The person is capable of abstract, logical and complex thought.

Sigmund Freud

Sigmund Freud developed the concepts of id, ego and superego as well as psychological defense mechanisms and five stages of growth and development. The id is an unconscious mechanism that operates in terms of instant gratification and instant pleasure; the ego is the person's sense of self that moderates and controls the id so the person can act in a legally and socially acceptable manner. The superego is the person's conscience. The superego develops as the result of age, cultural, parental and social factors.

The five stages of Sigmund Freud's stages of development are:

1. *The oral stage*
2. *The anal stage*
3. *The phallic stage*
4. *The latency stage*
5. *The genital stage*

Robert Havighurst

This theorist developed 6 age groups and the physical, psychological and social tasks associated with each. Robert Havighurst's age periods and related developmental tasks are as follows:

- *Infancy and Early Childhood*

    This age group is learning how to eat, walk and control elimination. The infant or young child establishes psychological stability, relationships with family, siblings and others and is also able to separate right from wrong with the development of the conscience.

- *Middle Childhood*

    The child further develops in terms of conscience, morality and values systems. Physical skills are further developed and reading, writing and basic math are learned.

- *Adolescence*

    During adolescence the teenager assumes feminine or masculine roles and they also develop more mature relationships with peers of both genders. During this age, the client will also think about their future occupational and educational goals and they also develop ethical guidelines for behavior.

- *Early Adulthood*

    Early adulthood is characterized with the selection of a mate, starting a family, managing the home and developing social and civic relationships.

- *Middle Age*

    The middle years are characterized with economic stability and adjusting to the changes of middle years, which include menopause and the "empty nest".

- *Later Maturity*

    During later years, older adults cope with retirement, a lower income level, losses of loved ones and changing physical health status.

Education on Genitourinary Cancers and Gastrointestinal Cancers

The Levels of Prevention

There are three levels of prevention, namely primary, secondary and tertiary levels of prevention.

Primary prevention and primary prevention activities aim to prevent the occurrence of infection, disease and dysfunction before it actually occurs. Secondary prevention and secondary prevention activities are designed in order to identify disorders and diseases, at the earliest possible time so that they can be treated. Tertiary prevention and tertiary prevention aim to return the affected individual, group or population to the highest possible level of functioning after the correction of a health problem such as an infectious disease.

Environmental Protection is an example of primary prevention. Some examples of primary prevention related to the environment include proper sanitation, clean water and a clean and uncontaminated food supply.

Health Promotion Activities

Education and counseling are examples. Nurses can, and should, educate and counsel individuals, groups and populations about the need for things like immunizations, hand washing and the need for clean water in underserved, undeveloped geographic areas.

Immunizations

Immunization programs for individuals as well as groups and populations such as infants, young children and those at risk for infections such as influenza, pneumonia and shingles are established and these recommended guidelines, as below, should be followed.

The CDC's recommended immunization schedule from the day of birth to 17 years of age can be viewed at:

http://www.aafp.org/patient-care/immunizations/schedules.html

The CDC's recommended immunization schedule for adults can be viewed at:

http://www.aafp.org/patient-care/immunizations/schedules.html

Some examples of secondary prevention are:

- *Health Assessments for Individuals, Groups and Populations*
- *Nurses perform complete and thorough assessments of individuals, groups of people and populations in order to determine things like risk factors, past medical history, strengths and weakness.*

Some examples of tertiary prevention are:

- *Follow up Care Relating to the Treatment Plan and the Medication Regimen*
- *Many clients need tertiary care in terms of follow up care and monitoring. For example, some medication regimens are long term and some clients stop taking their prescribed medications, like an antibiotic, when they are feeling better. Follow up is necessary to insure compliance and the prevention of complications.*

Restorative and Rehabilitation Care

The primary goal of rehabilitation is to maximize the client's physical, psychological, social, spiritual and vocational abilities and potential; restorative care aims to restore full functioning to clients who are affected with a debilitating disorder or dysfunction.

Rehabilitation care aims to maximize the client's potential functioning and to provide the client with the assistance necessary to adapt to, and cope with, a permanent dysfunction. It supports the restoration of lose function, the prevention of further dysfunction and complications and the optimization of the client's independence, abilities, self esteem, uniqueness and dignity.

Screening and Early Detection

Screening increases the chances of detecting certain cancers early on, when they are most curable. Generally speaking, the treatment and prognosis for cancer and other disorders is much more effective when the disease is found in its earliest stages.

There are different kinds of screening tests; these screening tests can consist of a physical exam, a medical history, laboratory tests, imaging procedures and genetic testing. Some of these tests have risks and others may have false positive and false negative findings, so screening tests and their results are used in context with other medical data and followed up with diagnostic procedures.

The U.S. Preventive Services Task Force (USPSTF) and other organizations provide screening guidelines for the following disorders and diseases in order to identify risk and health care problems before they occur or at their earliest stages.

The USPSTF recommends screening:

- *To reduce alcohol misuse by adults, including pregnant women, in primary care settings.*

- *Mammography, with or without clinical breast examination (CBE), every 1-2 years for women aged 40 and older.*

- *For cervical cancer in women who have been sexually active and have a cervix*

    The USPSTF recommends against routinely screening women older than age 65 if they have had adequate recent screening with normal Pap smears and are not otherwise at increased risk for cervical cancer and against Pap smear screening in women who have had a total hysterectomy for benign disease.

- *For all sexually active women aged 25 years and younger, and other asymptomatic women at increased risk for infection, for chlamydial infection.*

- *Adults for depression in practices that have systems in place to assure accurate diagnosis, effective treatment, and follow-up.*

- *For adults with hypertension or hyperlipidemia.*

- *To detect increased intraocular pressure and early primary open-angle glaucoma in adults; however, this evidence is not sufficient enough to determine the extent to which screening would reduce impairment in vision-related function or quality of life.*

- *Hearing impairments among those who are exposed to excessive occupational noise levels and the elders.*

- *For HBV infection in pregnant women at their first prenatal visit.*

- *For HCV infection for clients at risk for HCV infection*

- *For all persons at increased risk of HIV infection. Screening is recommended for all pregnant women at risk for HIV infection, including all women who live in states, counties, or cities with an increased prevalence of HIV infection. All patients should be counseled about effective means to avoid HIV infection.*

- *For Males 35 years and older and women aged 45 years and older for lipid disorders and treat abnormal lipids in people who are at increased risk of coronary heart disease should be routinely screened. Younger adults should be screened for lipid disorders, with total cholesterol (TC) and high-density lipoprotein cholesterol (HDL-C), if they have risk factors for coronary heart disease.*

- *Prostate specific antigen (PSA) testing or digital rectal examination (DRE) is effective.*

- *For all adults for tobacco use and to provide tobacco cessation interventions for those who use tobacco products. It is also recommended that all pregnant women get pregnancy related counseling for tobacco use.*

- *Among the elderly is recommended for those with diminished visual acuity using the Snellen visual acuity chart.*

- *Cleints and family members must also be educated about genitourinary cancers and gastrointestinal cancers.*

- *Among men and women 50 years of age or older for colorectal cancer. There are a number of screening tests that are used to detect polyups, cancer, or other problems of the colon and rectum. Those who are aged 50 or older are recommended to have a screening colonoscopy done; after which routine screening intervals are based on the client and the findings of the previous colonoscopy. Those with a higher-than-average risk of cancer in the color and/or rectum may need a colonoscopy more often than those without any known risk factors. Some of the other screening tests include a fecal occult blood test, sigmoidoscopy, colonoscopy, double-contrast barium enema and a digital rectal exam.*

The Genitourinary System

The genitourinary system consists of the kidney, ureters, bladder, urethra and the external genitalia. The kidney consists of the inner layer, or medulla and the outer portion referred to as the cortex. The kidney tubules and loops of Henle excrete urea, creatinine, drug metabolites and nitrogen, which are waste products. They also reabsorb and secrete water and substances like sodium, potassium, chloride, amino acids and glucose.

Cancer of the bladder and kidney alters urinary functioning and it may, at times, require urinary diversion.

Prostate Cancer

Prostate cancer is the second most commonly occurring cancer among American males. It is also the second leading cause of cancer death in men, lagging just after lung cancer.

The prostate-specific antigen test (PSA) is a screening tool for prostate cancer. Elevated PSA levels of more than 4.0 indicates that further testing and diagnosis is necessary. A positive biopsy is confirmative of prostatic cancer.

In most cases, prostate cancer is found first during a digital rectal exam or with a prostate specific antigen blood test. Prostate cancer in its early stages usually does not have any signs or symptoms

Testicular Cancer

Although rare, testicular cancer does occur, primarily among young males less than 35 years of age. Like breast cancer, self examination of the testes and a clinical examination of the testes on an annual basis may identify this form of cancer in its earliest stages.

Colorectal Cancer

Colorectal cancer is a common form of cancer found in developed nations. It can metastasize to other sites and it can lead to massive gastrointestinal bleeding and death.

Risk Factors

Colorectal cancer is associated with obesity, those over 60 years of age, cigarette smoking, ulcerative colitis, polyps, genetics, environmental factors, Crohn's disease, a diet poor in fiber and high in terms of refined fats, proteins and/or carbohydrates, estrogen and progesterone supplementation, and the long term use of NSAIDs.

Signs and Symptoms

Colon cancer, often asymptomatic, can present with bowel obstruction, abdominal pain, red rectal bleeding, weight loss, anorexia, malaise, bloating, black tarry stools, diarrhea and constipation.

Treatment

The treatment of colon cancer can include surgery (colon resection, colostomy) chemotherapy, and radiation, depending on the location and severity as well as the client's choices.

Cancer of the Stomach

Gastric cancer is a leading cause of cancer morbidity and mortality. The diffuse form of this adenocarcinoma has a higher mortality rate than the intestinal form. Metastasis most often affects the pancreas, spleen, liver, esophagus, lungs, bones and adjacent lymph nodes.

Risk Factor

Some of the risk factors associated with cancer of the stomach include cigarette smoking, H. pylori gastritis, a diet high in sodium and/or nitrates, a diet that is low in fresh vegetables and fruits, and possibly genetics.

Signs and Symptoms

Dyspepsia, nausea, often drastic weight loss, cachexia, bowel obstruction, epigastric pain, weakness and discomfort are common signs and symptoms.

Treatment

A combination of radiation and surgery with a I or Billroth II gastric resection is the typical treatment. These surgical procedures can lead to vitamin B12 deficiencies, dumping syndrome, malabsorption and duodenal reflux.

Nurse must monitor clients for complications like bowel obstructions and also address any nutritional challenges.

Cancer of the Esophagus

This form of cancer also has a high morbidity and mortality rate because it is typically not diagnosed until the entire esophagus is affected.

Risk Factors

Some of the risk factors include obesity, alcohol abuse, male gender, smoking, reflux disorders, foods contaminated with nitrosamines, and the African American race.

Signs and Symptoms

Some of the signs and symptoms are heartburn, odynophagia, which is substernal chest pain, weight loss, dysphagia, foul breath, regurgitation and anorexia.

Complications include metastasis, dysphagia, obstruction, pulmonary complications and weight loss. Post-surgical complications include bleeding, infection, and leakage of the anastomosis.

Treatment

Esophageal cancer is typically treated with a combination of surgery (total or subtotal esophagectomy or an esophagogastrostomy with gastric pull through), chemotherapy and radiation.

Parenteral or enteral nutrition, which are discussed under the nutrition section of this review, are often needed to sustain the client, particularly after surgery, in order to maintain good nutrition and optimal healing.

The client should be assessed for any complications and treated for pain associated with this disorder.

Cancer of the Pancreas

Most pancreatic cancers form in the head of the pancreas. This form of cancer rapidly progresses and death usually occurs from one to three years after diagnosis.

Risk Factors

Males, cigarette smokers, and those over 60 years of age are at risk. It also appears that cancer of the pancreas could be genetic.

The signs and symptoms include dull epigastric pain, jaundice, weight loss, anorexia and ascites.

Some of the complications associated with pancreatic cancer are malnutrition, pain and eventual death.

Treatment

A pancreatoduodenectomy is done when this cancer is diagnosed in the early stages, but most often, it is diagnosed in its later stages so the treatment typically consists of palliative radiation and chemotherapy for the relief of some of the symptoms.

Cancer of the Liver

Most cases of cancer of the liver are the result of metastasis from another site, although some cases can also be a primary site. Death usually occurs within 6 or 8 weeks after diagnosis when left untreated.

Risk Factors

The risk factors associated with primary site liver cancer include alcohol related and hepatitis B and/or C related liver disease. Liver cancer, as a secondary cancer site, occurs most often with cancer of the lung, kidney, breast, and other gastrointestinal sites.

Signs and Symptoms

Liver cancer can be asymptomatic or manifested with the typical signs and symptoms of liver disease and liver failure such as anorexia, weakness, fatigue, abdominal pain, and weight loss.

Treatment

Chemotherapy with high dose fluorodeoxyuridine and 5-fluorouracil is done when a liver resection is not a treatment option. This chemotherapy can be administered intravenously or directly into the liver using a hepatic arterial infusion.

Bowel Dysfunction

Diverticulitis and Diverticulosis

Diverticulitis is the inflammation of a diverticulum; and diverticulosis is the presence of diverticular. A diverticulum is a small pouch in the lining of the intestinal wall. This pouch can accumulate bacteria, stool, and other debris. It forms as a result of weakened colon musculature and herniations of the mucosal and submucosal layers of the colon. Thickening of the colon wall causes an increased intralumen pressure, which assists in the herniation process.

Diverticulum can form anywhere along the gastrointestinal tract, however, most cases occur in the sigmoid colon where pressures are greatest and the lumen is the most narrow. The greatest prevalence is among the adult population and those over 60 years of age..

Signs and Symptoms

Diverticular disease can be completely asymptomatic or it can manifest with the following:

- *Changes in bowel patterns, such as constipation*
- *Lower left quadrant cramping and pain*
- *Anorexia*
- *Nauseas and vomiting*
- *Bloating and feelings of fullness*
- *GI bleeding and occult blood in the stool*
- *Possible urinary tract symptoms secondary to the proximity of the inflammation*

- *Classical signs of infection (fever, chills and leukocytosis)*

Treatment

Conservative treatment without hospitalization is effective in most cases. Surgical intervention with an end to end anastomosis and a temporary colostomy may be indicated in most severe cases.

Inflammatory Bowel Disease

Inflammatory bowel disease consists of two similar but distinct disorders including Crohn's disease and ulcerative colitis. Both of these gastrointestinal disorders can possibly result from a combination of forces including genetic factors, environmental factors and immune system deficiencies. Additionally, both of these disorders are marked with periods of remission and periods of exacerbation.

Some of the differences between ulcerative colitis and Crohn's disease are:

- *The mucosal appearance has a cobblestone appearance with granulomas with Crohn's disease; and it appears edematous with shallow ulcerations and superficial bleeding among those affected with ulcerative colitis.*

- *The typical area of intestinal involvement is the left colon and rectum for ulcerative colitis and the right colon and distal ileum with Crohn's disease.*

- *The extent of involvement is noncontiguous and segmented with Crohn's disease; and it is contiguous and diffused with ulcerative colitis.*

- *The inflammation associated with Crohn's disease is transmural, and it is mostly mucosal among those with ulcerative colitis.*

Crohn's Disease

Crohn's disease is a chronic idiopathic inflammatory disease that affects the small and large intestines. It is also referred to as ileitis, regional enteritis, granulomatous colitis, transmural colitis, and ileocolitis. Crohn's disease is most commonly found among 30 to 50 year old adults who are Caucasian and/or Jewish.

The intestinal mucosa is thickened and edematous; ulcers in the wall of the intestines form in linear, longitudinal fashion, resembling a cobblestone road. Deep fissures may form in the bowel lining, forming a fistula or abscesses. The healing of these abnormalities cause constricted areas in the intestine.

The three phases of Crohn's disease are:

1. *The inflammatory phase*
2. *The fistulizing or perforation phase, and*
3. *The fibrostenotic (strictures forming during the healing) phase.*

Cigarette smoking can trigger an exacerbation.

Signs and Symptoms

The signs and symptoms of Crohn's disease include the classic ones of abdominal pain and diarrheas as well as streatorrhea, abdominal pain, a palpable upper lower quadrant mass, nausea, vomiting, anemia, weight loss and other symptoms that mimic appendicitis.

Treatment

Crohn's disease is treated with medications, dietary changes and surgical interventions, when a bowel obstruction is present.

The medications that are used include aminosalicylates, such as sulfasalzine, corticosteroids, which are immunosuppressive agents, antibiotics, monoclonal antibodies, such as infliximab, antidiarrhea agents, acid suppressants, antispasmotics and fat soluble vitamin supplementation.

Some surgical interventions include segmental resection with reanastomosis and strictureplasty.

Ulcerative Colitis

Ulcerative colitis is an idiopathic inflammatory disease of the mucosa and the submucosa of the colon and rectum, but it primarily occurs in the distal colorectal area. Ulcerative proctitis is the term used if only the rectum is involved.

This disorder continually inflames the area in a diffuse manner leading to shallow ulcerations and edema. Over time the area is affected with scar tissue, which leads to a loss of absorption and elasticity of the colon.

Because of the unknown etiology, only the symptoms and effects of the disease can be treated. Some theories indicate that genetics, immune disorders or hypersensitivity disorders are to blame.

Signs and Symptoms

The classic signs and symptoms are abdominal pain and diarrhea. Episodes of diarrhea, which are mixed with pus, blood and mucus, can occur as frequently as every hour during the acute phase of ulcerative colitis.

Other clinical manifestations include distention of the abdomen, weight loss, iron-deficiency, anemia, fever, dehydration, hypokalemia, nausea and vomiting.

Treatment

Medical treatment is supportive and it addresses the signs and symptoms.

During serious acute phases, the patient may need bed rest, a clear liquid diet, and IV fluid rehydration and electrolyte replacement. Total parenteral nutrition is indicated for cases of severe diarrhea, to restore a positive nitrogen balance.

Drug therapy can include sulfasalazine (Azulfidine), as the primary medication. Clients allergic to sulfa are treated with oral salicylates such as mesalamine or olsalazine. Corticosteroids, immunosuppressive drugs, purine drugs and antidiarrheal drugs are also used as indicated.

Surgery may be indicated if a toxic megacolon develops and there is a need to rest the colon with a temporary loop colostomy. A subtotal colectomy, an ileostomy, or a Kock pouch procedure can also be performed.

Genetic and Congenital Diseases

Congenital abnormalities or birth defects, most commonly occur within the first three months of gestational development. Birth defects affect how the body functions and/or how it appears. Some structural birth defects, such as a cleft lip, are neural tube defects that are clearly visible; other defects, such as heart defects are discovered with diagnostic testing. Birth defects often result from maternal exposures to some medications and chemicals. For example, fetal alcohol syndrome can result from maternal alcohol abuse and other birth defects can result from maternal infections during pregnancy.

At times, birth defects can be discovered and treated even before birth. Others can be treated with medical treatments, including surgical corrections, after birth.

Cryptorchidism

Cryptorchidism, also referred to as an undescended testicle, occurs when one or both of the testicles fail to move into the scrotum while the fetus is in utero. In most cases the only sign is an empty scrotum.

Most of the time the testicle will descend on its own within the first year of age, although if this does not occur, hormone injections, B-HCG or testosterone, may be given to try to bring the testicle into the scrotum. When these treatment options are not effective orchiopexy surgery is done to move the testicle(s) into the scrotum.

If it is found later in life, the testicle is not likely to function well and it could pose a risk for cancer, therefore necessitating the removal of the testicle.

Polyposis

Polyposis syndrome is one of many hereditary diseases. It is however a rare disease. Risk factors that can contribute to the formation of colon polyps include obesity, lack of exercise, uncontrolled type 2 diabetes, tobacco use, alcohol abuse, inflammatory bowel disease, 50 years of age or older, being African American a family history.

Signs and symptoms of colon polyps and possibly polyposis include rectal bleeding, stool color changes, bowel habit changes, pain, nausea, vomiting and iron deficiency anemia.

Treatment

Treatment for this rare disease is a total proctocolectomy, which is surgery to remove the colon and rectum.

Hirshprung's Disease

Hirshprung's disease affects the large intestine and results in difficulties passing stool. This is a congenital disease that is present at birth that results in missing nerve cells in part of or all of the colon.

Signs and Symptoms

There are varying degrees of severity, but when a newborn fails to have a bowel movement within the first 48 hours after birth it is usually a sign. There are cases, however, that do not present until later in life.

Other newborn symptoms include swelling in their abdomen, diarrhea, gas or constipation, and/or vomiting green or brown substances.

Later on, if the symptoms appear in an older child they can include the following:

- *Swelling in the abdomen*
- *Fatigue*
- *Excessive gas*
- *Inability to gain weight*
- *Chronic constipation*

Treatment

Treatment is performed through surgery to bypass the portion of the colon that is missing the ganglia nerve cells. The surgery removes the lining of the diseased portion of the colon and strips it away while attaching the normal colon to the anus from the inside. In some cases, such as in children who are extremely ill, the surgery is performed in a two step process.

Imperforate Anus

An imperforated anus, a congenital disorder, is an abnormal opening of the anus that is present at birth.

This rare problem is a result of abnormal development of the fetus and it has a varying signs and symptoms. In some cases the ending of the rectum is in a pouch and is not connected to the colon, and it other cases the rectum can open into other areas, such as the urethra, bladder, or genitals. There may also be stenosis of the anus or no anus at all.

Signs and Symptoms

The signs and symptoms include the following:

- *Anus opening that is missing or misplaced*
- *Stool that passes through the vagina, penis or other genital part*
- *Swollen abdomen*
- *No stool passed within the first 24-48 hours after a baby is born*

Treatment

Treatment includes surgery and in some cases a temporary colostomy may be needed.

Bladder Exstrophy

Bladder extrophy is when a baby is born with their bladder inside outside of its normal anatomical placement and sticking out of their abdomen. An abnormal separation of the pelvic bones is also present.

Treatment

Repair involves a series of two surgeries. The first surgery repairs the bladder; the second surgery, which may not occur for several weeks or even months after the first surgery, involves the attachment and fusion of the separated pelvic bones.

A catheter is used during the surgery and another one is placed in during the recovery time to promote healing.

Spina Bifida

Spina bifida is a neural tube defect that is characterized with a failure of vertebral column to close. It appears that low maternal folate levels may be a cause in addition to other factors such genetic, maternal diabetes and some medications such as valproate. It can be suspected in utero with an ultrasonography and with elevated maternal α-fetoprotein and/or the presence of large amounts of amniotic fluids.

This defect can vary greatly. Spina bifida can be occult with no signs of an anomaly or neurological deficits and it can also have a sac, which is referred to as spina bifida cystic, or even more severe as an open spine, referred to as rachischisis, with significant neurological losses and dysfunction distal to the deformity and the risk of mortality.

Signs and Symptoms

Some of the signs and symptoms are hydrocephalus, neurological deficits such as sensory losses and paralysis, muscular atrophy, loss of bladder and rectal sphincter control, neurogenic bladder, hydronephrosis, kyphosis, kidney damage and signs of hydrocephalus including increased intracranial pressure, apnea, stridor and swallowing problems.

Treatment

Depending on the severity of this deformity, some of the treatment options include surgical repair of the lesion, a ventricular shunt to relieve the hydrocephalus and other urological and orthopedic corrections as indicated.

Urinary Dysfunction

Interstitial Cystitis

Interstitial cystitis, which is also referred to as painful bladder syndrome, is a chronic condition that causes bladder pressure, bladder pain and in some cases pelvic pain.

Signs and Symptoms

Each person experiences different types of symptoms with this syndrome. Some signs and symptoms include the following:

- *Chronic pelvic pain*
- *Pain from sexual intercourse*
- *Pain while bladder fills and/or urinate*
- *Urinating frequently*
- *Constant urge to urinate*

The symptoms vary between patients and, in some cases, the symptoms mimic those of urinary tract infections, but in most cases bacteria are not present in urinalysis.

Treatment

Just as symptoms vary, so do treatments. Often times it is necessary to try different treatments until the patient finds relief. Treatment options include the following:

- *Physical therapy*
- *Medications, such as antihistamines, pentosan, tricyclic antidepressants, and nonsteroidal anti-inflammatories*
- *Nerve stimulation with a transcutaneous electrical stimulation unit (TENS) or sacral nerve stimulation*
- *Bladder distention*

- *Medications, such as dimethyl sulfoxide or Rimso-50, are administered directly in the bladder*
- *Surgical correction with fulguration, resection and bladder augmentation may be indicated*

Cystitis and Other Urinary Tract Infections

A urinary tract infection (UTI) is an infection in any part of the urinary system, which includes the kidneys, ureters, bladder and urethra. Most of the time UTI's involve the lower urinary tract, which includes the bladder and urethra. Women tend to suffer from UTIs more often than men, and can be extremely serious if they affect the kidneys.

Urinary tract infections don't always cause signs and symptoms, but when they do they may include a strong, persistent urge to urinate, dysuria, frequency, scant amounts of urine, urine that appears cloudy, urine that appears red or bright pink (gross hematuria), strong-smelling urine, pelvic pain among women and rectal pain among men.

Some evidence based guidelines for Catheter Associated Urinary Tract Infections (CAUTI) are provided by JCAHO as well as the CDC. The CDC's Compendium of Strategies to Prevent Healthcare-Associated Infections in Acute Care Hospitals can be found at http://www.shea-online.org/about/compendium.cfm and their Guideline for Prevention of Catheter-Associated Urinary Tract Infections can be found at:

http://www.cdc.gov/hicpac/cauti/001_cauti.html.

JCAHO, according to their 2015 National Patient Goal 7 recommends:

- *The use of an established protocol or policy/procedure for urinary catheter insertion that is consistent with established evidence based practice guidelines*
- *Limiting the use of and duration of indwelling urinary catheters to only those situations that are clinically necessary*
- *The use of strict aseptic technique during the insertion and maintenance of these catheters to maintain sterility*
- *The replacement of these catheter systems as needed*
- *The safe securing of the catheter to prevention urinary flow obstructions and to facilitate drainage*
- *The monitoring and measurement of catheter related urinary tract infections, prevention processes and outcomes in terms of established evidence based practices or best practices*
- *It is also recommended that all central venous catheters are removed as soon as clinically possible.*

Each type of UTI may result in more specific signs and symptoms, depending on which part of the urinary tract is infected. The table below summarizes these signs and symptoms.

Part Affected	Signs and Symptoms
Kidneys (pyelonephritis)	Upper back and side (flank) pain High fever Shaking and chills Nausea Vomiting Pus or blood present in the urine Strong urge to urinate Burning while urinating
Bladder (cystitis)	Pelvic pressure Lower abdomen discomfort Frequent, painful urination Blood in urine
Urethra (urethritis)	Burning upon urination

The treatment of urinary tract infections includes medications, such as sulfamethoxazole-trimethoprim, amoxicillin, nitrofurantoin, ampicillin, ciprofloxacin and levofloxacin.

Pain medication to numb the bladder and urethra may also be prescribed to relieve burning during urination. Additionally, fluids and the monitoring of renal function and urinary output are essential.

Pyelonephritis

Pyelonephritis, a kidney infection, is a specific type of urinary tract infection that begins in the urethra or bladder and travels up into the kidneys. Immediate medical attention is required, and if not treated or not treated effectively, this infection can permanently damage renal function and lead to sepsis.

The signs and symptoms include upper back and side flank pain, high fever, shaking and chills, nausea, vomiting, pus or blood in the urine, a strong urge to urinate and burning while urinating.

The first line of treatment is the use of antibiotics, and the type of antibiotic depends on the severity of the infection and the bacteria that are found in the urine. For severe infections it may be necessary to hospitalize the client so that they can receive intravenous antibiotics.

Urethritis

Urethritis is an inflammation of the urethra that can be caused by a virus, bacteria, injury, sensitivity to chemicals, and contraceptive creams, jellies and foams. It is most commonly seen among women during their reproductive years, males from 20-35 years of age and among those who have had multiple sexual partners and/or practice high risk sexual behaviors, such as unprotected sex, and who have a history of sexually transmitted diseases.

The signs and symptoms differ between men and women. In men, the signs and symptoms can include pain with intercourse or ejaculation, itching, tenderness, swelling of the penis or groin area, discharge from the penis, blood in urine and/or semen, dysuria, and frequent or urgent urination. Among women, the symptoms include vaginal discharge, pelvic pain, abdominal pain, dysuria, fever and chills, and a frequent or urgent need to urinate.

The treatment goals are aimed at preventing the spread of infection, eliminating the cause of infection and treating the symptoms. If an infection is present, antibiotics are given to the patient, and pain relievers, such as NSAIDs or pyridium, can be given as well.

If the cause is trauma or chemical irritants, treatment includes avoiding the source, and, while being treated, the patient must avoid sex or use condoms. The sexual partner(s) will also require treatment if the cause is infection.

Urinary incontinence

Urinary incontinence is an involuntary leakage of urine and a loss of bladder control. This is more common in women, due to childbirth, a short urethra, and menopause. As a result, women often have stress incontinence, which is urinary leakage that occurs when the person coughs, sneezes, or laughs. Cognitive impairments, decreased mobility, urinary tract infections, cerebrovascular accidents, spinal cord injury or other diseases and disorders can also lead to urinary incontinence.

Signs and Symptoms

The signs and symptoms are slightly different for the different types of urinary incontinence, as below:

Overflow incontinence: This type of incontinence occurs when the client is not able to fully empty their bladder during voiding as the result of a number of factors including weak bladder muscles, tumors that block urine flow, and constipation. It occurs most often among males.

Functional incontinence: This type of incontinence occurs most frequently among those who have cognitive dysfunction or severe physical disease. Complete uncontrollable bladder emptying occurs.

Stress incontinence: There is a small leakage of urine when the affected client coughs, laughs, or sneezes, which causes increased pressure in the abdomen. This type of incontinence results from weakened pelvic floor muscles.

Urge incontinence: This form of incontinence occurs as the result of an overactive bladder secondary to some bladder nerve damage. The client is simply not able to get to the bathroom quick enough after the urge to urinate occurs.

Treatment

Managing urinary incontinence includes bladder training, which is also referred to as continence training, pelvic muscle exercises, maintaining skin integrity and using external urinary drainage devices and briefs. Whenever possible, indwelling urinary catheters should be avoided because they can lead to infections.

Neurogenic Bladder

Neurogenic bladder results from a brain, spinal cord or neurological condition, in which one has problems controlling their bladder. Some diseases associated with this include stroke, spinal cord, Parkinson's disease, cerebral palsy, Alzheimer's disease, brain or spinal cord tumors and neurological disorders such as those that occur with some trauma. .

Signs and Symptoms

Urinary incontinence is the main symptom, although depending on the cause, one can also experience an overactive or underactive bladder.

Treatment

Treatments vary greatly depending on the cause. Some medications, such as anti-epileptic drugs, Botox, Gamma-Aminobutyric Acid (GABA) supplements and a variety of neurological system medications may be necessary. Some clients may need bladder training, including exercises, keeping a voiding diary etc. Some causes can be urinary tract infections, therefore cranberry juice and other treatments for infection can be helpful as well.

Other treatments include urinary catheters and in more severe cases surgery may be indicated.

Fecal and Urinary Diversions (Colostomy, Ileostomy, Urostomy)

Colostomy

A colostomy can be either temporary or permanent and may be performed on any part of the colon necessary. A temporary colostomy is performed when there is a diseased portion of the colon that needs time to heal. In these such cases a temporary colostomy can be used to allow time for that area of the colon to heal before reattaching the colon. A permanent colostomy is performed in cases with which the colostomy cannot be closed because the rectum may need to be removed or other health issues are present.

Types of Colostomies and Their Plan of Care

There are different types of colostomies, which include the following:

- *Ascending colostomy*

    This type of colostomy is used to divert the bowel to an opening in the wall of the abdomen, the surgeon rolls back the bowel into itself and stitches it to the abdominal wall. A pouch is usually worn to collect the stool and digestive enzymes

- *Loop transverse colostomy*

    With this type of colostomy a stoma is created by the surgeon with a distal opening and a proximal opening. The distal opening is used to expel mucus, whereas the proximal opening is used to expel stool. This allows the distal portion time to heal, and once that is done the colostomy can then be closed in many cases.

- *Double-barrel transverse colostomy*

    This type of colostomy that is extremely rare these days, but when it is done the surgeon divides the bowel completely; this leaves two stomas on the abdominal wall. One stoma is the proximal stoma which expels stool, and the other is the distal stoma which passes mucus. If they are both separated on the patient's abdominal wall the patient is required to wear a pouch over the proximal stoma and the distal stoma is covered with a piece of gauze, Vaseline gauze or a small pouch is used.

- *Descending and Sigmond colostomy*

    The descending colostomy stoma is just a few inches higher on the abdominal wall than the stoma for the sigmoid colostomy. The most common type of colostomy is the sigmoid colostomy which can be either temporary or permanent.

Appropriate Candidates for Irrigation

Most patients with colostomies are required to wear a pouch in order to collect the waste, and the pouch needs to be either emptied out or changed throughout the day and night, depending on how much waste the patient produces. Those who have an ostomy nearing the end of the intestinal tract and closer to the anus usually produce less waste a day when compared to clients who have the ostomy higher up in the intestinal tract, therefore, those with an ostomy higher up must empty or change their pouch more often than others.

Patients with colostomies who have the descending colon type or sigmoid colon type of ostomies may be candidates for not having to wear a pouch but instead use irrigation techniques.

Teach Irrigation Techniques

The goal of irrigation is to permit the client to be able to wear a gauze cap over the stomal opening rather than an ostomy pouch. Irrigation is done by placing a catheter into the stoma and flushing it out so the feces comes out into an irrigation sleeve and the patient can plan when to do it. Depending on the person and their food intake, it is usually done once a day or even every other day.

Instruct Patient In Dietary Modifications (E.G., To Prevent Constipation Or Reduce Gas)

After a colostomy the patient should be taught about the effects of different diets and what will be appropriate for them. Once they get approval of their doctor that they are healed enough to ingest solid foods, they can begin eating solid foods. For most patients this can take several days to a week or so.

Any foods that were a cause of gas before their colostomy will most likely be a cause of gas for the client after the colostomy. The patient might want to consider ingesting these types of food at home and in an environment where they will feel comfortable rather than in a public place where they may feel embarrassed with the gas production.

Each patient is different so for each one there will be some foods that are more likely to cause gas, diarrhea, constipation, indigestion or odor in their urine than others. These affects can vary in degree. Patients should be urged to try a small amount of something at home and see how it affects them before ingesting a larger amount outside of the comforts and privacy of their own home. An important note, however, is to encourage the client to drink plenty of water and completely chew their food.

Prepare Patient for Reanastamosis and Takedown

Just as colostomy surgery, the reversal of the colostomy can be down either with open surgery or laparoscopically. The patient's colon is cleaned and emptied prior to the surgery using a cleansing enema, flushing the colon with tempid water, medication or a combination of one of more of these interventions. The surgical procedure can commence only after the patient's colon has been thoroughly cleaned out.

The procedure is performed by making several small incisions in the patient's abdomen, which are used to insert the surgical equipment and the laparoscope. The part of the intestine that was sewn into the wall of the abdomen is cut after lifting the abdomen wall. This is then stapled back to where it was originally taken from during the initial colostomy surgery. This site can be either the rectum or a part of the small intestine. The stitches or sutures are placed and the area is bandaged for the healing process.

Ileostomy

An ileostomy, similar to a colostomy, is performed when there is a difficulty passing stool through the anus. The difference between the two is that with an ileostomy the entire colon and rectum are removed and a stoma is created to allow waste to be expelled via the small intestine into a disposable pouch. An ileostomy is almost always permanent except when the rectum is not removed.

This surgery is most commonly seen among clients who are affected with Crohn's disease, ulcerative colitis, familial polyposis, and in those with certain types of cancer.

The waste expelled into the bag will tend to be watery or soft and green in color, which is because of the diversion or removal of the colon. The ostomy bag is external and must be worn all the time.

It is important that the patient is made aware of the risk of dehydration and that they need to drink plenty of clear fluids daily.

Prepare Patient for Reanastamosis And Takedown

A reversal, which is rare, may be performed if the colon has recovered and it was not removed. If it is recovered then the intestines are reattached and normal functioning will resume; if the colon was removed then a pouch attaches to the anus and waste is passed like before the colostomy but simply without the colon.

In the beginning the patient may have to defecate up to 12 times a day and they may experience watery stool, difficulty controlling their stool and may need to wear disposable diapers for a time while they heal and the body adjusts to this diversion.

Urostomy

A urostomy, which is also referred to as a urinary diversion, is indicated in a variety of different instances. For example, clients affected with a ureter blockage due to kidney stones or a tumor, cancer, bladder extrophy, neurogenic bladder, and interstitial cystitis may require a surgical urostomy.

There are several types of urostomy, including the following:

- *Ileal conduit*
- *Neobladder*
- *Indiana punch*

- *Miami pouch*
- *Nephrostomy*

Patients should to be taught about self-care, as discussed above, so that they can be able to live a normal life after this body altering procedures. A medical alert bracelet should be worn by all patients.

Instruct Patients in:

Fluid Modifications

The patient should be instructed that they should consume at least six to eight glasses of water a day. This is extremely important to help prevent bacterial growth, to reduce the formation of salt, and to keep their urine at its proper acid level.

Mucus Management

Urine, under normal conditions contains shreds of mucus, but if the mucus clogs the pouches' drain spout it is necessary for the patient to consume more fluids in an effort to unclog the spout. The patient can also be instructed how to order Marlen Muco-Sperse, which is used to dissolve clogged mucus.

Manage Stents

Teach Patients Signs and Symptoms of Urinary Tract Infections

As previously detailed, urinary tract infections don't always cause signs and symptoms, but when they do they may include a strong, persistent urge to urinate, a burning sensation when urinating, passing frequent, small amounts of urine, urine that appears cloudy, urine that appears red or bright pink (gross hematuria) which is a sign of blood in the urine, strong-smelling urine, pelvic pain, in women, and rectal pain, in men.

Obtain Urine Specimens

Whenever the patient needs to supply a urine sample or specimen, a trained health care provider can collect it directly from the stoma by using a catheter.

Continent Fecal and Urinary Diversions

Instruct Patient Regarding:

Signs and Symptoms of Pouchitis

Signs and symptoms of pouchitis include abdominal pain, cramps, strong urge to have a bowel movement, and increased number of bowel movements.

Ileal Pouch Anal Anastamosis (IPAA)

This procedure eliminates the need for a permanent stoma. This surgery removes the large bowel completely, while a small bowel is connected to the anus. A small portion of the small bowel is made to use as an internal pouch and serve to function as the rectum. Patients are therefore able to maintain control of their bowel habits, due to the creation of a new storage place for the stool. Patients are also continue to eliminate waste through their anus.

Fistulas and Percutaneous Tubes and Drains

Anal Abscess, Fistulas And Fissures

Anal abscesses, fistulas and fissures	These disorders occur as the result of trauma or infection Pain, constipation, swelling, tenderness, throbbing, pruritis and erythema can occur	Incision and drainage Fistulotomy Fostiectomy Stool softeners and analgesics

Percutaneous Tubes and Drains

Percutaneous drains are used I many situations, such as with a large infection, bowel fluid leakage, drainage of the urinary system if a blockage is present, which is known as nephrostomy, for bile drainage, etc.

There are risks and/or complications that can occur, although the procedure is fairly safe. Risks include:

- *Infection*
- *Bowel injury*
- *Blood infection*
- *Excessive bleeding*

There are safety precautions that need to be taught including caring for the drain, flushing the drain, bandage and dressing care etc.

Continence Care

General Principles of Assessment

Obtain history regarding the following to identify high risk patients:

Rectocele

A bulging of the front wall of the rectum into the back wall of the vagina, is referred to as a rectocele. This is actually quite common, and usually results from a thinning in the rectovaginal septum, as well as a weak pelvic floor. There usually are not symptoms that present, and there are other organs that can also bulge into the vagina, mimicking this, such as the bladder or the small intestine.

Signs and Symptoms

There are usually no symptoms, but if the rectocele is large it may be more noticeable. Usually it is noticed during a routine examination.

If symptoms are present they include constipation, difficulty passing bowels, a need to assist in bowel movement, straining etc. Symptoms to the vagina include dyspareunia, full feeling vagina and vaginal bleeding.

Treatment

Rectoceles do not always need treatment, unless they are severe. Sometimes a high fiber diet or stool softener can be the best treatment. In severe cases surgery may be indicated.

Prostatitis

Prostatitis is an inflammation of the prostate gland which can result from an infection. It can be chronic or acute. The types of prostatitis are acute bacterial prostatitis, chronic bacterial prostatitis and chronic nonbacterial prostatitis which is sometimes referred to as chronic pelvic pain syndrome.

The signs and symptoms of prostatitis include frequent urinary tract infections, urinary urgency and frequency, pelvic pain, burning upon urination and the other signs of infection such as fever and chills.

The treatment of prostatitis includes intravenous antibiotics, pain relief and fluids for the acute bacterial form; fluids and perhaps low dose long term antibiotic therapy treat chronic bacterial prostatitis; and pain relief and fluids are used for chronic nonbacterial prostatitis.

Neuromuscular Conditions

As mentioned earlier, neuromuscular conditions are those that affect the peripheral nervous system. The small intestine can be affected, known as hamartomatous condition, mimics clinically inflammatory bowel disease.

Obstruction

Bowel Obstructions

Bowel obstructions can affect all people at any age. Bowel obstructions occur as a result of either intestinal lumen narrowing or impaired peristalsis that is usually neurogenic in nature.

The most common causes of bowl obstructions are post-surgical adhesions, which narrow the lumen and .an inguinal hernia that is incarcerated. Other factors include tumors, foreign bodies, fecal impaction, gallstones, hematomas, strictures and congenital adhesive banding.

Bowel obstructions are classified as mechanical and non-mechanical as well as complete and incomplete. Mechanical obstructions arise from extraintestinal disorders or a blockage inside the intestinal lumen. Mechanical obstructions occur as the result of adhesions, volvulus, which is intestinal twisting, hernias, tumors, gallstones, fecal impactions and strictures that occur secondary to chronic inflammatory bowel disease.

Non-mechanical obstructions occur as the result of diminished peristalsis, as occurs with a paralytic ileus and losses of nervous system innervations as a result of disorders, such as Parkinson's diseases and Hirschsprung's disease.

Bowel contents accumulate above the obstruction, regardless of the cause. This causes increased capillary permeability and bowel edema. As a result, plasma leaks into the peritoneal space thus disrupting fluid and electrolyte balances.

Signs and Symptoms

The signs and symptoms of the bowel obstruction depend on the location of the obstruction. The Table below summarizes the signs and symptoms of large and small intestinal bowel obstructions.

Signs and Symptoms	Small Intestine	Large Intestine
Vomiting	Copious and frequently	Rare

Pain	Intermittent, cramping colicky pain	Low degree of cramping
Onset	Rapid onset	Gradual onset
Abdominal Distention	Minimal amount	Greater distention
Bowel Movement	Less constipation	Pronounced constipation

Other signs and symptoms can include diffuse abdominal tenderness or rigidity, absent or hyperactive bowel sounds, fever, hypotension and tachycardia.

Treatment

Fluid and electrolyte imbalances are corrected with IV fluid and electrolyte replacements; prophylactic antibiotics are sometimes used to prevent infection; and bowel decompression is relieved with a nasogastric tube with suctioning. Other interventions include motility medications for a nonmechanical obstruction.

Surgical interventions are performed with a variety of techniques, many of which can be performed endoscopically. Some surgical procedures that are used include the correction of any adhesions, bowel resection with reanastomosis and the placement of a temporary colostomy.

Infection

Infectious/Inflammatory Conditions

The Chain of Infection

The chain of infection includes the agent, the reservoir, the environment, the mode of transmission, the portal of entry, the portal of exist and the susceptible host.

The Causative Agent: Bacteria, Viruses, Fungi, Prions And Parasites

There are a wide variety of microorganisms which can cause infections and diseases among humans and there are also a wide variety of microorganisms that do not lead to infections and diseases, in fact some are highly beneficial to humans in terms of health. It is the pathogenic, or disease causing, agents that infection control aims to eliminate.

The ability of a pathogenic microorganism to cause disease depends on a number of factors including their pathogenicity, virulence and the infective dose.

Pathogenicity

Pathogenicity is the ability of the agent to cause disease. Pathogenicity is quantified as the ratio of the number of people who develop disease and the total number of people exposed to it.

Virulence

How severe and intense the microbe is. Some are highly virulent and others have a low level of virulence.

Infective dose

The infective dose refers to the amount of the agent that is necessary to lead to an infection. Some agents need a higher dosage than others in order to infect the person.

Bacteria

Bacteria can be categorized and classified in several ways including their morphology and their reactions to some laboratory tests. Bacteria are singular cell beings that appear as spirals, rods, spheres and other shapes. Some are pathogenic, lead to disease and release tissue damaging toxins; others are highly beneficial to the body. Some examples of bacteria include streptococcus, staphylococcus and Escherica coli.

Bacterial shapes and morphologies include spherical or round shapes (cocci), spiral shaped (spirochetes), rod shaped (bacilli), and even as cubes and tetrahedral shapes. They also form and cluster into different formations.

Some bacteria are classified as gram positive because they react to a gram stain; these microbes have thick walls containing teichoic acid and peptidoglycan. Others are classified as gram negative because they do not react to a gram stain. These microbes, more common than gram positive bacteria, have thinner walls than gram positive bacteria; these walls are comprised of peptidoglycan and a lipid membrane which includes lipoproteins and lipopolysaccharides, which are endotoxins.

Bacteria are also differentiated by their ability to resist color changes when subjected to a staining procedure in the laboratory. Acid fast bacteria resist decolorization when stained with a Ziehl-Neelsen or Kinyoun stain, for example.

Bacterial Growth

phase in this sequential order.

1. *The lag phase of bacterial growth is characterized with the bacteria's acclimation to the new environment and a period of slow growth. The rate of biosynthesis is high because the bacteria need these proteins for future, rapid growth.*

2. *The log phase, often referred to as the exponential phase, consists of a period of rapid and continuous growth until one or more of the nutrients needed to grow is exhausted.*

3. *The stationary stage, which results from depleted nutrients, is marked with a halt in growth and metabolic activity.*

4. *The death stage is the end of the bacteria's life. There are no nutrients left at all.*

Viruses

Viruses, which are much smaller than bacteria, have three parts including its RNA, DNA and long molecules which comprise its genetic composition; their protein coat and an outer coating contain lipids.

Viruses can have a wide host range and be capable of infecting many species; or it can have a narrow host range that limits it to only some species.

Viruses, like bacteria, can be categorized and classified in several ways. For example, they can be categorized according to the host cell that they can infect. Viruses can be plant viruses, fungal viruses and animal viruses. They can also be classified according to their shape. Viruses come in several shapes including icosahedral and helical shapes as well as more intricate and complex forms. They can also be categorized according to their nucleic acid composition and their method of replications. These classifications consist of:

- *DNA viruses which include both single and double stranded DNA viruses*

- *RNA viruses which include single and double stranded RNA viruses, negative sense and positive sense viruses*

- *Reverse transcribing viruses including double stranded reverse transcribing DNA viruses, single stranded reverse transcribing RNA viruses and retroviruses*

The six stages of virus growth include the attachment, penetration, uncoating, replication, self-assembly and release, in sequential order.

1. *The attachment stage occurs when the virus attaches to a receptor on the host's cellular surface. Some are very specific and limited in terms of their abilities to attach; they have a low or limited host range.*

2. *The penetration stage occurs when the virus enters the host's cell. This process is also referred to as viral entry.*

3. *The uncoating phase involves the removal of the viral capsid, or coating thus allowing the virus's nucleic material into the host cell.*

4. *The replication stage is characterized with the replication and multiplication of the genome.*

5. *The self-assembly phase follows the replication stage. During this phase, the maturation and modifications of the viral proteins occurs*

6. *The release of the virus from the host cells, with lysis, occurs during this stage. Now, the cell is killed with this lysis.*

Fungi

There are an enormous number of fungi in our natural environment including those in the soil, plant life and on human beings. Fortunately, the vast majority of fungi are harmless, however, there are some that can lead to serious infections among humans, particularly when they are immunocompromised.

Fungi have mutualistic, antagonist, and commensal symbiotic relationships with other organisms, including humans. Mutualistic symbiotic relationships benefit both the virus and the organism it is attached to; antagonistic symbiotic relationships harm the fungi's host; and commensal symbiotic relationships neither harm nor benefit the fungus or the host.

Although fungi in the world of botany can be categorized and classified in many ways, fungi that affect human beings are typically classified as superficial, cutaneous, subcutaneous and systemic.

Superficial fungal infections affect the skin's epidermis and the hair. These infections can often occur among healthy people. An example of a superficial fungal infection is tinea capitis which is often referred to as ringworm of the scalp because it takes on the appearance of a worm despite the fact that it is caused by a fungus.

Cutaneous fungal infections include invasive hair and nail infections that go beyond the epidermis. An example of a cutaneous fungal disease is athlete's foot, or tinea pedis.

Subcutaneous fungal infections can infect all layers of the skin to the muscles and the fascia. These fungal infections, often serious, typically result from a deep puncture wound.

Systemic fungi infections are typically highly virulent and they can spread to virtually all organs of the body. Those with immunosuppression as the result of HIV, chemotherapy and metastatic cancer are at greatest risk. Some examples of systemic fungal infections include aspergillosis, candidiasis and cryptococcosis.

Prions

A prion is not a living organism; it is defined as an abnormal folding of normal cellular, or prion, proteins. Some of the infectious diseases associated with prions include encephalopathy, including "mad cow disease, Creutzfeldt-Jacob disease, and other rare diseases such as kuru, or fatal familial insomnia.

At the current time, it is believed that humans become infected when they ingest teprion that can be found in the soil or in dead animals.

Prions and prion diseases primarily affect the brain and neural tissue; these infections are associated with a high morbidity and mortality rate without a possible cure. Prions can be destroyed only with sterilization.

Parasites

A parasite is an organism that lives on or in a host and gets its food from or at the expense of its host. Parasites can cause disease in humans. Some parasitic diseases are easily treated and some are not. The burden of these diseases often rests on communities in the tropics and subtropics, but parasitic infections also affect people in developed countries.

Some examples of parasitic infections include giardia, tapeworms, pin worms, lice infestations, maggot infestation and scabies.

Cancer

Neoplastic Diseases

Bladder Cancer/Carcinoma

Bladder cancer is classified based on how the bladder's abnormal cells grow. For example, papillary tumors are attached to a stalk and appear like warts and non-papillary or sessile tumors are flat, more invasive, have more serious outcomes, but they are not as common.

The exact cause is unknown, but cigarette smoking, chemical exposure, chemotherapy, radiation therapy, and chronic bladder infections are some things that increase the risk for bladder cancer.

Signs and Symptoms

Signs and symptoms of bladder infection include weight loss, incontinence, urinary urgency and frequency, pain with urination, fatigue, blood in the urine and abdominal pain.

Treatment

Treatment for bladder cancer depends upon the stage of the cancer, the severity of the symptoms and the patient's overall health. For stage 0 and 1, treatment includes surgery to remove the tumor without the removal of rest of the bladder, and chemotherapy or immunotherapy placed directly into the bladder. For stage 2 and 3, treatments include a radical cystectomy, removal of adjacent lymph nodes, followed by chemotherapy and radiation therapy. Chemotherapy is used to shrink the tumor before surgery as well as after the radical cystectomy. When clients choose not to have surgery or they cannot have surgery, a combination of chemotherapy and radiation is indicated. Patients with stage 4 tumors have a very poor prognosis, therefore, surgery is not an option, but chemotherapy may be considered.

Prostate Cancer/Carcinoma

The risk factors associated with prostate cancer include males over 65 years of age, a familial history, some genetic changes and an African American ethnicity.

Signs and Symptoms

Symptoms include pain accompanying ejaculation, low back pain, and difficulties urinating, such as starting or stopping the stream, or dribbling.

Treatment

Treatment for prostate cancer depends on the stage of the cancer and client choices. Some treatment options include radiation, surgery, hormone therapy, chemotherapy and a combination of two or more treatment strategies.

Renal Cell Carcinoma

Renal cell carcinoma is a type of kidney cancer that begins in the tubules of the kidney.

Signs and Symptoms

Symptoms include weight loss, flank pain, varicocele, blood in the urine, back pain, abdominal pain and swelling, visual problems, pallor, and, among females, excessive hair growth.

Treatment

Treatment options include nephrectomy, which may include removal of the bladder, surrounding tissues or lymph nodes, hormone treatments, and a pharmacological regimen of interleukin. Chemotherapy and radiation therapy, in most cases, are not effective treatment options.

Testicular Cancer/Carcinoma

Testicular cancer can occur in one or both of the testes. It is most commonly seen in men who are between the ages of twenty and thirty-nine, those who have had a undescended testicle at the time of birth, those who have a family history of testicular cancer and those who have had an abnormal testicle development

Signs and Symptoms

Symptoms of testicular are pain, testicular swelling, lumps in one or both testicles, the testicular area, and/or groin area.

Treatment

Treatment options include surgery, chemotherapy, and/or radiation therapy, and regular follow-up care. Some treatments can cause the patient to become infertility; therefore those who wish to have children should consider sperm banking before treatment begins.

Wilms Tumor

Wilms' tumor is a rare type of kidney cancer, in which a tumor(s) can develop on one or both kidneys. Children are more likely to be affected, although adults can be affected as well.

Signs and Symptoms

The signs and symptoms include hematuria, a fever with an unknown cause and a lump in the abdomen.

Treatment

Surgery to remove the tumor, chemotherapy, radiation and biologic therapy are the treatment options.

Urinary Neuromuscular Conditions

Neuromuscular conditions and diseases are those that affect the peripheral nervous system. For example, neuromuscular disorders are conditions that affect both muscles and nerves that are responsible for controlling the bladder. These disorders can make it difficult to empty one's bladder, or can cause one to experience bladder spasms.

As the result of urinary tract abnormalities, changes can occur in the bladder or urethra, which in turn can cause incontinence problems.

Urinary Obstruction

Obstructive uropathy is a condition in which a blockage in a ureter causes urine to flow back into the kidneys instead of urination. There are a variety of different causes, such as pressure on the kidney(s), pelvic fracture(s), kidney, bladder, colon or ureter cancer, kidney stones, blood clots, nervous system disorders, pregnancy, enlarged prostate, and more.

Signs and Symptoms

This can occur quickly or take some time to progress, and the amount of pain and the exact location can vary from person to person. The most common symptoms include fever, nausea and vomiting.

Other symptoms include kidney swelling or tenderness, difficulty urinating, blood in the urine, slow urine, feeling the bladder is not empty, and feeling the urge to urinate more frequently.

Treatment

The main goal of treatment is to remove the obstruction. There are different approaches depending on the individual case, and they include surgery to remove polyps, tumors or scar tissue that may be present, and in some cases a stent can be used to treat the obstruction.

Endocrine Conditions

Hyperparathyroidism

An increase in the secretion of parathyroid hormone (PTH), which regulates normal serum levels of calcium, is known as hyperparathyroidism. The kidneys and bones are affected by the increase in PTH, which results in the following pathophysiologic changes:

- *Formation of renal calculi and the deposit of calcium in soft tissues*

- *Bone decalcification resulting from an increased release of calcium and phosphorus by the bones*

- *An increase in the risk of metabolic acidosis and hypokalemia resulting from increased bicarbonate excretion and decreased acid excretion by the kidneys*

- *An increase in the risk of hypercalcemia and hypophosphatemia resulting from increased reabsorption of calcium and excretion of phosphate by the kidneys*

Signs and Symptoms

There are several signs and symptoms associated with hyperparathyroidism. These include the following:

- *Bone pain to the back, joints and shins*
- *Muscle weakness*

- *Muscle atrophy*
- *Pathologic fractures, which occur in women*
- *Renal calculi*
- *Polydipsia*
- *Polyuria*
- *Nausea*
- *Constipation*
- *Pancreatitis*
- *Peptic ulcers*
- *Abdominal pain*
- *Arrhythmias*
- *Hypertension*
- *Paresthesias*
- *Depression*
- *Psychosis*
- *Acidosis*
- *Weight loss*

Treatment

Decreasing of the elevated serum calcium levels are what the treatment of hyperparathyroidism focuses on. In mild cases, the patient should avoid immobilization, thiazide diuretics, large doses of vitamins A and D, antacids that contain calcium and calcium supplements, they are also urged to keep active and drink fluids. In severe cases intensive treatment with IV saline and hospitalization is required. For short-term treatment medications that inhibit bone reabsorption and reduce hypercalcemia, such as zoledronate, which is known as Zometa, alendronate, which is known as Fosomax and pamidronate, which is known as Aredia, may relieve bone pain. Primary hyperparathyroidism is treated by a surgical removal of the parathyroid glands affected by hyperplasia or adenoma.

Hypoparathyroidism

Abnormally low PTH levels results in hypoparathyroidism.

Signs and Symptoms

The signs and symptoms include the following:

- *Increased intracranial pressure*
- *Psychosis*
- *Hyperactive reflexes*
- *Mood disorders, such as irritability depression and anxiety*
- *Paresthesias, such as lips, hands and feet*
- *Arrhythmias*
- *Abdominal cramps*
- *Malabsorption*
- *Hair loss*
- *Brittle nails*
- *Dry, scaly skin*
- *Tetany or convulsions*
- *Carpopedal spasms*
- *Muscle spasms*
- *Facial grimacing*

Treatment

Increasing calcium levels are focused on with the treatment of hypoparathyroidism. In order to reduce tetany, IV calcium gluconate is given immediately. Increased dietary calcium, vitamin D therapy and supplemental calcium are included in long-term therapy.

Hyperthyroidism

A disorder caused by an excessive delivery of thyroid hormones (TH) to the peripheral tissues, is known as hyperthyroidism, which is also referred to as thyrotoxicosis or overactive thyroid. As a result of tumors that stimulate thyroid secretion, the discontinuation or excessive use of anti-thyroid medications and the deterioration of pre-existing hyperthyroid state, due to toxemia, diabetic ketoacidosis (DKA), trauma or infection, hyperthyroidism can occur.

There are two types of spontaneous hyperthyroidism, which depending on the type and severity of the disease, will present or produce a variety of signs and symptoms. These two types are Grave's disease and toxic nodular goiter. A thyroid storm or crisis, which is a life-threatening emergency, can be precipitated by severe hyperthyroidism and can be triggered by minor trauma or stress.

Signs and Symptoms

There are several signs and symptoms associated with hyperthyroidism; some examples of these are as follows:

- *Smooth and warm skin*
- *Hair may become fine*
- *Loss of hair in the scalp, eyebrow, axillary or pubic areas*
- *Heat intolerance*
- *Insomnia*
- *Palpitations*
- *Increased sweating*
- *Increased appetite, but loses weight*
- *Hypermotile bowels and diarrhea*
- *Emotional instability*

Treatment

Reduction of the TH levels is the principal goal of treatment. For young patients with small glands and a mild form of the disease, using anti-thyroid medications are most beneficial. In a patient with a large gland or multinodular goiter, surgery to reduce thyroid hormone release may be indicated. For patients that are twenty-one years of age or older that do not have heart disease, the treatment of choice is radioactive iodine therapy. Prevention of a thyroid storm or crisis is the second goal of treatment. In doing so, the patient is educated on proper dosing of medication, which includes taking anti-pyretics as prescribed and to seek care if there is any sign of infection. In order to prevent the condition from worsening, fluids are to be replaced as needed.

Hypothyroidism

This endocrine disorder can result from primary, secondary and tertiary thyroid failures such as occurs with Hashimoto's disease, a thyroid stimulating hormone deficiency and deficient thyrotropin releasing hormone, respectively. Hashimoto's disease is the most common cause of hypothyroidism in the United States.

Other risk factors are neck radiation therapy, diabetes type 1, Addison's disease, pernicious anemia, amiodarone and/or lithium therapy and/or a family or personal history of thyroid disease.

Signs and Symptoms

The many signs and symptoms of hypothyroidism include decreased T3 and T4 levels accompanied with elevated TSH levels constipation, hoarseness of the voice, pallor, dry skin, stiff muscles, edema, anorexia, weight gain, menstrual alterations, bradycardia, cardiac enlargement and anemia.

The most serious of all complications is myxedema coma, a severe case of hypothyroidism, which presents with coma, respiratory failure, cardiac failure, decreased cardiac output, edema, especially around the feet, eyes and hands, adrenal insufficiency, severe hypothermia, and other signs of severe hypothyroidism.

Treatment

The replacement of the thyroid hormone is the primary treatment; a subtotal thyroidectomy may be necessary for large goiters.

Myxedema coma mandates the immediate intravenous administration of levothyroxine sodium, glucose and corticosteroids. At times, intubation, mechanical ventilation and cardiovascular support are indicated.

Thyroiditis

An inflammation of the thyroid gland is known as thyroiditis, which is usually the result of a viral infection. This is an acute disorder, which can become chronic. If it becomes chronic, this can result in a hyperthyroid state due to repeated infections destroying gland tissue.

Signs and Symptoms

Thyroiditis can in some cases be difficult to diagnose due to the fact that many of the signs imitate symptoms of other disorders. When thyroid cell damage is slow and chronic, common symptoms occur, which include the following:

- *Constipation dry skin*
- *Depression*
- *Feeling 'fuzzy-headed'*
- *Weight gain*
- *Fatigue*

There are other rare symptoms, such as decreased concentration, vague aches and pains and swelling of the legs.

Treatment

The treatment for thyroiditis depends on the type that is diagnosed. Examples of treatments are immediate hormone replacement, which prevents or corrects hypothyroidism and generally prevents the gland from getting bigger, bed rest, non-steroidal anti-inflammatory medications, steroids, which are uses to reduce inflammation and control palpitations, and beta-blockers, which are used to lower the heart rate and to reduce tremors.

Diseases of the Adrenal Glands

Corticoadrenal Insufficiency

Addison's disease, also referred to as adrenal cortisol insufficiency, is a chronic adrenocortical insufficiency, which is caused by a primary deficiency of the adrenal cortex. It occurs primarily among women and adults under the age of sixty, but it can occur at any age. It is also associated with cancer, tuberculosis or AIDS which affects the adrenal glands.

Signs and Symptoms

This disorder has a primary and secondary form. The primary form is marked by is marked with hyperkalemia, hypotension, hyponatremia darkened skin pigmentation and an insufficient mineralocorticoid levels, dehydration, renal failure, shock and death.

Secondary adrenal insufficiency is NOT characterized with insufficient mineralocorticoid levels, but there is a slight hyperpigmentation and a mild degree of water retention and low serum sodium levels secondary to this retention.

Other signs and symptoms include fatigue, muscular aches, hypoglycemia, weight loss, confusion, nausea, vomiting, anorexia, diarrhea, menstrual changes, tremors and joint pain.

Treatment

Intravenous fluids, steroids, and rest are used for adrenal crisis; and hydrocortisone, prednisone, prednisolone, methylpredinisolone or dexamethasone is used to treat primary and secondary cortisol deficiency.

The most serious complication of Addison's disease is adrenal hemorrhage septicemia which is an emergency situation which is treated with aggressive antibiotic therapy, intravenous vasopressors and large doses of steroids

Cushing Syndrome

Cushing's syndrome, also known as hypercortisolism, is a chronic hypersecretion of glucocorticoids from the adrenal cortex. The risk factors include a pituitary tumor and female gender between 30 and 50 years of age especially when the person has taken long term steroids, as often occurs after an organ transplant or when steroids are used as an adjunct to chemotherapy.

Signs and Symptoms

This disorder affects many bodily functions because the metabolism of proteins, carbohydrates and fats is altered. Altered carbohydrate metabolism is characterized with hyperglycemia secondary to impaired insulin utilization, and hepatic gluconeogenesis. Some of these signs and symptoms include muscular weakness and wasting, osteoporosis, bone pain, pathological fractures, purple striae, thin, fragile skin and bruising related to the loss of collagen as the result of altered protein metabolism. Altered fat metabolism can result in a moon face, buffalo hump of the back and a pendulous abdomen.

Other signs and symptoms include compromised Inflammatory and immune responses which places the person at risk for serious infections, acne, oligomenorrhea, amenorrhea, excessive androgen which can lead to hirsutism, impotence and libido changes, altered water and mineral metabolism as characterized by hypertension, hypochloremia, weight gain, edema, metabolic alkalosis, osteoporosis, and increased calcium reabsorption. Hematological changes including high red blood cell counts, increased hematocrit and hemoglobin, leukocytosis, eosinopenia and lymphopenia. Mental and emotional responses, such as psychosis, emotional liability, anxiety, depression, and memory losses may occur.

Treatment

Surgical interventions include an adrenalectomy, removal of an adrenal cortex tumor, and a hypophysectomy to remove any pituitary tumor when this is the cause.

Stereotactic irradiation is also done for patients who have a small adenoma and medications can include mitotane, aminoglutethemide or metyrapone.

Diseases of the Pituitary Gland

Acromegaly

When sustained GH hypersecretion begins during adulthood, acromegaly, which literally means enlarged extremities, occurs, most commonly due to pituitary tumors.

Signs and Symptoms

Bone and connective tissue continue to grow, as a result of constant stimulation. For example, the voice deepens, the tongue enlarges, the maxilla lengthens and the forehead enlarges. Other manifestations that can occur include diabetes, impaired glucose tolerance, visual disturbances, seizures, congestive heart failure, hypertension, headache and peripheral nerve damage due to entrapment of nerves.

Treatment

Treatment that halts excessive GH production may be able to relieve secondary bone and connective tissue growth, which arthralgias develop. Surgical removal or irradiation of the pituitary tumor can be used to treat acromegaly, of which a transfrontal or transsphenodial surgical procedures are most commonly used. Suppression of the anterior pituitary gland and decreased GH levels can be achieved through the use of octreotide (Sandistatin).

Gigantism

When GH hypersecretion begins before puberty and the closure of epiphyseal plates, gigantism occurs.

Signs and Symptoms

Body proportions are relatively normal even though the person becomes abnormally tall, often exceeding a height of seven feet tall (213 cm). This condition is most often a result of a tumor.

Treatment

Due to an improvement in both diagnosing and treating this condition, it is rare today. Patients require interventions to help in coping with both emotional and physical changes. They will also need to prevent complications that involve other organs and functions of the endocrine system.

Diabetes Insipidus

As a result of ADH insufficiency, brain tumors or infections, pituitary surgery, renal and organ failure and cerebral vascular accidents diabetes insipidus can occur. It is also a complication of closed head trauma with increased intracranial pressure. There are two major types of diabetes insipidus, and they are as follows:

1. *Nephrogenic diabetes insipidus, which is a disorder where there is no sensitivity by the renal tubules to ADH. This can be related to renal failure or it can be familiar in origin.*

2. *Neurogenic diabetes insipidus, is a disorder that can be idiopathic or result from the hypothalamus and pituitary gland, which can be from trauma, irradiation or cranial surgery.*

Signs and Symptoms

An excretion of large amounts of dilute urine, which is known as polyuria, in some instances as much as 12 L/day, is caused by a deficit of ADH. The patient drinks large volumes of water due to their excessive thirst, which is known as polydipsia, but if the patient cannot replace all the fluid, they can then become hypernatremic and dehydrated.

Symptoms will present three to six days after the initial injury and can last for seven to ten days in a patient with diabetes insipidus that is caused due to a cerebral injury. The symptoms of diabetes insipidus will usually disappear if the increased intracranial pressure is relieved.

Diabetes insipidus can however be a chronic illness and it would then require lifelong care and treatment.

Treatment

If possible, the correcting the underlying causes of diabetes insipidus can be a treatment for this disorder. Other possible treatments include replacing the ADH hormone, increasing oral fluids and administering IV hypotonic fluids. The treatment of choice is administering desmopression acetate orally, intranasally or parenterally.

Dwarfism

Dwarfism is short stature that results from a number of genetic and medical conditions such as achondroplasia, Turner's syndrome, poor nutrition and a growth hormone deficiency.

There are two types of dwarfism. They are:

1. *Disproportionate dwarfism.*

    Some bodily parts are small and others are larger and normal in terms of size. Bone development is impaired with disproportionate dwarfism.

2. *Proportionate dwarfism.*

    The body is equally proportionately small without parts that are larger or smaller than others.

Signs and Symptoms

The primary sign is an adult height of less than 4 feet and 10 inches with the average height of those affected with dwarfism is about 4 feet.

Treatment

Treatments do not increase height, but they can lessen the risk of some complications related to this disorder. Some surgical procedures can help to correct problems with bones among those affected with disproportionate dwarfism. For example, limb lengthening surgery may be done. Other treatments can include growth hormone administration if the dwarfism is caused by a growth hormone deficiency.

Pituitary Adenoma

Pituitary adenomas are noncancerous pituitary gland tumors that can be classified according to their size, their histological composition and the associated impaired function(s).

Size classifications include microadenomas of less than 10 mm in size, macroadenomas of greater than 10 mm in size, a Stage I microadenoma which is less than 1 cm in size and without any sella expansion, a Stage II macroadenoma which is larger than 1 cm and has possible extension above the sella, a Stage III macroadenoma that has invaded the floor or the suprasellar area, and a Stage IV macroadenoma which destroys the sella.

Histological classifications can include basophilic, chromophobic and acidophilic adenomas as based on whether or not the cells take up a tinctorial stain in the laboratory.

Signs and Symptoms

Some of the signs and symptoms include visual field and peripheral vision losses, hemianopsia, increased intracranial pressure, headaches, psychiatric manifestations such as depression, hostility and emotional instability, acromegaly, or gigantism, which results when the anterior pituitary gland overproduces the growth hormone, Cushing's syndrome, the hypersecretion of adenohypophyseal hormones such as luteinizing hormone, follicle stimulating hormone, growth hormone, prolactin, thyrotropin and adrenocorticotropic hormone, pituitary apoplexy and diabetes insipidus.

Treatment

Some of the treatment options, as based on the size and type of the pituitary tumor include bromocriptine, quinagolide, octreotide or carbergoline to shrink the tumor, radiation therapy and surgery.

Diabetes Mellitus (Type 1 And Type 2)

Diabetes mellitus is a chronic systematic disease that alters carbohydrate, protein and fat metabolism. It is the most common disease of the endocrine system. There are several different types of diabetes mellitus, which include the following:

Type 1 diabetes mellitus, which is also known as insulin dependent diabetes mellitus, is associated with toxic chemicals, abnormal antibodies that attack the islet of Langerhans cells, some viruses and histocompatibility antigens. This type of diabetes mellitus can be induced genetically and when ninety percent of the pancreatic beta cells have been destroyed, it will then cause symptoms to present.

Type 2 diabetes mellitus, which is also known as non-insulin dependent diabetes mellitus, is associated with obesity. It has different causes than type 1 diabetes, such as defects in insulin secretion and action. Eighty percent of diabetic patients have this type of diabetes.

Gestational diabetes mellitus, causes, during pregnancy, glucose intolerance and it usually disappears after the baby is delivered, but it can turn into either type 1 or type 2 diabetes.

Other types, which are associated with disorders, such as certain genetic syndromes, insulin receptor disorder, endocrinopathies and pancreatic disease, and the use of drugs or chemicals, such as lithium, furosemide, epinephrine, corticosteroids and glucagon.

Signs and Symptoms

There are several classic signs and symptoms associated with diabetes mellitus including polyuria, polydipsia, polyphagia, weight loss, fatigue and somnolence.

Treatment

There are several different types of treatment associated with diabetes mellitus, and they are as follows:

- *Insulin*:

    There are different types of insulin which are prescribed depending on the patient's needs. Protamine zinc and ultralente insulin is used for a patient requiring long acting therapy. This type of insulin starts to work at 4-8 hours, peaks at 16-18 hours and lasts for more than 36 hours. Neutral protamine hagedon (NPH), globin zinc or lente insulin is used for patients who require intermediate therapy. This type of insulin begins to work at 1-4 hours, peaks at 6-12 hours and lasts for 12-24 hours. Regular, crystalline zinc and semilente insulins are used for patients who require short acting therapy. They begin to work in less than 1 hour, peak at 2-7 hours and lasts for 4-16 hours.

- *Diet:*

  In order to control the number of calories and the amount of carbohydrates that are ingested, the patient should be involved with diet therapy. Distribution of calories should be maintained by the patient over a twenty-four hour period. The patient may use an exchange system, which groups foods that can be substituted for one another. For increased activity, the diet should be modified.

- *Oral anti-diabetic agents*:

  Some diabetic patients are prescribed oral anti-diabetic medications, such as tolazamide and acetohexamide, which are intermittent-acting agents, that are used to enhance both types of insulin secretion, glipizide and glyburide, which stimulate insulin release and should be administered once or twice daily and have no anti-diuretic effect, chlorpropamide, which is a long-acting agent used in patients who have low basal insulin secretion, but can secrete, with food intake, sufficient insulin, and tolbutamide, which is a short-acting agent used in patients who have elevated basal insulin secretion, but cannot, with food intake, produce sufficient insulin.

- *Physical exercise*:

  Patients are encouraged to follow a consistent exercise program. The exercise should be performed when glucose levels are high, if the patient is exercising when glucose levels are low they will need to increase their intake of carbohydrates. Exercising helps blood vessels to perform more effectively, maintain normal cholesterol levels, lower blood glucose levels and may reduce the amount of insulin they may need to take.

Acute Complications of Diabetes

Hypoglycemia

Hypoglycemia, or low blood glucose, is defined as a blood glucose level that is less than 70 mg/dL.

Signs and Symptoms

Hypoglycemia has a variety of signs and symptoms, which include early and late signs as well as minor and severe signs and symptoms. Some of the early warning signs and symptoms of diabetic hypoglycemia include dizziness, headache, slurred speech, sweating, anxiety, shakiness, irritability and hunger.

Severe symptoms occur if the early warning signs are not treated. These severe late signs and symptoms include the following:

- *Blurry or double vision*
- *Drowsiness*
- *Convulsions and seizures*
- *Unconsciousness*
- *Difficulty speaking or slurred speech*
- *Confusion*
- *Clumsiness or jerky movements*
- *Muscle weakness*
- *Agitation*
- *Coma*

Treatment

Early recognition of the symptoms of hypoglycemia can generally be treated by oral ingestion of glucose tablets or consuming sugar, which can include eating candy or fruit juice. If the client is unable to orally ingest sugar an injection of glucagon can be administered or intravenous glucose can be given.

Hyperglycemia

Hyperglycemia, or high blood glucose, is defined as a fasting (8hour) blood glucose level that is more than 180 mg/dL. Despite the fact that hyperglycemia leads to complications and chronic diabetes disorders, it, unlike hypoglycemia is not life threatening.

Signs and Symptoms

Hyperglycemia symptoms do not occur until the client's blood glucose level exceeds 200 mg/dL. It can take several days or even weeks for them to develop at that point, but the longer those levels stay elevated the more several the symptoms become and the greater the risk for the damaging long term complications of hyperglycemia.

The early signs and symptoms include headache, fatigue, blurred vision, excessive thirst and frequent urination. If these early symptoms are left untreated, ketones, or toxic acids, will build up in the client's blood and urine. This buildup of ketones is referred to as ketoacidosis, which is fully described below.

Treatment

A client can help to keep their blood glucose levels within a normal range by exercising regularly, taking their medications as directed and adjusted by their physician, maintain a diabetic meal plan, check their blood glucose levels regularly and adjust their insulin doses accordingly to prevent hyperglycemia.

Diabetic Ketoacidosis

Signs and Symptoms

The signs and symptoms of diabetic ketoacidosis usually develop quickly, often within 24 hours. These include:

- *Nausea and vomiting*
- *Abdominal pain*
- *Weakness or fatigue*
- *Shortness of breath*
- *Fruity-scented breath*
- *Confusion*
- *Excessive thirst*
- *Frequent urination*

Some symptoms can be noticed only through urine and blood tests, which can be performed at home as well as in a healthcare facility. In the blood, the client can detect high blood sugar levels or hyperglycemia and in the urine test high ketone levels can be detected.

Treatment

Clients diagnosed with diabetic ketoacidosis may be treated in the emergency department or they may have to be admitted to the hospital for treatment. Treatment includes a three-step process, which includes the following:

- *Rehydration, which includes oral or intravenous fluids to dilute the excess sugar in the client's urine and to replace fluids that have been lost from excessive urination*

- *Replacement of electrolytes, which are delivered intravenously to replace the electrolytes lost. This replacement prevents any short term or long term complications that can adversely affect the client's heart, muscles and nervous system. e cells to function properly*

- *Insulin therapy, which is delivered intravenously until the client's blood sugar level falls below 240 mg/dL and is no longer acidic*

Once these symptoms are addressed and the client's body chemistry returns to normal the physician will try to figure out what caused the diabetic ketoacidosis. Additional treatments may then be necessary. For example, if a bacterial infection was the cause antibiotics are necessary. The physician will also determine if there is any risk for a heart attack, and if so, the client may need a complete cardiac assessment.

Hyperglycemic Hyperosmolar Nonketotic Syndrome (HHNS)

Signs and Symptoms

Initial signs and symptoms of hyperglycemic hyperosmolar nonketotic syndrome (HHNS) include fever, convulsions, lethargy, nausea, weight loss, coma, weakness, confusion, increased thirst and frequent urination.

If left untreated, other symptoms can develop over a period of days to weeks, including speech impairments, loss of feeling or function of one's muscles and dysfunctional movement.

Treatment

The treatment of hyperglycemic hyperosmolar nonketotic syndrome includes intravenous fluids with potassium, intravenous insulin and other medications to correct any problems relating to the client's blood pressure, urinary output, level of hydration and circulation.

Lipid Disorders

Hypercholesterolemia

Hypercholesterolemia is high blood cholesterol; although not a disease itself, it can be secondary to many diseases and it can also contribute to many forms of diseases such as cardiovascular disease. There are no symptoms of hypercholesterolemia other than a blood test that measures it.

The first line of treatment includes lifestyle changes, such as a low cholesterol diet and exercise. If the lifestyle changes are made but the cholesterol, especially the LDL, remains high, medication may be indicated.

Medications include statins, such as Lipitor, Lescol, Altoprev, Mevacor, Pravachol, Crestor, and Zocor, bile-acid binding resins such as Prevalite, Welchol and Colestid, cholesterol absorption inhibitors such as Zeita and combination cholesterol absorption inhibitors like Vytorin.

Hypertriglyceridemia

High level of triglycerides in the blood is associated with the development of atherosclerosis and other cardiovascular disease.

In most cases the patient will be asymptomatic, but some forms of primary hypertriglyceridemia can present with symptoms such as eruptive xanthoma, lipemia retinalis, hepatosplenomegaly and neurological alterations; acute pancreatitis occurs in patients with a triglyceride level above 1000 mg/dl.

Lifestyle changes are recommended for people with mild to moderately high levels of triglycerides. These changes can include the restriction of fat and carbohydrates in the patient's diet; patients with high levels of triglycerides typically are given medications such as fibrates.

Sexual/Reproductive Function

Alterations of Sexual Function

Alterations of sexual functioning can be impacted by a number of forces, or factors, such as sexual desire disorders like a hypoactive sexual desire or a sexual aversion, sexual arousal and erectile dysfunction, orgasmic disorders, satisfaction alterations and problems, and sexual pain disorders including:

- *Dypareunia, which is pain during and after sexual intercourse*
- *Vaginismus, which is involuntary vaginal muscle spasms which impedes penetration and causes pain*
- *Vulvodynia, which is burning that is located in the vulva*
- *Vestibulitis, which is severe pain with touch or an attempted vaginal penetration*

Sexuality and Illness

The loss of sexual desire is quite common among clients who are affected with a disease or disorder such as cancer and diabetes. Both men and women may not experience orgasms in the same manner that they had in the past. For example, some patients may need more time to reach an orgasm and others may need more stimulation than they usually do, in order to have an orgasm.

Often times, men have erectile problems and women experience vaginal dryness and pain; therefore, they may just give up on sex all together. Women who experience vaginal dryness, discomfort or pain during pregnancy can try vaginal lubrications to help and, in some cases, a vaginal dilator can resolve the problem. Men who are experiencing erectile dysfunction can discuss an assistive device, such as a penile implant or a pump as a helpful intervention.

A patient who is receiving chemotherapy may have to exercise some caution with oral and vaginal sex because some of the toxic chemicals used in the treatment can be found in the vaginal fluids and semen. Therefore, these patients should use condoms and/or dental dams during any sexual activities.

Sexual activity after all surgery often leaves the patient either too uncomfortable or just unable to engage in sexual activity for a brief period of time. Cancer patients with a weakened immune system, which can lead to potential problems with sexual activity, may experience vaginal bleeding or genital discomfort that may limit their sexual activity.

Interventions for Sexual Disorders

Patients who experience difficulties regarding their sexuality are encouraged to seek help from the nurse, and/or the professional interventions with a sex therapist or psychologist. The patient can benefit highly through medical attention and counseling.

Patients may also patient education about their changes in sexuality in terms of their problem, the common occurrence of this problem and ways that the client can cope with, and correct, their sexual concerns. Unfortunately, due to the stigma attached to sexual dysfunction and counseling for it, many patients are too embarrassed to discuss their problems so they do not take advantage of these services. There are also numerous books and publications on the subject that can overcome the barrier associated with verbalizing these concerns with their healthcare provider.

There is a plethora of information on the Internet, but as all other topics on the Internet, it is important to verify this information in terms of its validity and soundness. There are blogs and self-help groups that meet in person and on the internet that can also be very helpful to some patients because these support groups encourage the client to verbalize their concerns and also help the client to see that they are not alone. Other people are experiencing similar situations.

Patients who experience difficulties in their sex lives have choices. There are a variety of things, such as medications, surgery and assistive devices that can be helpful, depending on what problems the patients is experiencing. For example, an assistive device, such as a penile implant can be used for men with erectile dysfunction, lubricators and vaginal dilators can be used to help to ease the pain or discomfort a woman may be experiencing when they are having vaginal intercourse.

No matter what type of situation the patient is in, such as married, dating or looking, they should to be prepared for discussions regarding illness and sexual activity. A partner accepting of the illness and how it may affect their sexual life is important for both the patient and the partner.

These discussions should be open and honest. Partner education often proves to be extremely helpful and it should always be encouraged. As a couple there may be many obstacles to overcome, but with the help and guidance of a nurse, counselor and/or sex therapist, any issues and questions can be discussed and, in most cases, concerns, problems and issues can be worked out.

Functional and Mental Status and Environment

The term mental health can have many definitions. For example, mental health can be defined as successful adjustments and coping with the stressors of everyday life in a manner that is acceptable to society and healthy for the client. On the other hand, mental illness is defined as the societal view of what is not appropriate in terms of behavior; and it can also be defined as the lack of effective adjustments and coping skills to deal with the stressors of everyday life in an acceptable manner and healthy manner.

Some of the factors that impact on the development of mental health include genetic makeup (inheritance), life circumstances, such as good physical health and friends, and nurturing during the early years of life.

Signs and Symptoms

Commonly occurring signs and symptoms of mental illness are not as clear and objective as the signs and symptoms of a physiological disorder. Generally speaking, the signs and symptoms of mental disease can include social withdrawal, changes in personal habits like grooming and hygiene, abnormal changes in mood, changes in thought processes, and other behaviors.

Risk Factors Associated With Mental Illness

Populations at Risk

Adolescents are often adversely affected with sexual identity issues, peer pressure, illicit drug use and bullying.

New patents often experience stressors relating to the transition from being a couple to being parents with great responsibilities, possible loss of financial income, anxiety regarding the child's wellbeing, concerns that they are not adequate parents, the baby's constant demands and needs, as well as some conflicts and ambivalence about accepting the pregnancy and the newborn.

Older adults may be at risk because of social isolation, grief/loss after the death of a spouse, friend, or another loved one, fear of declining physical and mental abilities, actual physical and mental declines, reduced income, and relocation to another level of care like an assisted living or long term care healthcare facility.

Gender

Women are at risk for mental illness as the result of domestic violence, hormonal changes as occurs after pregnancy, internal, intrapersonal conflicts about the roles they wish to fulfil, including that of a full time career person, homemaker, single parent, etc.

Other Illnesses and Disorders

The physically and cognitively impaired are at risk for mental illness because they affected with social isolation, lack of independence, poor quality of life, impaired self-image, societal stigma and the lack of meaningful relationships.

Social Forces

The homeless and refugees have stressors such as financial uncertainty, poverty, poor social status, the loss of self-esteem and self-worth, and other stressors.

Classifications of Mental Illness

- *Anxiety disorders, such as obsessive disorders, phobias and panic disorders*
- *Sleep disorders*
- *Eating disorders*

- *Mood disorders, such as bi-polar disease and depression*
- *Schizophrenia and other psychotic disorders, such as paranoid or catatonic-type schizophrenia*
- *Sexual and gender identity disorders*
- *Cognitive disorders, such as dementia and delirium*
- *Impulse control disorders*
- *Substance abuse disorders, such as alcohol abuse or drug dependence*
- *Personality disorders, such as dependent personality and antisocial personality*

The American Psychiatric Association's (APA) Diagnostic and Statistical Manual of Mental Disorders (DSM) contains four major categories of mental illness. Each of these four broad categories contain hundreds of related mental health disorders and their characteristics.

The APA's four major categories are:

1. Mood disorders

    These disorders affect the client's mood. These disorders are also referred to as mood affective disorders.

2. Behavioral disorders

    Clients with behavioral disorders typically exhibit hostility, aggression and defiance. These people can experience problems at home, at school, at work, and in other social settings as a result of their behaviors.

3. Thought disorders

    These clients have disordered thoughts. They have serious problems with thinking, feeling and behavior.

4. Mixed disorders

    These disorders have features of more than one of the above.

Mental illness can also be categorized, or classified, as temporary, episodic and chronic. For example, a single self-limiting minor depression is classified as a temporary mental illness. Bipolar disease and schizophrenia are considered episodic mental illnesses. The client with an episodic mental illness will have episodes of normal life interspersed with the symptoms of the mental illness. Examples of a chronic mental illness are permanent, irreversible dementia and nonrelenting, continuous problems with disorders like bipolar disease and schizophrenia.

Assessing Family/Caregiver Dynamics And Social Support Systems

The nurse must thoroughly, completely and accurately assess each member of the family, the dynamics within the family unit and other social support systems that can be helpful to the patient.

All families are unique and different, and all members of the family unit are also unique and different in terms of their physical, social, emotional, intellectual, spiritual, and occupational dimensions, strengths and weaknesses.

Some families have all members of the family who are physically, socially, emotionally, intellectually and occupationally able and willing to support the patient and assist in their care. Most families, however, are not this fortunate.

Members of the family may simply not want to help and support the client; others may not be physically or emotionally capable of caring for their loved one. For example, an elderly woman with multiple health problems and profound emotional and cognitive problems, like dementia, cannot care for her sick husband.

Still other family members may be geographically distant from their loved one with a disease or disorder so they, even when they are physically, emotionally, and cognitively able to support the client, cannot support the needs of the client because geographic distance prohibits this involvement. Similarly, the "sandwich generation", that has children and parents to care for, may be employed and not able to leave their job and continue to support themselves while caring for a sick family member.

In these cases, the nurse, often in collaboration with a social worker, will identify resources within the community that can assist the client. Some of these community support systems may include civic and religious groups, governmental agencies and services like Meals on Wheels and medically necessary transportation.

Differentiate and Manage Types of Urinary Incontinence

Teach patients to foster healthy bladder and bowel habits:

Dietary and Fluid Management

In some cases alcohol, caffeine or acidic foods need to be cut out of one's diet in order for them to regain control of their bladder.

Factors Affecting Voiding

The volume and characteristics of urine produced and the manner in which it is excreted can be affected by a variety of factors.

Age

Second to respiratory infections, urinary tract infections are the second most common infection among children. Newborns and young infant boys are the most commonly affected population as the result of obstructions and malformations of the urinary system.

As children grow older urinary tract infections are seen more often among young girls as the result of poor wiping habits that result in stool contaminating the urethra. It is important that girls are taught to wipe from front to back, which can help to avoid this stool contamination.

Older adults can experience problems in urinary elimination due to the aging process. Older men can have enlarged prostate glands, which can lead to urinary incontinence and urinary retention because they may be unable to empty their entire bladder.

Older women, such as those who have already experienced menopause, can experience urgency and stress incontinence as a result of a decrease in perineal tone and support of the bladder, vagina and supporting tissues.

Psychosocial Factors

There are some people who can be able to have their micturition reflex stimulated under certain conditions. These conditions can include factors such as normal positioning, privacy, enough time and in some cases running water is needed. When clients are not able to have these factors present, they may be unable physically to relax enough to be able to void. Some client's may feel anxious or rushed and therefore are unable to void as well.

Fluid and Food Intake

Foods that are high in sodium can cause a client to retain water and therefore leave them unable to void. In most cases if the fluid intake is increased a client should be able to have an increase in fluid output as well. Inhibiting the production of antidiuretic hormone, which can be achieved through ingestion of fluids, such as alcohol, can help to increase fluid output.

Medications

There are a number of medications that can affect the body's normal urination process. In particular, medications that affect the autonomic nervous system can interfere and they can cause retention of fluids. Prevention of reabsorption of water and electrolytes from the tubules of the kidney into the bloodstream is seen with diuretics and this increases urine formation. The color of the urine can also be altered by certain medications.

Muscle Tone

Clients with poor bladder muscle tone often times require the use of a retention catheter for a long period of time. The muscle tone is the pelvic region can also affect a client's ability to store and empty urine.

Pathologic Conditions

Urine formation and excretion can be affected by a variety of diseases or pathogens. The ability of the nephrons to produce urine can be affected by diseases of the kidney. Renal failure is one of these conditions, it causes the kidneys to stop produces urine altogether. Blood flow to the kidneys can be affected by heart and circulatory disorders, such as shock, heart failure or hypertension. This interference with blood flow can cause problems with urine production. Vomiting and diarrhea can cause the body to lose abnormal amounts of fluid, which results in water being retained by the kidneys and therefore urine output decreases. Processes that interfere with the urine flow from the kidneys to the urethra can affect urinary excretion. Hypertrophy of the prostate can impair urination and bladder emptying, because it can obstruct the urethra.

Urinary Disorders

Polyuria

Polyuria is an excessive amount of urine produced by the kidneys, which can occur among those with a history of diabetes mellitus, diabetes insipidus and kidney disease. It can cause the person to become dehydrated, Thirst and weight loss as a result of excessive fluid loss.

Oliguria

Oliguria is a less than normal amount of urinary output. Oliguria can result from a decrease in fluid intake, excessive fluid loss, impaired blood flow to the kidneys or it could even be a sign of renal failure.

Anuria

Anuria is a lack of the production of urine.

Dysuria

Dysuria is painful or difficult urination. It can result from a urinary tract infection and trauma.

Urinary Incontinence

Urinary incontinence is an involuntary leakage of urine and a loss of bladder control. This is more common in women, due to childbirth, which can cause trauma to the pelvic floor, a shorter urethra, and menopause. As a result, women often have stress incontinence, which is urinary leakage that occurs when the person coughs, sneezes or laughs.

Cognitive impairments, decreased mobility, urinary tract infections, cerebrovascular accidents, spinal cord injury or other diseases and disorders can lead to urinary incontinence.

Urinary Retention

Urinary retention is a condition in which urine accumulates in the bladder, which can result in over distention of the bladder. It often occurs when the client is not able to completely empty their bladder.

Treatment choices are, in most cases, began with the least invasive, and has the lowest chance of experiencing any complications. For example, exercise should be tried before the decision to perform surgery. In some cases it may be necessary to perform minimally invasive surgery.

Type of Incontinence	Treatment Interventions
Stress	Surgery
	Pelvic floor physiotherapy
	Anti-incontinence devices
	Medications
Urge	Changes in diet
	Pelvic floor exercises
	Behavioral modification
	Medications
	New types of surgical interventions

Functional	Treatment of the underlying cause
Overflow	Catheterization regimen or diversion
Mixed	Anticholinergic drugs and surgery

Emptying Maneuvers And Bladder And Bowel Training Program

Double voiding, which entails urinating then waiting a few minutes and trying to go again. It is a practice that can be used to help one to learn or teach themselves to empty their bladder more completely and also to avoid overflow incontinence.

Delaying voiding after the urge to go arises. It should be started slowly and working up to longer periods of time, over time. A patient can begin with a ten minute weight initially and move up from there.

Some interventions include maintaining adequate fluid intake and maintaining normal voiding habits. If these actions aren't successful, a cholinergic drug to stimulate bladder contractions and to facilitate more complete bladder emptying can be used. Crede massage is used if the client has a flaccid bladder. This massage includes the manual pressing on the bladder.

The first steps in treating urinary retention include maintaining adequate fluid intake, maintaining normal voiding habits and giving the client needed assistance with toileting. If these actions aren't successful, then the doctor may prescribe a cholinergic drug, which can be helpful in stimulating bladder contractions and allowing more complete bladder emptying. If the client's bladder is flaccid, then the Crede's maneuver can be used. Crede massage includes manual pressing on the bladder. If there is no improvement after these interventions, it may be necessary to catheterize the client.

Managing urinary incontinence includes bladder training, which is also referred to as continence training, pelvic muscle exercises, maintaining skin integrity and using external urinary drainage devices and briefs. Whenever possible, indwelling urinary catheters should be avoided because they can lead to infections.

Teach and/or perform the following management techniques:

- *Pelvic Floor Exercises*

    Kegel's exercises to strengthen and relax the bladder as well as other pelvic floor muscles. bladder training, which is also referred to as continence training, pelvic muscle exercises, maintaining skin integrity and using external urinary drainage devices and briefs. Whenever possible, indwelling urinary catheters should be avoided because they can lead to infections.

    To perform Kegel exercises, contract the muscles that you would normally use to stop the flow of urine. Hold the contraction for three seconds, then relax for three seconds. Repeat this pattern 10 times. As your muscles strengthen, hold the contraction longer, gradually working your way up to three sets of 10 contractions every day.

- *Electrical Stimulation*

    One of the tools used to help strengthen the pelvic floor muscles is to insert electrodes into the vagina and rectum temporarily for electric stimulation. The gentle stimulation may need to be repeated several times and up to months. It has helped with a variety of problems including stress and urge incontinence.

- *Biofeedback*

    Biofeedback is a method of treatment in which the patient is able to use monitoring devices to help consciously control physical processes that are normally controlled automatically. For example, temperature, heart rate, sweating, blood pressure, muscle tension and sweating can be controlled.

    Specially trained physiotherapists teach simple exercises that can increase anal muscle strength. People learn how to strengthen pelvic floor muscles, sense when stool is ready to be released and contract the muscles if having a bowel movement at a certain time is inconvenient.

    It has been shown that biofeedback can help patients with chronic pain, sleep difficulties and it can help to improve the patient's overall quality of life.

Vaginal Weights

Vaginal weights, which are also known as vaginal cones, are a medical device that is made in a specific design and shape to exercise the muscles in the pelvic floor. These are used to help strengthen and restore the muscles to help in the management and treatment of urinary stress incontinence.

- *Pessaries*

Pessaries are another tool helpful for patients with incontinence problems. The pessary is a stiff ring, which is inserted into the vagina to help hold up the bladder. It is used to prevent urine from leaking, and it is effective most commonly in women with a prolapsed bladder or uterus.

- *Urge suppression techniques (e.g., quick flicks)*

There are many different types of urge suppression techniques, which are discussed earlier in this review. Quick flicks is another exercise that can help keep the pelvic floor muscles tight and allow for more control over one's bladder, and urine output. It is a series of rapid contractions and releases, which are performed by quick tightening of the muscles, lifting them up, and letting them go. These exercises are repeated a number of times, several times a day.

- *Environmental Modifications*

There are different choices of environmental modifications that can help with urinary issues. Each patient has different needs and what works for one patient may not work for another. Options include the following:

- *Bedside Commode.*

This can be helpful for patients who are able to, either with some help or alone, be able to get out of bed, but may not be able to use the toilet, to use a portable commode that can be set close to their bed, and has handrails to assist. It is vital that the commode is kept clean and dry for the patient, as there can be a variety of problems if they are not emptied and kept clean throughout the day.

- *Urinal.*

Urinals are available for those who are unable to get out of bed whenever they wish to urinate. If they feel the urge to urinate and no one is there to help them to the toilet, they can use a urinal in bed. Just as with the commode it is vital that the urinal is emptied, cleaned and washed often. Some patients require that the amount of urine be measured and recorded.

Clothing.

Special clothing is available for patients to allow for easier removal or access when needing to urinate or defecate.

Catheterization

A catheter is used for patients who are incontinent and cannot fully empty their bladder, as well as other reasons, such as uncontrolled bladder, those who are injured and can't get up to use the restroom, etc. It involves using a soft tube and putting in the urethra to empty the bladder into an attached bag. The intermittent type is inserted several times a day, whereas the indwelling type stays in place until such time that the patient is no longer in need of that.

Urinary catheterization for residual urine may be used, as well as an indwelling urinary catheter, however, whenever possible, catheterization should be avoided in order to prevent urinary tract infections.

Toileting Programs

Trips are planned to go to urinate every two to four hours, rather than waiting for the urge to go.

The "Knack"

The knack is not only strong pelvic muscles, but it incorporates timing with it. Just as other exercises, and pelvic exercises need to be practiced, so does this. It is important to teach patients the knack method, and encourage them to practice the exercises often.

The knack helps to close the urethra more effectively, and therefore women with leakage problems or dribbling problems can train to prevent them. They should be taught to practice the knack exercises just before coughing, sneezing, laughing or any other activity in which they normally have difficulty with leaking.

The following in the complete knack process and exercises that should be taught and followed by patients:

- *Sit away from the back of the chair or stand tall with your chest lifted and the normal inward curve in your low back. You can even do this on the toilet.*
- *Lift and squeeze the muscles in and around all three pelvic openings (urethra, vagina and anus) immediately before you cough, sneeze or lift.*
- *Contract around all three pelvic openings at once, with a strong inward lift and squeeze of your pelvic floor muscles*
- *Maintain this pelvic floor muscle contraction as you do a small cough*
- *After you cough, relax your pelvic floor muscles back to normal resting level.*

- *Progress this exercise with a more forceful cough, or repeating a couple of coughs in a row maintaining your pelvic floor contraction throughout as you do so.*

Recommend pharmacologic treatment

Medications commonly used to treat incontinence include the following:

- *Anticholinergics*

These medications can calm an overactive bladder and may be helpful for urge incontinence. Examples of these types of medications include oxybutynin (Ditropan XL), tolterodine (Detrol), darifenacin (Enablex), fesoterodine (Toviaz), solifenacin (Vesicare) and trospium (Sanctura).

- *Mirabegron*

Used to treat urge incontinence, this medication relaxes the bladder muscle and can increase the amount of urine your bladder can hold. It may also increase the amount you are able to urinate at one time, helping to empty your bladder more completely.

- *Alpha blockers*

In men with urge or overflow incontinence, these medications relax bladder neck muscles and muscle fibers in the prostate and make it easier to empty the bladder. Examples include tamsulosin (Flomax), alfuzosin (Uroxatral), silodosin (Rapaflo), terazosin (Hytrin) and doxazosin (Cardura).

- *Topical estrogen*

Applying low-dose, topical estrogen in the form of a vaginal cream, ring or patch may help tone and rejuvenate tissues in the urethra and vaginal areas. This may reduce some of the symptoms of incontinence.

Recommend surgical treatment and prepare patient for procedures

There are several surgical procedures that can be used to treat the problems that cause urinary incontinence, but these are used if the other treatment options fail. These procedures include the following:

- *Sling procedures,* which is used to treat stress incontinence, involves creating a pelvic string from strips of the client's body tissue, mesh or synthetic material. The sling is made to go around the patient's urethra and the bladder neck. This is used to help to keep the urethra closed when the client coughs, sneezes, laughs, etc.

- *Prolapse surgery,* which can be used in women with mixed incontinence and pelvic organ prolapse. The surgery can include a combination of prolapse surgery and a sling procedure.

- *Bladder neck suspension*, which is performed during general or spinal anesthesia because it involves an abdominal incision, provides support for the patient's bladder neck and urethra.

- *Artificial urinary sphincter*, which are particularly helpful for men whose incontinence is associated with treatment of prostate cancer or an enlarged prostate gland. This surgery involves implanting a fluid filled ring around the bladder neck to keep the urinary sphincter shut, until such time as the patient needs to urinate. The patient has a valve implanted under their skin, which when pressed causes the ring to deflate, and therefore allows the urine from their bladder to be able to flow.

Urinary Retention

Urinary retention occurs when urine accumulates in the bladder and it causes bladder distention. It occurs when the client is not able to completely empty their bladder and 200 to 250 ml, or 10% of the bladder capacity, is retained. Some of the conditions associated with urinary retention include prostate cancer, benign prostatic hypertrophy, a urethral tumor and other forms of obstruction and muscular dysfunction.

Signs and Symptoms

Clients with acute urinary retention can experience pain or discomfort, an urge to urinate with no urinary output, abdominal bloating, a weak flow of urine, and urinary leakage between voiding.

Treatment

Some interventions include maintaining adequate fluid intake and maintaining normal voiding habits. If these actions aren't successful, a cholinergic drug to stimulate bladder contractions and to facilitate more complete bladder emptying can be used. Crede massage is used if the client has a flaccid bladder. This massage includes the manual pressing on the bladder.

Urinary catheterization for residual urine may be used, as well as an indwelling urinary catheter, however, whenever possible, catheterization should be avoided in order to prevent urinary tract infections.

Manage other types of voiding disorders:

Post-Prostatectomy Incontinence

Immediately following a radical prostatectomy the majority of men experience problems with incontinence. It usually only lasts a short time and is fairly mild. It is usually gone by three months, but can last for up to six months or a year.

Detrusor Hyperactivity With Impaired Contractility

This is a common, but unrecognized cause of incontinence is elderly patients. In such cases the patient's bladder is overactive, but empties in an ineffective way. Due to the fact that it is often unrecognized and treated as another form of bladder dysfunction or incontinence is the very reason why there is very little known about it, but it is starting to now be noticed and further information and treatments can be developed as an understanding is also developed.

Detrusor Sphincter Dyssynergia

Detrusor sphincter dyssynergia is when the detrusor muscle of the bladder contracts at the same time that the sphincter muscle of the urethra contracts. This therefore results in an obstruction of the normal urinary outflow.

Mixed Incontinence

Mixed incontinence occurs when a patient experiences more than one type of incontinence. The different types of incontinence are explained in another section of the review.

Nocturia

Nocturia is when one awakens from sleep throughout the night to pass urine, or excessive urination at night. This is often an early sign or a subtle clue that the patient may have an important systemic disease. This can also be a symptom of benign prostatic hyperplasia and/or an overactive bladder.

Types of Bowel Dysfunction

Review symptom profile to identify type of bowel dysfunction:

Constipation

Constipation is defined as fewer than three bowel movements a week that are hard and dry usually indicates constipation. It impacts on many palliative care and hospice clients as the result of immobility, the aging process, and medications such as opioids.

Signs and Symptoms

Signs and symptoms of constipation include the following excessive straining, hard stools, and abdominal fullness.

Treatment

Pharmacological interventions include bulk additives, suppositories and enemas; at times manual finger evacuation may be necessary to prevent impaction. Dietary increases of fiber, increased fluids and activity can prevent episodes of constipation.

Fecal Impaction

A fecal impaction is a large lump of dry, hard stool that remains stuck in one's rectum. It most commonly occurs among clients who have had long term constipation.

Signs and Symptoms

Common symptoms include rectal bleeding, abdominal cramping and bloating, sudden episodes of watery diarrhea, straining when trying to pass stools, and small, semi-formed stools. Other possible symptoms include lower back pain, rapid heartbeat or lightheadedness from straining to pass stool, and a loss of bladder control.

Treatment

Treatment includes the removal of the impaction with a mineral oil enema and/or digital disimpaction. In some rare cases surgery may be indicated.

Bowel Incontinence

Bowel incontinence, also known as fecal incontinence, is defined as the inability to control one's bowel movements, which then in turn cause stool or feces to leak out of the rectum unexpectedly and uncontrollably. This leakage can range from this slight leakage to a complete loss of bowel control.

There are certain types of cancer, such as cancers to the anus and rectum, in which the client is more likely to experience this. It is quite embarrassing for the client and the situation should always be handled with respect and dignity.

Signs and Symptoms

In most cases bowel incontinence only occurs when a client is experiencing diarrhea, but there are cases of recurrent or chronic fecal incontinence. Other conditions that can accompany bowel incontinence are gas, bloating, and constipation.

Treatment

Bowel incontinence can, in some cases, be treated according to its cause. For example, anti-diarrheal drugs, laxatives and medications that slow down peristalsis may be indicated. Adding fiber to the diet is also helpful, since fiber adds bulk and solidity to the stool.

If the bowel incontinence is linked to muscular damage, exercise to improve anal sphincter control as well as biofeedback, bowel training and sacral nerve stimulation may be indicated. Some surgical interventions are a sphincteroplasty, the correction of a rectal prolapsed and sphincter replacement.

Diarrhea

Diarrhea is loose, watery stools that occur on a frequent basis. Episodes of diarrhea can be acute and short lived, and it can also be long term and the effect of a disease process such as a gastrointestinal infection and chronic disorders like Chron's disease and inflammatory bowel disease. Additionally, many medications can lead to diarrhea.

Signs and Symptoms

The signs and symptoms include frequent loose and watery stools, abdominal cramps and/or pain, fever, bloating, and bloody stools.

Treatment

Most of the time diarrhea will pass on its own in a couple of days with the help of over the counter remedies.

Fluid and electrolyte balances must be monitored and maintained, particularly among the elderly, infants and young children. It is suggested that the client attempt to maintain the fluid balance with dietary fluids, however, when this is not successful, intravenous fluids and electrolytes like potassium and sodium may be indicated.

Factors That Affect Defecation

There are several factors that affect defecation. These factors include the level of development, diet, activity, psychological factors, defecation habits, medications, diagnostic procedures, anesthesia and surgery, pathologic conditions and pain.

Fecal Elimination Problems

Common problems with fecal elimination include constipation, which is having fewer than three bowel movements a week, fecal impaction, which is a mass or collection of hardened feces within the folds of the rectum, diarrhea, bowel incontinence, which refers to the inability to control fecal and gaseous discharges through the anal sphincter, and flatulence, which results from swallowed air, gas that diffuses between the bloodstream and the intestine, or action of bacteria on the chyme in the large intestine.

Promoting Regular Defecation

The following are interventions that can help clients to defecate on a regular basis:

- *Positioning*
- *Exercising*
- *Nutrition and fluids. Fiber and fluids are helpful.*
- *Timing*
- *Privacy*
- *Enemas*

Depending on the age and medical condition of the client the enema can be small to large in volume. The enema can be high, which means it is able to enter the large intestine and remove feces from as much of the colon as possible, or they can be low, which means that the enema will clean the rectum and sigmoid colon only.

There are four types of enemas as follows:

- *Cleansing Enema*

    Cleansing enemas are used to remove feces. The usual reason for this type of enema is to prevent eliminate the presence of feces during surgery, to prepare the intestine for diagnostic tests, such as visualization tests like a colonoscopy, and to remove feces in a client experiencing constipation or impaction.

- *Carminative Enema*

    A carminative enema is used to primarily expel flatus. With this type of enema the fluid in the rectum expels gas. When the gas is expelled, the rectum and colon distend and allow for peristalsis to be stimulated.

- *Retention Enema*

    With a retention enema, an oil solution or medication is introduced into the rectum and sigmoid colon and stays there for an hour to three hours. This type of enema is used to soften the feces as well as to lubricate the rectum and anal canal. This helps the feces to be passed in a more comfortable fashion.

- *Return-Flow Enema*

    A return-flow enema, which is also known as a Harris flush, is also used to expel flatus. The fluid is inserted into the rectum and sigmoid colon in order to stimulate peristalsis. Often times this type of enema is performed five or six times to expel flatus completely and allow the abdominal distention to be relieved.

Prevention Strategies to Maintain Optimal Bowel Function:

Lifestyle Modifications (E.G., Diet, Fluids, Exercise)

Food and fluids consumed affect the consistency of one's stool. If constipation is causing fecal incontinence, increasing fluid intake is recommended, whereas if diarrhea is occurring, than the stool can be bulked up and less watery by ingesting high fiber foods. Exercise is another component to having better control over one's bowel movements.

This is discussed earlier in the review as well.

If fecal incontinence is caused by muscle damage, recommending a program of exercise and other therapies to restore muscle strength should be done. These treatments can improve anal sphincter control and the awareness of the urge to defecate.

Kegel exercises are discussed earlier in the review.

Skin Protection

Keeping the skin around a patient's anus clean and dry, can help to avoid extra discomfort from fecal incontinence. Recommendations to help a patient relieve anal discomfort and any odor that may accompany fecal incontinence include the following:

- *Washing with water*

    Gently wash the area with water after each bowel movement. Showering or soaking in a bath also may help. Soap should be avoided, as it can dry and irritate the skin, and any rubbing with dry toilet paper, should also be avoided. Using pre-moistened towelettes or wipes, with no alcohol added, should be recommended as alternatives to take the place of dry paper and soap.

- *Dry thoroughly*

    Air drying, if the time permits, is the best way to dry. If time does not permit patting the area dry is an alternative.

- *Use cream or powder*

    Keeping the skin from being in direct contact with feces allows for avoidance of irritated skin. This can be achieved through the use of moisture-barrier skin. Anal discomfort can also be avoided by using cornstarch or non-medicated talcum powder.

- *Loose clothing and cotton under garments*

    Skin problems can become worse if airflow is restricted, such as with tight clothing. Soiled undergarments should always be changed right away.

In some instances medical treatments cannot fully eliminate incontinence in a patient, therefore products, such as disposable adult diapers and/or absorbent pads, can be used to keep the patient's clothing dry. These should be changed as soon as possible after they are wet.

Practice test for CWOCN

1. **Select the risk factor that is paired with the type of cancer that it is most associated with.**

   a) Epstein-Barr virus: Cancer of the stomach.
   b) Epstein-Barr virus: Throat cancer.
   c) Helicobacter pylori: Cancer of the liver.
   d) Helicobacter pylori: Cancer of the stomach.

2. **Select the statement that is accurate and true relating to Chron's disease.**

   a) The typical area of intestinal involvement is the left colon and rectum.
   b) The extent of involvement is diffuse throughout the entire small intestine.
   c) The extent of involvement is segmented.
   d) The inflammation is mostly mucosal and bacterial in nature.

3. **Select the type of dermatitis is correctly paired with its symptoms.**

   a) Atopic-dermatitis: An itchy red rash on the folds of the skin which leaks and crusts over.
   b) Contact dermatitis: Usually causes dandruff, and referred to as cradle cap in infants.
   c) Dyshidrotic dermatitis: A red rash with yellowish oily scales usually on the scalp and face.
   d) Seborrheic dermatitis: A red rash that presents in either the genital regions or between the toes.

4. **Select the pressure ulcer stage that is accurately paired with its description. .**

   a) Stage I: The ulcer is an open wound; the epidermis and part of the dermis is damaged or lost.
   b) Stage II: The loss of skin usually exposes some amount of fat; the bottom of the wound may have some yellowish dead tissue.
   c) Stage III: The wound is open; the ulcer, in only some rare cases, appears red when touched.
   d) Stage IV: The wound may expose muscle, bone, and tendons, and the damage often extends beyond the primary wound.

5. **Your 67 year old female client has vaginal pressure, feelings that the bowel has not been emptied after a bowel movement, pain during intercourse and pain with defecation. What would you recommend as initial treatment for this client?**

   a) Kegal exercises and increasing fiber and fluid intake
   b) A posterior colporrhaphy
   c) A supportive mesh
   d) A surgical rectovaginal septum strengthening

6. Which disorder does your type 2 diabetic patient most likely have when the blood glucose levels are extremely high without the presence of ketones?

    a) Diabetic hyperglycemic hyperosmolar syndrome
    b) Diabetic hypoglycemic hyperosmolar syndrome
    c) Ketotic hyperglycemic hyperosmolar coma
    d) Ketotic hyperglycemic hypomolar coma

7. The dermis layer of skin at a regular birth is:

    a) 20% of adults
    b) 40% of adults
    c) 60% of adults
    d) 80% of adults

8. Cool atrophic skin is associated with:

    a) Arterial insufficiency.
    b) Non-arterial insufficiency.
    c) Diabetic neuropathy.
    d) Non-diabetic neuropathy.

9. Select the phase of wound healing that matches the period during which it is seen.

    a) Hemostasis: Occurs between day five and day twenty
    b) Inflammation: Occurs from day one to day four
    c) Maturation: Occurs after the twenty-first day
    d) Proliferative/granulation: Occurs within moments after the injury

10. Select the correctly paired descriptive term that can be used to describe a wound.

    a) An open wound: Indicative of tunneling
    b) Closed Wound: Seen with a surgical incision
    c) Attached or unattached edges: Indicative of granulation
    d) Healing ridge: Seen with dehiscence or ulcerations

11. What is the normal value of albumin?

    a) <1.5 g/dL
    b) <2.0 g/dL
    c) = 3.5 – 5.5 g/Dl
    d) >5.5 g/dL

12. The protein, transferrin at a level of 185 mg/dL is considered to be in what range?

    a) Normal values
    b) Mild deficiency
    c) Moderate deficiency
    d) Severe deficiency

13. Albumin is produced by the:

    a) Gallbladder.
    b) Kidneys.
    c) Stomach.
    d) Liver.

14. Your client's albumin level abruptly decreased to <3.2. This client is:

    a) At risk for morbidity and death.
    b) Not at risk for morbidity and death.
    c) Unable to produce albumin.
    d) Highly anemic.

15. What test is used to measure the abilities of the kidneys to constitute or dilute urine after serum changes?

    a) BUN-creatinine ratio
    b) Blood urea nitrogen
    c) Serum osmolality
    d) Urine specific gravity

16. What is the normal value for the blood urea nitrogen (BUN)?

    a) 1-6mg/dL
    b) 7 – 23 mg/dL
    c) 24-105 mg/dL
    d) 106-320 mg/dL

17. What test is used to measure ion concentrations with dehydration levels increase?
    a) Serum Sodium
    b) BUN-Creatnine Ratio
    c) Blood Urea Nitrogen (BUN)
    d) Serum Osmolality

18. **A factor of malunutrition includes low body weight, which is:**

    a) 60% of body weight for their age
    b) 70% of body weight for their age
    c) 80% of body weight for their age
    d) 90% of body weight for their age

19. **The body mass index is calculated by:**

    a) Dividing the height of the client by the weight of the client in terms of pounds.
    b) Dividing the weight of the client by the height of the client in terms of meters.
    c) Multiplying the weight of the client by 31.5% and adding in the height of the client.
    d) Multiplying the height of the client by 2.864% and subtracting .005 for each pound of weight.

20. **Obesity occurs when:**

    a) Energy consumed exceeds the energy expended.
    b) Energy expended exceeds the energy consumed.
    c) Energy consumed is equal to the energy expended minus 10%.
    d) 10% of the energy consumed is equal to or greater than the energy expended.

21. **What is the normal percentage of immature neutophil bands?**

    a) 0-3%
    b) 1-3%
    c) 12-16%
    d) 50-625%

22. **What can cause an increase in immature neutrophils?**

    a) Infection
    b) Malnutrition
    c) Obesity
    d) An acute virus

23. **What can cause enoinophils to decrease?**

    a) Obesity
    b) Malnutrition
    c) Over eating
    d) An acute infection

24. What type of topical agent is made of a fast-drying solvent that is applied approximately every 14 days?

   a) Moisture barrier ointments
   b) Moisture barrier pastes
   c) Solid skin barriers
   d) Skin sealants

25. The water used for hydrotherapy should be:

   a) 34 degrees C
   b) 37 degrees C
   c) 42 degrees C
   d) 46 degrees C

26. Select the type of dressing that is correctly paired with its example and description.

   a) Bioactive dressing: Gauze; allows for observation of the wound
   b) Interactive dressing: Chitosan; allows the wound to stay permeable to water and oxygen
   c) Reactive dressing: Hyrocolloids; includes substances that directly allow for wound healing
   d) Traditional dressing: Tulle, gauze; primarily used as a protective cover for the wound

27. What form of debridement is used to control hypergranulation tissue?

   a) Chemical cauterization
   b) Sharp wound debridement
   c) Surgical debridement
   d) Mechanical debridement

28. Which methods of wound culturing are invasive?

   a) Swab and aspirate
   b) Aspirate only
   c) Tissue biopsy
   d) Aspirate and tissue biopsy

29. Hyperbaric oxygenation treatment increases the availability of oxygen to tissues by:

   a) 10 to 20 times
   b) 30 to 40 times
   c) 60 to 80 times
   d) 90 to 100 times

Trivium Test Prep

30. Which protein is necessary for the growth and migration of cells?

    a) Platelets
    b) Growth factors
    c) Macrophages
    d) Ovarian follicles

31. Your client has a wound that is difficult to heal; the healing is less than 30% over a four week period of time. Which treatment is now indicated?

    a) Negative pressure wound therapy
    b) Amputation of the affected area
    c) Growth factor treatment
    d) Sterilization

32. Which of the following is the term used for an inflammation of tissue that is accompanied with edema and pronounced erythema?

    a) Eschar
    b) Cellulitis
    c) Amorphous
    d) Necrosis

33. What is eschar?

    a) The formation of new blood vessels and capillaries
    b) The removal of necrotic tissue
    c) Dark brown or black leathery necrotic tissue
    d) A wound that is lacking a defined form

34. What is the term used for impermeable to air or liquids?

    a) Occlusive
    b) Amorphous
    c) Cellulitis
    d) Debridement

35. During which of the four stagess of pressure ulcers does the ulcer appear as a shallow, pinkish-red, basin-like wound or as an intact or ruptured fluid-filled blister?

    a) Stage I
    b) Stage II
    c) Stage III
    d) Stage IV

36. What stage(s) of pressure sores will heal within several weeks to months with conservative care?

    a) I
    b) I and II
    c) II and III
    d) III and IV

37. According to the four point check for edema, moderate pitting to approximately 4mm for 10-15 seconds is which level?

    a) 1
    b) 2
    c) 3
    d) 4

38. When evaluating for peripheral arterial disease, the ankle-brachial examination is performed with:

    a) A blood cuff and stethoscope.
    b) A Doppler device, a thermometer and a blood cuff.
    c) A Doppler device, blood pressure cuff and a stethoscope.
    d) A thermometer, a Doppler device and a stethoscope.

39. The degree of the disease can be calculated by dividing the brachial systolic by the ankle systolic. If the calculation of your client's brachial systolic divided by the ankle systolic is 0.25, this means:

    a) Severe disease and ischemia.
    b) That the limb is in threatening condition.
    c) Borderline perfusion.
    d) Minor disease with no chance of infection.

40. You have just divided the brachial systolic by the ankle systolic and the calculation is 0.65. This indicates:

    a) Borderline perfusion.
    b) Normal, asymptomatic.
    c) Critical limb-threatening condition.
    d) Severe disease, ischemia.

41. What test is used to find the appropriate amputation site for a client with hypoxic limbs?

    a) Monofilament test
    b) Transcutaneous oxygen pressure (TcPO2)
    c) Pressure relief test
    d) Damaged tissue removal

42. **Select the following test results from the transcutaneous oxygen pressure test that is correctly paired with its significance.**

    a) 40mm Hg: Means there is marked ischemia
    b) 20-40 mm: Hg means there is marked ischemia
    c) <20 mm: Means there is an adequate amount of oxygenation for healing
    d) 40mm Hg: Means there is an adequate amount of oxygenation for healing

43. **What type of dermatitis is also referred to as cradle cap?**

    a) Contact dermatitis
    b) Suborrheic dermatitis
    c) Atopic dermatitis
    d) Venous dermatitis

44. **Which type of wrap is reusable and used for ambulatory clients with an ankle brachial index of >0.5 - <0.8?**

    a) Short-stretch wrap
    b) Unna's boot
    c) Single layered wrap
    d) Layered wraps

45. **A direct result of neuropathy that weakens the muscles of the foot and reduces sensations is known as:**

    a) Charcort changes.
    b) Arterial insufficiency.
    c) Perfusion.
    d) Necrotic tissue.

46. **Treatments used for lymphadema include the following EXCEPT for:**

    a) Light exercise
    b) Ice applications
    c) Wrapping the area effected
    d) Keeping the effective area still at all times

47. **The chain of infection in correct sequential order is the:**

    a) The agent, the reservoir, the environment, the mode of transmission, the portal of entry, the portal of exist and the susceptible host.
    b) The reservoir, the agent, the environment, the mode of transmission, the portal of entry, the portal of exist and the susceptible host.
    c) The reservoir, the environment, the agent, the mode of transmission, the portal of entry, the portal of exist and the susceptible host.
    d) The reservoir, the mode of transmission, the environment, the agent, the portal of entry, the portal of exist and the susceptible host.

48. You are caring for a middle age client who has cancer and is no longer able to work outside of the home. Although the client is doing relatively well in terms of his physical, psychological and social condition, he is no longer able to work. What fact about this client is accurate?

    a) This client is not considered healthy, according to a functional model of wellness, because the client is no longer able to be employed.
    b) This client is considered healthy, according to the health-illness continuum, because the client expresses physical, psychological and social wellbeing.
    c) This client is considered healthy, according to a functional model of wellness, because the client expresses physical, psychological and social wellbeing.
    d) This client is not considered healthy, according to the optimal wellness theory, because the client is no longer able to be employed.

49. Select the health and wellness theory that is correctly paired with its description.

    a) High – Level Wellness Model: The components of wellness are the physical, social, emotional, intellectual, spiritual, occupational and environmental components of health.
    b) Seven Components of Wellness: high level wellness in a very favorable environment, emergent high level wellness in an unfavorable environment, protected poor health in a favorable environment, and poor health in an unfavorable environment.
    c) Health-Illness Continuum: Disease occurs as the result of the interrelationships among the agent, the host and the environment.
    d) Health Belief Model: This model can predict whether or not a person will engage in screening tests

50. Which theorist developed the Health-Illness Continuum?

    a) Ryan and Travis
    b) Clark and Leavell
    c) Rodenstock and Becker
    d) Braddick and Devall

51. The client's level of motivation and commitment is impacted by many factors including emotions, affect, behavior specific cognitions, the client's prior experiences, personal characteristics, feelings of self-efficacy and the support of others according to which model of health and wellness?

    a) Seven Components of Wellness
    b) The Dimensions Model
    c) Pender's Health Promotion Model
    d) The Agent – Host – Environment Model

52. **Madeleine Leininger supports which of the following nursing modes of intervention?**

    a) Cultural practices and cultural respect
    b) Self-care agency
    c) Cultural care restructuring and repatterning
    d) Universality

53. **Who is responsible for the five-stage process containing knowledge, persuasion, decision, implementation and confirmation?**

    a) Rogers
    b) Leininger
    c) Neumann
    d) Henderson

54. **Select the dimension of health that is correctly paired with its description.**

    a) Biophysical: Physical looks, lifestyle choices and contaminated water supply
    b) Psychological: Coping and mental health
    c) Behavioral: Air pollution and contaminated water supplies
    d) The physical environment: Lifestyle choices like exercise and good nutrition

55. **During which phase of the nursing process does data get organized and validated with the client by the nurse?**

    a) Assessment
    b) Analysis
    c) Evaluation
    d) Planning

56. **You are determining the outcomes of patient care for your client. Which phase of the nursing process are you using?**

    a) Evaluation
    b) Diagnosis
    c) Planning
    d) Discharge

57. **All nursing diagnoses must minimally contain:**

    a) The problem and the etiology.
    b) The problem and the expected outcome.
    c) The etiology and defining characteristics.
    d) The etiology and the expected outcome.

58. When the client states that they are in "severe, crushing pain", it is an example of:

    a) Objective data.
    b) Extraneous data.
    c) Subjective data.
    d) Terminal data.

59. Nocicetive pain:

    a) Can be somatic or radicular.
    b) Is acute pain originating in the spinal cord.
    c) Can be neuropathic or visceral.
    d) Is chronic pain originating in the spinal cord.

60. Your client has had a compression spinal injury and is complaining about sharp and severe. What type of pain is this client most likely experiencing?

    a) Peripheral neuropathic pain
    b) Central neuropathic pain
    c) Insidious and sporadic pain
    d) Somatic, visceral pain

61. Select the type of pain that is accurately paired with its description.

    a) Acute pain: More easily locatable than chronic pain
    b) Acute pain: More likely to be relieved completely than chronic pain
    c) Chronic pain: Often accompanied with increased sympathetic activity
    d) Chronic pain: More easily locatable than acute pain

62. The International Association for the Study of Pain describes pain as:

    a) An objective experience.
    b) A personal experience.
    c) An existential experience.
    d) A behavioral reaction.

63. Which fact about pain is most accurate?

    a) Behavioral pain cues are consistent among age groups.
    b) Sedation is the most effective mode of pain management.
    c) Pain is best assessed with patient self reports.
    d) Pain is a combination of cognition and behavior.

64. Which of the following disorders is associated with peripheral neuropathic pain?

    a) Transmandibular joint malalignment
    b) Increased intracranial pressure
    c) Post amputation phantom pain
    d) Ocular damage

65. Your client is complaining of dull, diffuse and aching pain. Which nerve fibers are most likely transmitting this pain?

    a) Unmyelinated C nerve fibers
    b) Heavily myelinated C nerve fibers
    c) Thinly myelinated A delta fibers
    d) Heavily myelinated A delta fibers

66. Select the pain management term that is correctly paired with its definition or description.

    a) Addiction: It can occur with or without physical dependence.
    b) Addiction: A combination of both psychological and physical dependence
    c) Pseudoaddiction: A drug seeking behavior where the person feigns pain
    d) Physical dependence: It is often associated with amphetamines

67. Which type of decision making, within the nurse-client relationship, is the most beneficial to the client?

    a) Patient sovereignty decision making because it includes the client
    b) Shared decision making because the client gets the professional support of the nurse
    c) Paternalistic decision making because the nurse, as the expert, insures that the client makes the correct decision
    d) Caring decision making, because the client and their loved ones are included

68. Which organization developed the Pain Ladder?

    a) The World Health Organization
    b) The American Nurses Association
    c) The National Board for Certification of Hospice and Palliative Nurses
    d) The American Board for Certification of Hospice and Palliative Nurses

69. The PQRST method of pain assessment is useful to nurses in order to insure that all pain related data is collected and assessed. What does PQRST stand for?

    a) Pain level, quality, radiation, sensation and timing
    b) Provocation, quality, region, severity and triggers
    c) Provocation, quantity, radiation, severity and triggers
    d) Pain level, quantity, region, sensation and timing

70. Your department is considering the use of a standardized pain management scale. What priority consideration should go into the selection of the best possible scales?

    a) Its ease of use
    b) Its applicability to all age groups
    c) Its validity and reliability
    d) Its cost

71. **The McGill Pain Questionnaire consists of:**

    a) Affective, sensory and evaluative descriptors of pain.
    b) Sensory determinations in regards to pain and pain management.
    c) Levels adjusted and evaluated in regards to a group of clients in pain.
    d) Affective and sensory adjustments for clients in mild to severe pain.

72. **A pain management tool, or scale, is considered reliable when it:**

    a) Can be used by different people with the same results.
    b) Actually measures what it is supposed to measure.
    c) Can be used by different people with the different results.
    d) Accessible and ready to use by all pain management nurses.

73. **Select the neonatal and/or pediatric pain scale that is accurately paired with its description.**

    a) The Face, Legs, Activity, Crying, Consolability Scale (FLACC): A total score of 5 indicates severe pain at the highest possible level.
    b) The CRIES Pain Scale: Represents the toddler's Crying, Required vital signs, Increased medication, Expression, and sleep patterns.
    c) The Children's Hospital of Eastern Ontario Scale (CHEOPS): This pain scale measures pain with behaviors such as cries, facial expressions, torso movement, verbalizations, touching the affected area of the body, and the positioning of the legs.
    d) The Neonatal Infant Pain Scale (NIPS): Scale that documents only infants between 0-12 months of age.

74. **Your client informs you that they are taking vitamin D supplementation for pain. What should you tell this client in terms of using vitamin D for pain relief?**

    a) Vitamin D is a fat soluble vitamin so there are no dangers associated with mega doses and over dosages.
    b) Vitamin D should always be taken with calcium because vitamin D needs calcium for absorption.
    c) Professional literature indicates that high levels of vitamin D increase, and not decrease, pain.
    d) Professional literature indicates that low levels of vitamin D are associated with increased levels of chronic pain.

75. **Why does anxiety interfere with healthful sleep?**

    a) Anxiety disrupts stage IV sleep but it does not interfere with sleep induction.
    b) Anxiety disrupts stage IV sleep but it does not interfere with sleep maintenance.
    c) Anxiety leads to autonomic responses and the anticipation of danger..
    d) Even low levels of anxiety precipitate nightmares and other sleep disorders.

76. **As you are planning care with the client, your client asks you about cognitive behavioral therapy and its usefulness in terms of pain management. How would you respond to this client's question?**

    a) "Cognitive behavioral therapy addresses the here and now of a person's perceptions and behaviors in relationship to pain."
    b) "Cognitive behavioral therapy has not been found to be effective for chronic or acute pain."
    c) "Cognitive behavioral therapy is a kind of psychotherapy that explores underlying repressed thoughts."
    d) "Cognitive behavioral therapy is conducted in groups such as a peer support group for those in chronic pain."

77. **How many behavioral and physical measurements are included in the Cries Pain Scale?**

    a) Five
    b) Six
    c) Seven
    d) Eight

78. **A major difference among side effects, adverse effects and allergic responses to medications includes the fact that:**

    a) Adverse effects cannot be prevented, but allergic responses and side effects can be.
    b) Side effects and adverse responses cannot be prevented, but allergic reactions can be.
    c) Allergic responses cannot be prevented but adverse effects and side effects can be.
    d) Side effects cannot be prevented, but adverse responses and allergic responses can be.

79. **When should a differential assessment of a wound be done?**

    a) During the initial assessment
    b) Once the doctor has seen the patient
    c) After the etiology is documented and approved by the treating physician
    d) Four hours after the wound occurs

80. **The R in the SMARTTA framework stands for:**

    a) Reliable
    b) Realistic
    c) Real
    d) Renewable

81. Expected outcomes, and goals, must be within a timeframe that is realistic, achievable, trackable and:

    a) Measurable.
    b) Strong.
    c) Confirmed.
    d) Projected.

82. Which age group, according to Erik Erikson, is charged with the developmental challenge of autonomy, self-control and will power versus shame, doubt and a low tolerance for frustration?

    a) Toddler
    b) Preschool child
    c) School age child
    d) Adolescent

83. The chain of infection in correct sequential order is the:

    a) The agent, the reservoir, the environment, the mode of transmission, the portal of entry, the portal of exist and the susceptible host.
    b) The reservoir, the agent, the environment, the mode of transmission, the portal of entry, the portal of exist and the susceptible host.
    c) The reservoir, the environment, the agent, the mode of transmission, the portal of entry, the portal of exist and the susceptible host.
    d) The reservoir, the mode of transmission, the environment, the agent, the portal of entry, the portal of exist and the susceptible host.

84. Whose theory of development most accurately describes why infants and toddlers are at risk for the aspiration of foreign bodies?

    a) Stella Chess
    b) Robert Havighurst
    c) Sigmund Freud
    d) Roger Gould

85. Which of the following is a factor intrinsic to the pathogen that impacts on the ability of a pathogenic microorganism to cause disease?

    a) The susceptibility of the host
    b) Its virulence
    c) Its mode of transmission
    d) The immune status of the host

86. Select the phase of viral growth that is accurately paired with its characteristic.

   a) The Attachment Stage: The virus enters the host's cells.
   b) The Penetration Stage: The virus attaches to a receptor on the host's cellular surface.
   c) The Uncoating Stage: The viral capsid is removed which allows it nucleic material to enter the bodily cells.
   d) The Uncoating Stage: The viral capsid is hardened which allows it nucleic material to enter the bodily cells.

87. Select the age group correctly paired with behavioral cues associated with pain.

   a) Adults: Relate their pain because they know that they will be given narcotics.
   b) The Adolescent: May ignore and deny pain because it is viewed as a sign of weakness and they may also fear pain because of what it can mean
   c) The School Age Child: Not able to describe and identify the location of their pain in any manner.
   d) Toddlers and Preschool Children: Begin to describe pain, its intensity and its location.

88. Select the phase of bacterial growth that is accurately paired with its characteristic.

   a) The Stationary Phase: Growth and metabolic activity decreases.
   b) The Death Phase: The bacteria is not acclimating to its new environment
   c) The Lag Phase: The bacteria are without any nutrients at all.
   d) The Log Phase: The growth rate slows down.

89. Select the level of prevention that is accurately paired with its description.

   a) Quadriary prevention: The prevention of disease
   b) Primary prevention: Screening
   c) Tertiary prevention: Restoration of function
   d) Secondary prevention: Monitoring compliance with quarantine

90. You are teaching your client's visitors about the proper donning of a gown and gloves. What domain of learning are you teaching?

   a) Wound care and ostomy education
   b) Cognitive
   c) Affective
   d) Psychomotor

91. Which teaching strategy is most appropriate when teaching a client's visitors about the proper donning of a gown and gloves?

   a) Discussion
   b) Demonstration
   c) Reading material
   d) Role playing

92. The five types of sounds that are elicited during percussion are:

a) Flatness, resonance, hyperresonance, tympany and dullness.
b) Hyperresonating, dullness, flatness, resonating and tympany.
c) Dullness, flatness, resonating, timbre and hyperresonance.
d) Timbre, hyperresonance, resonance, depth and flatness.

93. Select the breath sound that is accurately paired with its description.

a) Rales: Crackling and rattling
b) Tubular: Squeaky and high-pitched
c) Vesicular: Low pitched and snoring like
d) Friction rub: Resonant and susurrating

94. The S3 sound:

a) Is heard early during diastole when the heart's ventricle is compressed and not compliant.
b) Indicates a left ventricular problem when heard during inspiration from a horizontal position.
c) Is typically considered normal among pregnant women, some children and young adults.
d) Indicates a right ventricular problem when heard during inspiration from a horizontal position.

95. Your female client's laboratory test results have just been delivered to the client care unit. This client's erythrocyte sedimentation rate is 10 millimeters per hour, their C reactive protein is 8 mg/L, and their blood viscosity is $3 \times 10-3$. What would you suspect?

a) The absence of infection
b) The presence of a mild infection
c) The presence of a moderate infection
d) The presence of a severe infection

96. Select the neonatal and/or pediatric pain scale that is accurately paired with its description.

a) The Face, Legs, Activity, Crying, Consolability Scale (FLACC): A total score of 5 indicates severe pain at the highest possible level.
b) The CRIES Pain Scale: Represents the toddler's Crying, Required vital signs, Increased medication, Expression, and sleep patterns.
c) The Children's Hospital of Eastern Ontario Scale (CHEOPS): This pain scale measures pain with behaviors such as cries, facial expressions, torso movement, verbalizations, touching the affected area of the body, and the positioning of the legs.
d) The Neonatal Infant Pain Scale (NIPS): Scale that documents only infants between 0-12 months of age.

97. Your client has a murmur that is loud and audible with minimal stethoscope to chest contact. What grade is this murmur?

   a) Grade 2
   b) Grade 3
   c) Grade 4
   d) Grade 5

98. Which of these medications is used for the treatment of scabies?

   a) Atovaquone-proguanil
   b) Metronidazole
   c) Ivermectin
   d) Pyrantel pamoate

99. Which term best describes the nurse's application of research findings into practice?

   a) Benchmarking practice
   b) Evidence based practice
   c) Professional decision making
   d) Critical thinking practice

100. Although antimicrobials should be used as based on the site of the infection, the host, and whenever possible, based on a definitive diagnosis of the infection and the offending pathogen, at times what type of antimicrobial therapy is sometimes indicated?

   a) Therapeutic use
   b) Prophylactic use
   c) Empiric use
   d) Tentative use

101. What are the three phases of the perideath process in correct sequential order?

   a) Preparation for death, the death itself and after death
   b) Onset, peak, duration and death
   c) Preparation for death, onset of symptoms and death
   d) Onset, duration, peak and death

102. The PQRST method of pain assessment is useful to nurses in order to insure that all pain related data is collected and assessed. What does PQRST stand for?

   a) Pain level, quality, radiation, sensation and timing
   b) Provocation, quality, region, severity and triggers
   c) Provocation, quantity, radiation, severity and triggers
   d) Pain level, quantity, region, sensation and timing

103. Which epidemiological model consists of the agent, host and environment?

   a) The Web of Causation
   b) The Wheel of Causation
   c) The Determinants of Health
   d) The Epidemiological Triad

104. As part of your performance improvement and quality assurance program you review your entire infection control program in terms of its completeness and accuracy. What are you studying as part of this review?

   a) Outcomes
   b) Processes
   c) Structures
   d) Administrative tools

105. Electrolytes and fluids are transported through the body with:

   a) Active transport processes.
   b) Passive transport processes.
   c) Both active and passive transport processes.
   d) None of the above.

106. Your client will be having a Billroth II surgical procedure. What should the nurse include in this client's teaching plan?

   a) Things, including foods, which can increase vitamin A
   b) Things, including foods, which can increase calcium levels
   c) Dumping syndrome signs and symptoms
   d) The effect of a Billroth II in the palliation of peptic ulcers

107. Select the client with the type of nursing system, according to Dorothea Orem's Self Care theory.

   a) A 54 year old client in a coma: Wholly compensatory nursing system
   b) An infant: Supportive nursing system
   c) A 76 year old client who is able to perform all self care independently: Supportive-educative nursing system
   d) A 23 year old client with leukemia who needs some assistance with personal hygiene: Wholly compensatory nursing system

108. You are teaching your client about the proper care of a new colostomy. What domain of learning are you teaching?

   a) Pedagogy
   b) Cognitive
   c) Affective
   d) Psychomotor

109. Culture impacts on what aspects of the teaching/learning process?

   a) Communication and terminology use
   b) Tolerance for low lighting and communication
   c) The ambient temperature of the room and stress levels
   d) Teaching strategies and terminology use

110. Which is a motivator?

   a) High stress
   b) No stress
   c) Moderate stress
   d) Low stress

111. The force of facilitators must be stronger than the barriers to change according to which theory or concept?

   a) Havelock's Six Phases of Planned Change
   b) Lewin's Forced Field Analysis
   c) Roger's Innovation-Decision Process
   d) Chaos Theory

112. Your client has terminal cancer and the client's daughter has expressed extreme sorrow about their mother and their mother's condition. What type of loss is this daughter most likely experiencing?

   a) Perceived loss
   b) Anticipatory loss
   c) Actual loss
   d) Profound loss

113. Which theorist has 5 phases of bereavement as shock, awareness of the loss, conservation and withdrawal, healing or the turning point and renewal?

   a) Sander
   b) Kubler-Ross
   c) Engel
   d) Piaget

114. The primary purpose of feeling guilty is to:

   a) Punish the person for a wrongdoing.
   b) Change behaviors.
   c) Facilitate amends.
   d) Serve spiritual wellness.

115. Whose theory of grieving includes the unique phase of bargaining?

a) Engel's
b) Sander's
c) Maslow's
d) Kubler Ross's

116. As you are caring for a client with type 2 diabetes, the client expresses concerns about the acute complications of diabetes. What should you teach this client about?

a) The role of good blood glucose control in terms of preventing hyperglycemic hyperosmolar nonketotic coma
b) The role of good blood glucose control in terms of preventing neuropathy and nephropathy
c) The role of regular exercise in terms of preventing peripheral neuropathy
d) The role of regular exercise in terms of preventing diabetic retinopathy

117. The fourth sequential step of the evaluation process is:

a) Data collection relating to the expected outcome
b) Data analysis and comparison of the data to the outcomes
c) Relating the interventions to the expected outcomes
d) Concluding about the client's problem status

118. Which is an appropriate expected outcome for a client who is taking an opioid for pain?

a) The client will maintain adequate oxygenation
b) The client will express a decrease in their pain
c) The nurse will assess for pain before the administration of the opioid
d) The nurse will assess for pain before and after the administration of the opioid

119. You have completed a full assessment of your client. You will now be establishing priorities. What phase of the nursing process includes establishing priorities?

a) Diagnosing
b) Priority setting
c) Planning
d) Implementation

120. You are caring for an adolescent with multiple traumas including a thermal burn on the anterior and posterior aspects of both legs and the posterior aspect of the left arm. How would these burns be categorized?

   a) An 18 % burn
   b) A 22.5% burn
   c) A 27.5% burn
   d) A 36 % burn

- ## Answer Key

1. D
2. C
3. A
4. D
5. A
6. A
7. C
8. A
9. B
10. B
11. C
12. B
13. D
14. A
15. D
16. B
17. D
18. D
19. B
20. A
21. B
22. A
23. D
24. D
25. B
26. D
27. A
28. C
29. A
30. A
31. A
32. B
33. C
34. A
35. B
36. B
37. B

38. C
39. B
40. D
41. B
42. D
43. B
44. A
45. A
46. D
47. A
48. A
49. D
50. A
51. C
52. C
53. A
54. B
55. A
56. A
57. A
58. C
59. A
60. B
61. B
62. B
63. C
64. C
65. A
66. A
67. B
68. A
69. B
70. C
71. A
72. A
73. C
74. D
75. C
76. A
77. A
78. B
79. A
80. B
81. A
82. A
83. A
84. C
85. B
86. C
87. D

88. A
89. C
90. D
91. B
92. A
93. A
94. C
95. A
96. C
97. D
98. C
99. B
100. C
101. A
102. B
103. D
104. C
105. C
106. C
107. A
108. D
109. A
110. C
111. B
112. B
113. A
114. B
115. D
116. A
117. D
118. B
119. C
120. B

Exclusive Trivium Test Tips

Here at Trivium Test Prep, we strive to offer you the exemplary test tools that help you pass your exam the first time. This book includes an overview of important concepts, example questions throughout the text, and practice test questions. But we know that learning how to successfully take a test can be just as important as learning the content being tested. In addition to excelling on the CWOCN, we want to give you the solutions you need to be successful every time you take a test. Our study strategies, preparation pointers, and test tips will help you succeed as you take the CWOCN and any test in the future!

Study Strategies

1. Spread out your studying. By taking the time to study a little bit every day, you strengthen your understanding of the testing material, so it's easier to recall that information on the day of the test. Our study guides make this easy by breaking up the concepts into sections with example practice questions, so you can test your knowledge as you read.
2. Create a study calendar. The sections of our book make it easy to review and practice with example questions on a schedule. Decide to read a specific number of pages or complete a number of practice questions every day. Breaking up all of the information in this way can make studying less overwhelming and more manageable.
3. Set measurable goals and motivational rewards. Follow your study calendar and reward yourself for completing reading, example questions, and practice problems and tests. You could take yourself out after a productive week of studying or watch a favorite show after reading a chapter. Treating yourself to rewards is a great way to stay motivated.
4. Use your current knowledge to understand new, unfamiliar concepts. When you learn something new, think about how it relates to something you know really well. Making connections between new ideas and your existing understanding can simplify the learning process and make the new information easier to remember.
5. Make learning interesting! If one aspect of a topic is interesting to you, it can make an entire concept easier to remember. Stay engaged and think about how concepts covered on the exam can affect the things you're interested in. The sidebars throughout the text offer additional information that could make ideas easier to recall.
6. Find a study environment that works for you. For some people, absolute silence in a library results in the most effective study session, while others need the background noise of a coffee shop to fuel productive studying. There are many websites that generate white noise and recreate the sounds of different environments for studying. Figure out what distracts you and what engages you and plan accordingly.
7. Take practice tests in an environment that reflects the exam setting. While it's important to be as comfortable as possible when you study, practicing taking the test exactly as you'll take it on test day will make you more prepared for

the actual exam. If your test starts on a Saturday morning, take your practice test on a Saturday morning. If you have access, try to find an empty classroom that has desks like the desks at testing center. The more closely you can mimic the testing center, the more prepared you'll feel on test day.
8. Study hard for the test in the days before the exam, but take it easy the night before and do something relaxing rather than studying and cramming. This will help decrease anxiety, allow you to get a better night's sleep, and be more mentally fresh during the big exam. Watch a light-hearted movie, read a favorite book, or take a walk, for example.

Preparation Pointers

1. Preparation is key! Don't wait until the day of your exam to gather your pencils, calculator, identification materials, or admission tickets. Check the requirements of the exam as soon as possible. Some tests require materials that may take more time to obtain, such as a passport-style photo, so be sure that you have plenty of time to collect everything. The night before the exam, lay out everything you'll need, so it's all ready to go on test day! We recommend at least two forms of ID, your admission ticket or confirmation, pencils, a high protein, compact snack, bottled water, and any necessary medications. Some testing centers will require you to put all of your supplies in a clear plastic bag. If you're prepared, you will be less stressed the morning of, and less likely to forget anything important.
2. If you're taking a pencil-and-paper exam, test your erasers on paper. Some erasers leave big, dark stains on paper instead of rubbing out pencil marks. Make sure your erasers work for you and the pencils you plan to use.
3. Make sure you give yourself your usual amount of sleep, preferably at least 7 – 8 hours. You may find you need even more sleep. Pay attention to how much you sleep in the days before the exam, and how many hours it takes for you to feel refreshed. This will allow you to be as sharp as possible during the test and make fewer simple mistakes.
4. Make sure to make transportation arrangements ahead of time, and have a backup plan in case your ride falls through. You don't want to be stressing about how you're going to get to the testing center the morning of the exam.
5. Many testing locations keep their air conditioners on high. You want to remember to bring a sweater or jacket in case the test center is too cold, as you never know how hot or cold the testing location could be. Remember, while you can always adjust for heat by removing layers, if you're cold, you're cold.

Test Tips

1. Go with your gut when choosing an answer. Statistically, the answer that comes to mind first is often the right one. This is assuming you studied the material, of course, which we hope you have done if you've read through one of our books!

2. For true or false questions: if you genuinely don't know the answer, mark it true. In most tests, there are typically more true answers than false answers.
3. For multiple-choice questions, read ALL the answer choices before marking an answer, even if you think you know the answer when you come across it. You may find your original "right" answer isn't necessarily the best option.
4. Look for key words: in multiple choice exams, particularly those that require you to read through a text, the questions typically contain key words. These key words can help the test taker choose the correct answer or confuse you if you don't recognize them. Common keywords are: *most*, *during*, *after*, *initially*, and *first*. Be sure you identify them before you read the available answers. Identifying the key words makes a huge difference in your chances of passing the test.
5. Narrow answers down by using the process of elimination: after you understand the question, read each answer. If you don't know the answer right away, use the process of elimination to narrow down the answer choices. It is easy to identify at least one answer that isn't correct. Continue to narrow down the choices before choosing the answer you believe best fits the question. By following this process, you increase your chances of selecting the correct answer.
6. Don't worry if others finish before or after you. Go at your own pace, and focus on the test in front of you.
7. Relax. With our help, we know you'll be ready to conquer the CWOCN. You've studied and worked hard!

Keep in mind that every individual takes tests differently, so strategies that might work for you may not work for someone else. You know yourself best and are the best person to determine which of these tips and strategies will benefit your studying and test taking. Best of luck as you study, test, and work toward your future!

Made in the USA
Lexington, KY
04 December 2019